Cover and Title Page: Nathan Love

www.mheonline.com/readingwonders

Copyright © 2016 McGraw-Hill Education

All rights reserved. No part of this publication may be reproduced or distributed in any form or by any means, or stored in a database or retrieval system, without the prior written consent of McGraw-Hill Education, including, but not limited to, network storage or transmission or broadcast for distance learning.

Send all inquiries to:
McGraw-Hill Education
2 Penn Plaza
New York, NY 10121

ISBN: 978-0-02-132635-8
MHID: 0-02-132635-5

Printed in the United States of America.

8 9 LMN 24 23   C

ELD
Companion Worktext

Program Authors

Diane August

Jana Echevarria

Josefina V. Tinajero

Unit 1

CHANGES

The Big Idea
How can changes transform the way people look at the world? 12

Week 1 • Perspectives 14

More Vocabulary 16
Shared Read Cow Music | Genre • Realistic Fiction 18
Respond to the Text 22
Write to Sources 24

Week 2 • Alliances 26

More Vocabulary 28
Shared Read Drumbeat of Freedom | Genre • Historical Fiction 30
Respond to the Text 34
Write to Sources 36

Week 3 • Environments ... 38

More Vocabulary 40
Shared Read The Secret World of Caves   Genre • Expository 42
Respond to the Text 46
Write to Sources 48

Week 4 • Dynamic Earth ... 50

More Vocabulary 52
Shared Read The Monster in the Mountain
  Genre • Narrative Nonfiction 54
Respond to the Text 58
Write to Sources 60

Week 5 • Using Money ... 62

More Vocabulary 64
Shared Read Making Money: A Story of Change
  Genre • Informational and Persuasive Article 66
Respond to the Text 70
Write to Sources 72

Unit 2

Excursions Across Time

The Big Idea
What can we gain from reading about past civilizations? 74

Week 1 • Contributions — 76

More Vocabulary 78
Shared Read Empire of the Sea Genre • Expository 80
Respond to the Text 84
Write to Sources 86

Week 2 • Democracy — 88

More Vocabulary 90
Shared Read The Democracy Debate Genre • Expository 92
Respond to the Text 96
Write to Sources 98

Socrates

Week 3 • Ancient Societies 100

More Vocabulary 102
Shared Read Yaskul's Mighty Trade   Genre • Historical Fiction 104
Respond to the Text 108
Write to Sources 110

Week 4 • Influences 112

More Vocabulary 114
Shared Read Cusi's Secret   Genre • Historical Fiction 116
Respond to the Text 120
Write to Sources 122

Week 5 • Past and Present 124

More Vocabulary 126
Shared Read "Ozymandias"   Genre • Poetry 128
Respond to the Text 132
Write to Sources 134

Unit 3

Accomplishments

The Big Idea
What does it take to accomplish a goal? 136

Week 1 • Common Ground — 138

More Vocabulary 140
Shared Read The Rockers Build a Soccer Field
Genre • Realistic Fiction 142
Respond to the Text 146
Write to Sources 148

Week 2 • Transformations — 150

More Vocabulary 152
Shared Read Facing the Storm Genre • Realistic Fiction ... 154
Respond to the Text 158
Write to Sources 160

Week 3 • Inspiration 162

More Vocabulary 164
Shared Read Jewels from the Sea   Genre • Narrative Nonfiction 166
Respond to the Text 170
Write to Sources 172

Week 4 • Milestones 174

More Vocabulary 176
Shared Read Marian Anderson: Struggles and Triumphs
Genre • Biography 178
Respond to the Text 182
Write to Sources 184

Week 5 • A Greener Future 186

More Vocabulary 188
Shared Read Is Your City Green?
Genre • Informational and Persuasive Article 190
Respond to the Text 194
Write to Sources 196

Unit 4

Challenges

The Big Idea
How do people meet challenges and solve problems? 198

Week 1 • Changing Environments 200

More Vocabulary 202
Shared Read The Day the Dam Broke Genre • Expository 204
Respond to the Text 208
Write to Sources 210

Week 2 • Overcoming Challenges 212

More Vocabulary 214
Shared Read She had to Walk Before She Could Run
Genre • Biography 216
Respond to the Text 220
Write to Sources 222

Week 3 • Standing Tall 224

More Vocabulary 226
Shared Read Treasure in the Attic   Genre • Drama 228
Respond to the Text 232
Write to Sources 234

Week 4 • Shared Experiences 236

More Vocabulary 238
Shared Read My Visit to Arizona   Genre • Realistic Fiction 240
Respond to the Text 244
Write to Sources 246

Week 5 • Taking Responsibility 248

More Vocabulary 250
Shared Read "Hey Nilda"   Genre • Poetry 252
Respond to the Text 256
Write to Sources 258

Unit 5

Discoveries

The Big Idea
How can discoveries open up new possibilities? 260

Week 1 • Myths — 262

More Vocabulary 264
Shared Read Thunder Helper   Genre • Myth 266
Respond to the Text 270
Write to Sources 272

Week 2 • Personal Strength — 274

More Vocabulary 276
Shared Read Journey to Freedom   Genre • Historical Fiction 278
Respond to the Text 282
Write to Sources 284

Week 3 • Innovations 286

More Vocabulary 288
Shared Read The Science of Silk Genre • Expository 290
Respond to the Text 294
Write to Sources 296

Week 4 • Breakthroughs 298

More Vocabulary 300
Shared Read Light Detectives Genre • Expository 302
Respond to the Text 306
Write to Sources 308

Week 5 • Exploration 310

More Vocabulary 312
Shared Read Tools of the Explorer's Trade
  Genre • Informational and Persuasive Article 314
Respond to the Text 318
Write to Sources 320

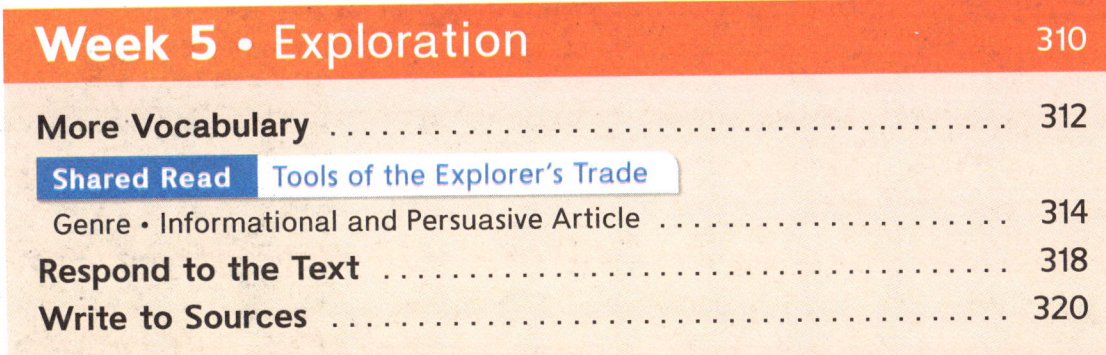

Unit 6

Taking Action

The Big Idea
When is it important to take action? 322

Week 1 • Resources — 324

More Vocabulary 326
Shared Read | The Fortunes of Fragrance | Genre • Expository 328
Respond to the Text 332
Write to Sources 334

Week 2 • Witnesses — 336

More Vocabulary 338
Shared Read | The Great Fire of London
Genre • Narrative Nonfiction 340
Respond to the Text 344
Write to Sources 346

Week 3 • Investigations — 348

More Vocabulary 350
Shared Read Researcher to the Rescue   Genre • Expository 352
Respond to the Text 356
Write to Sources 358

Week 4 • Extraordinary Finds — 360

More Vocabulary 362
Shared Read Messages in Stone and Wood   Genre • Expository ... 364
Respond to the Text 368
Write to Sources 370

Week 5 • Taking a Break — 372

More Vocabulary 374
Shared Read "How Many Seconds?"   Genre • Poetry 376
Respond to the Text 380
Write to Sources 382

THE BIG IDEA

How can changes transform the way people look at the world?

TALK ABOUT IT

Weekly Concept Perspectives

? Essential Question
How do new experiences offer new perspectives?

>> *Go Digital*

 What can you tell about a Tlingit clanhouse from the photo? Write words in the chart to describe the house.

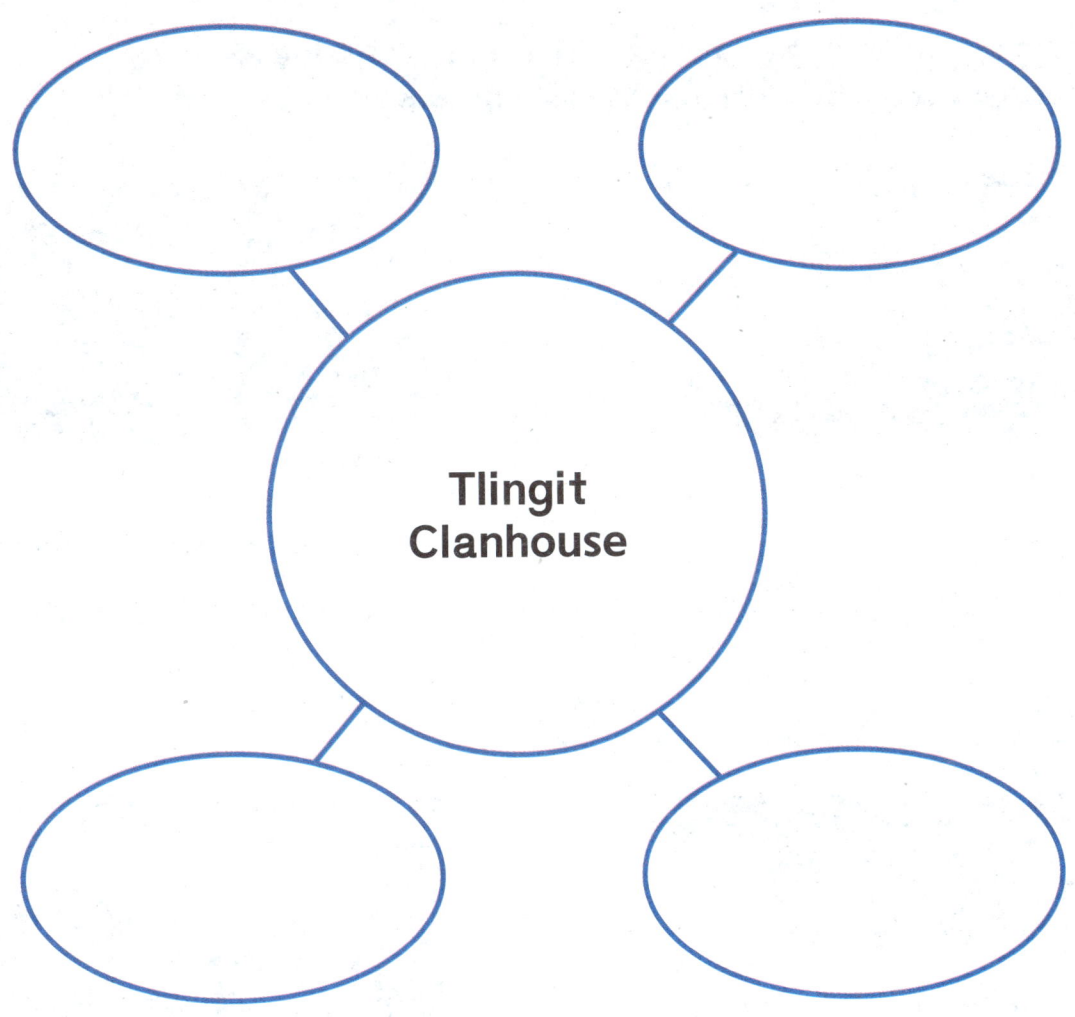

Discuss how seeing a Tlingit clanhouse changes your view of what houses look like. Use words from the chart. You can say:

A Tlingit clanhouse is _____ my house because it has

_____.

More Vocabulary

 Look at the picture and read the word. Then read the sentence. Talk about the word with a partner. Write your own sentence.

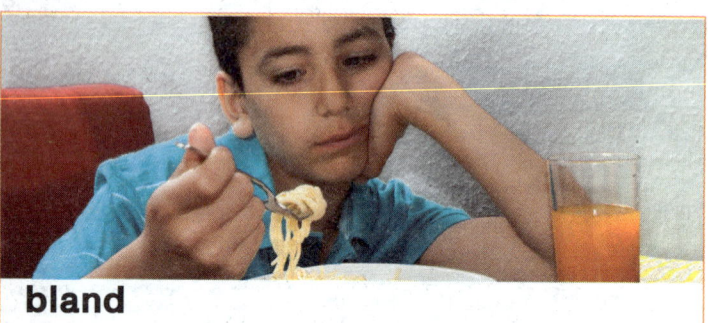
bland

David thinks the pasta tastes **bland**.

I think _____ is a *bland* food.

glumly

The sad child walked **glumly** in the hallway.

I sometimes walk *glumly* when _____

_____.

expecting

Robert is **expecting** a letter from his friend.

Today, I am *expecting* _____

_____.

overwhelmed

The worker feels **overwhelmed** at his job.

I feel *overwhelmed* when _____

_____.

16

thrilled

The winners of the game were **thrilled**.

Another word for *thrilled* is _____

_____.

unattractive

A town looks **unattractive** with a lot of trash.

A park looks *unattractive* with _____

_____.

Words and Phrases
Phrasal Verbs

clam up = to become silent or quiet
Frank <u>clams up</u> when the teacher asks him a question.

wander off = to walk away in no particular direction
The dog will <u>wander off</u> if he's not on a leash.

Read the sentences below. Write the phrasal verbs that mean the same as the underlined words.

Monique sometimes <u>becomes silent</u> when she meets new people.

Monique sometimes _____ when she meets new people.

The young boy might <u>walk away</u> from his parents.

The young boy might _____ from his parents.

» Go Digital Add these phrasal verbs to your New Words notebook. Write a sentence to show the meaning of each.

Text Evidence

Shared Read   Genre • Realistic Fiction

1 Talk About It

Read the title. Talk about what you see. Write your ideas.

What does the title tell you?

_____
_____
_____
_____

What are the characters doing?

_____
_____
_____
_____
_____
_____

Take notes as you read the story.

COW Music

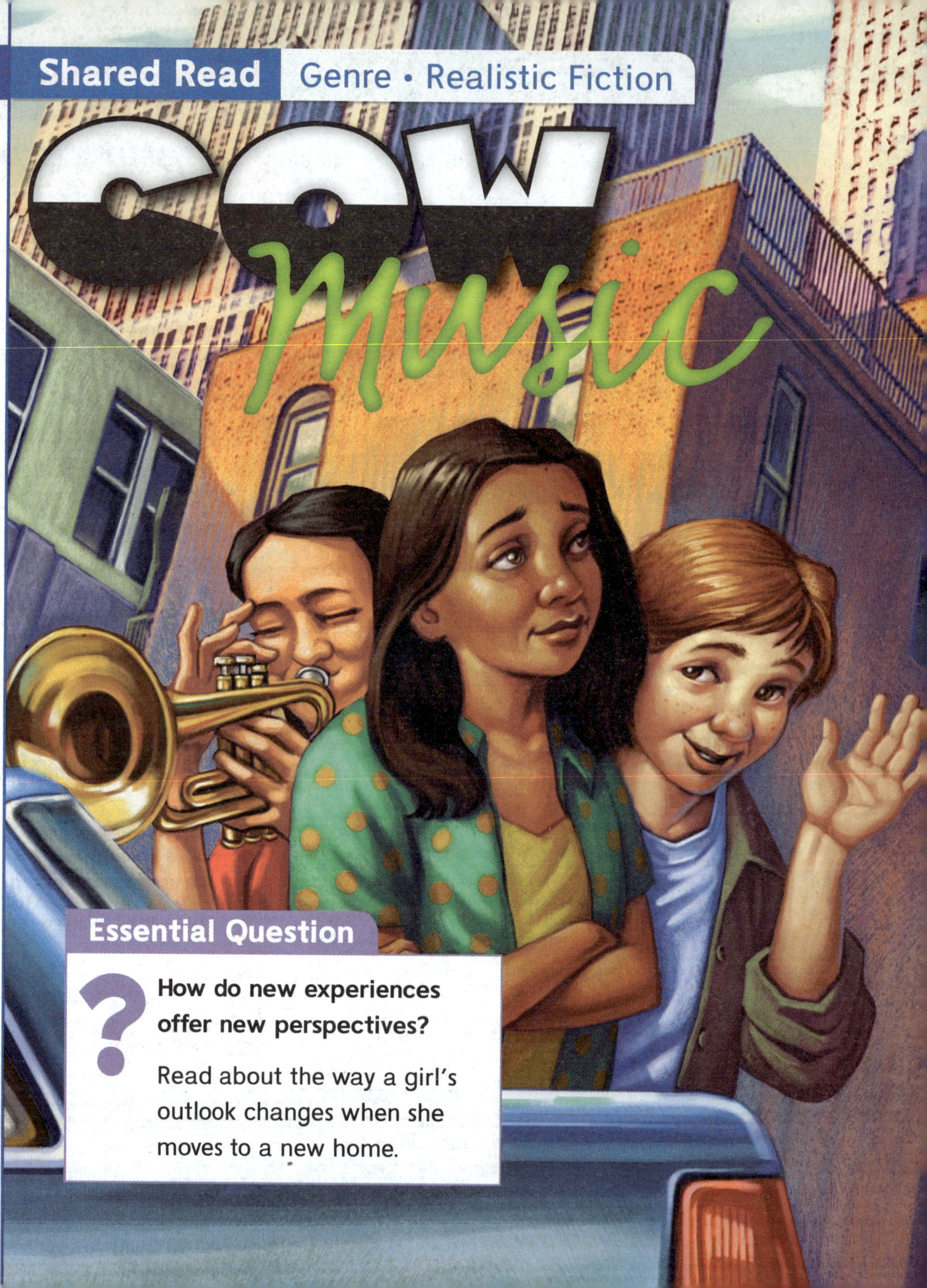

Essential Question

? How do new experiences offer new perspectives?

Read about the way a girl's outlook changes when she moves to a new home.

18

Farewell to Me

I crammed one last box into the back seat and slammed the car door. It felt as if I were slamming the door on my whole life. At first, I was **thrilled** when Mom told me she'd gotten a fantastic new job as a veterinarian at an animal hospital. Then, because she always saves the bad news for last, she told me the really heinous part. The hospital wasn't in our city; it was miles away in the middle of nowhere. And I'm definitely *not* a country girl.

I slouched against the car, taking a last look at our building. To most people, it probably just looks like any other old apartment house, but I love every grimy brick. Soon I'd be staring at piles of hay.

Just then, I heard a **bright** blast of music and saw my best friends, Hana and Leo, come charging up to me. While Hana played a cool riff on her trumpet, Leo sang, "We will miss you, Celia . . . At least you won't be in Australia." I raised my eyebrows.

Laughing, Leo said, "Hey, *you* find something to rhyme with *Celia*!"

"You guys are utterly indispensable!" I blurted out. "How will I live without you?"

"Ever hear of texting?" asked Hana, punctuating her question with a loud trumpet honk. I jumped into the car fast so no one could see me tear up. As Mom pulled away, I waved goodbye to my friends, my neighborhood, and my life.

We rode a while in silence, and I wedged my violin case beneath my legs for comfort. Leo, Hana, and I had been writing songs for our band, but that was all over now. "Don't think of this as an ending," Mom said, with her knack for reading my mind. "It's an exciting beginning, and we're on the threshold of a breathtaking new adventure."

"Yeah, it'll be great. I couldn't be happier," I said **glumly**.

"Don't be sarcastic, *mija*," Mom said. "It's so **unattractive**."

Text Evidence

❶ Comprehension
Character, Setting, Plot

Reread the first three paragraphs. Circle the names of four characters, or people in the story. Draw a box around the word that tells the setting, or where they are.

❷ Specific Vocabulary

The word *bright* has many meanings. It can mean "full of light," "having a bold color," and "lively and happy." Read the first sentence in the third paragraph.

In this sentence, *bright* means

_____.

❸ Sentence Structure

Read the last sentence in the sixth paragraph. *As* is a conjunction, or connecting word. It shows that two things happen at the same time. Underline the two things that happen at the same time.

Text Evidence

1 Comprehension

Character, Setting, Plot

Read the first and second paragraphs. Underline words that name things in the new setting. Draw a box around the word in the fifth paragraph that tells the new setting.

2 Talk About It

What does Celia think about everything in the country? How do you think she feels about her new home? Justify your answer.

_____

_____

3 Sentence Structure

Read the first sentence in the last paragraph. Underline the main part of the sentence that tells what Celia did. Circle the other part of the sentence that tells what she was doing as she wandered off.

Being attractive wasn't a big goal at the moment, but annoying Mom wasn't either. So I clammed up and looked out the window as crowded, exciting city streets turned first into **bland** suburban shopping strips and then into endless, boring trees and fields of corn.

"Look: cows!" Mom said, as we cruised past some black-and-white blotches in a pasture.

"Sure, they seem sweet," I said, "but I bet they have a mean streak when you're not looking."

"It's normal to be a bit phobic about unfamiliar things," Mom said, in her best patient-parent tone. "But you don't need to be afraid of cows. They're harmless."

"Harmless . . . and boring," I thought to myself. "Like everything in the country."

Not So Bad?

We finally arrived at our new home, a two-story wooden farmhouse. It had a crooked roof, a rickety front porch, and too many places for bats to hide. "Would you mind if I don't go in yet?" I asked.

Mom looked **overwhelmed**. She just nodded and said I could go explore. I felt a glimmer of hope, a small hint that country life might turn out okay. Mom never let me go out alone in the city, so maybe a bit more freedom would be one consolation of living here.

I wandered off, clutching my violin and not paying attention to where I was going. It didn't matter; it was all just a blur of green and brown. I imagined that a big Saturday night here meant sitting around talking about corn . . . or watching it grow.

Suddenly I heard something I wasn't **expecting**—a blaring, jazzy tune. I pushed through some corn only to come face-to-face with an enormous cow. Then another hot jazz riff floated through the air. I spun around and saw a tall kid playing a beat-up old saxophone in the clearing. His music was fantastic, and he didn't dress the way I figured a country kid would. Where were the muddy dungarees and plaid bandana? This guy was wearing clothes that made him look cool, like a famous performer.

Not Bad at All!

I couldn't resist, so I took out my violin and began to play along. The boy looked surprised, but he didn't miss a beat. We improvised a cool duet, and by the end—no kidding—the big cow's tail was swishing to the rhythm. "I'm Jason," he said when we finished. "I play out here because the cows don't complain when I mess up. You must be Celia. My dad said you were moving in. I can't believe you play violin! I've been looking for someone to write songs with."

I looked at Jason and his dented sax, the cheerful cow and tall corn, the majestic trees in the distance, and the sun shining in the brilliant blue sky. I could feel my perception of country life already changing, and I had a feeling it would change a lot more.

Make Connections

Talk about how Celia's first experience in her new home gives her a new perspective.
ESSENTIAL QUESTION

Describe a time when trying something new or unfamiliar changed your perspective.
TEXT TO SELF

Text Evidence

1 Specific Vocabulary

Read the first sentence in the second paragraph. If you can't resist doing something, you enjoy it and really want to do it. What thing couldn't Celia resist?

_____

_____

2 Comprehension
Character, Setting, Plot

Circle the name of a new character in the story. Why is this character happy to meet Celia? What does he say? Underline the two sentences that tell you.

3 Talk About It

How do you think Celia feels about the country at the end of the story? Justify your response.

_____

_____

_____

Respond to the Text

Partner Discussion Work with a partner. Answer the questions. Discuss what you learned about "Cow Music." Write the page numbers where you found text evidence.

What is Celia's opinion about the country at the beginning of the story?

As she says goodbye, Celia feels _____.

As she and her mother drive to their new home, Celia thinks _____.

Text Evidence

Page(s): _____

Page(s): _____

What is Celia's opinion in the middle of the story?

When her mother lets her explore, Celia _____.

Text Evidence

Page(s): _____

What is Celia's opinion at the end of the story?

After Celia and Jason talk, Celia decides _____.

Text Evidence

Page(s): _____

Group Discussion Present your answers to the group. Cite text evidence to justify your thinking. Listen to and discuss the group's opinions about your answers.

Write Review your notes about "Cow Music." Then write your answer to the Essential Question. Use text evidence to support your answer. Use vocabulary words from this week's reading in your writing.

How does Celia's opinion about the country change because of her experiences?

As she says goodbye to her friends, Celia _____.

As she and her mother drive to the country, Celia _____
_____.

When her mother lets her explore, Celia _____
_____.

After she meets Jason, Celia _____
_____.

Share Writing Present your writing to the class. Discuss their opinions. Think about what the class has to say. Did they justify their claims? Explain why you agree or disagree with their claims.

I agree that _____.

I disagree with _____ because _____.

23

Write to Sources

Teresa

Take Notes About the Text I took notes on the idea web to answer the question: *What was Celia's mood on the car ride to the country?*

pages 18–21

Detail
Celia rode a while in silence.

Detail
Celia said glumly, "Yeah, it'll be great. I couldn't be happier."

Main Idea
Celia was not in a good mood on the car ride.

Detail
Her mom asked Celia not to be sarcastic.

Detail
Celia said the cows were harmless and boring, like everything in the country.

Write About the Text I used notes from my idea web to write an email from Celia's mom, Mia, to her friend, Paula, describing Celia's mood on the car ride to the country.

Student Model: Narrative Text

Hello Paula,

Celia and I drove from the city to the country today. Unfortunately, Celia was not in a good mood on the car ride. At the beginning of the trip, she rode a while in silence. I told her that we were starting a new adventure. She responded to me glumly. She said, "I couldn't be happier." I asked her not to be sarcastic. Later, as we drove past cows in a pasture, she said cows were boring, like everything else in the country. I hope she feels happier soon.

Your friend,

Mia

TALK ABOUT IT

Text Evidence
Draw a box around a sentence that comes from the notes. Did Teresa use this information as the main idea or a detail? Why?

Grammar
Circle a past-tense verb. Why does Teresa use past-tense verbs to write the e-mail?

Condense Ideas
Underline the sentence with the word *glumly*. How can you combine this sentence with the sentence after it to condense the ideas?

Your Turn

Write an email from Celia to her friend Hana about how her perception of the country has changed.

>> Go Digital!
Write your response online. Use your editing checklist.

TALK ABOUT IT

Weekly Concept Alliances

? Essential Question
Why do people form alliances?

›› Go Digital

 What are the brothers doing in the photo? What do they agree to do? What do they want? How does an alliance help them? Write words in the chart to explain.

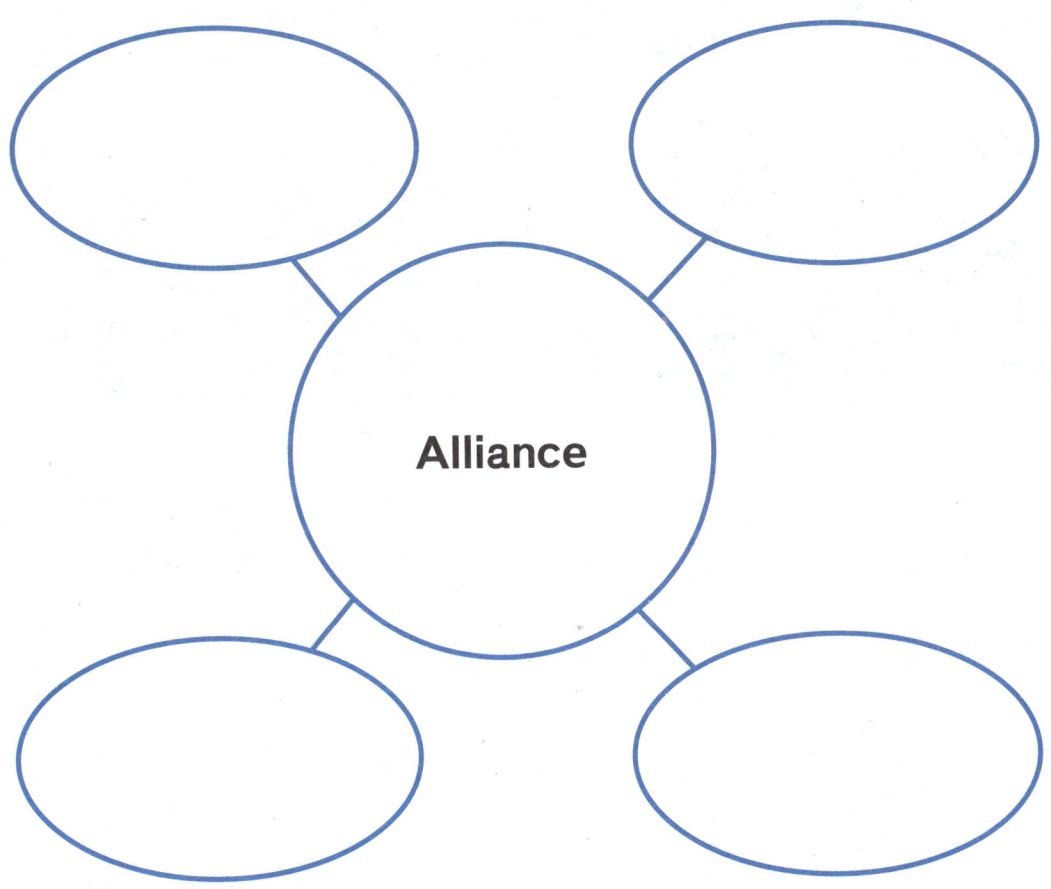

Discuss the alliance the brothers have made. Use words from the chart. Complete these sentences.

The brothers show they agree by _____.

They will _____ to get _____.

Working together helps them _____.

27

More Vocabulary

 Look at the picture and read the word. Then read the sentence. Talk about the word with a partner. Write your own sentence.

barely

Jordan **barely** won the final race.

I *barely* won _____

_____.

involved

The volunteers are **involved** in cleaning up the beach.

I would like to be *involved* in _____

_____.

loyalty

The dog shows **loyalty** to its owner.

I show my *loyalty* to _____ when I

_____.

resolve

The runner has the **resolve** to finish the race.

I have the *resolve* to _____

_____.

sympathetic

Fran is **sympathetic** to the new student.

I am *sympathetic* to _____

_____ .

wary

He is **wary** of flying in an airplane.

I am *wary* of _____

_____ .

Words and Phrases
stand and *stand by*

stand = a group of plants
The animals hid in a <u>stand</u> of trees.

stand by = to do nothing
We will <u>stand by</u> until the train leaves.

Read the sentences below. Write the word or words that mean the same as the underlined words.

I saw a <u>group</u> of sunflowers by the road.

I saw a _____ of sunflowers by the road.

Please <u>do nothing</u> until the firefighters arrive.

Please _____ until the firefighters arrive.

» Go Digital Add these words to your New Words notebook. Write a sentence to show the meaning of each.

Text Evidence

Shared Read | Genre • Historical Fiction

1 Talk About It

Read the title. Talk about what you see. Write your ideas.

What does the title tell you?

_____

_____

_____

What do you notice about the soldier in the illustration?

_____

_____

_____

What do you notice about the girl in the illustration?

_____

_____

_____

Take notes as you read the story.

Drumbeat of Freedom

Essential Question

? Why do people form alliances?

Read how a brother and sister form an alliance with a soldier in the War of Independence.

On a cold December evening in 1777, the deep blue curtain of night had begun to drop over the snow-covered hills and fields of Valley Forge, Pennsylvania. As always at this time, Sarah Bock lit a lantern and walked to the barn to check on the animals. Though she had only just turned twelve, she shouldered many responsibilities on her family's farm.

As she crossed the yard, Sarah could see smoke rising above the encampment **barely** a mile away. She had often wondered about General George Washington and his Continental Army wintering there. The soldiers faced great adversity during this bitterly cold winter. They were poorly clothed, and many were hungry or ill.

Sarah hurried toward the barn to seek refuge from the wind that bit at her cheeks. She took a shortcut through a stand of spindly trees. Their thin branches could barely support the weight of the snow. Suddenly, she saw something that made her heart leap to her throat. A trail of footprints led from the trees to the barn. Some were smudged with blood.

When Sarah reached the barn, she took a few **wary** steps inside. All at once, the lantern's glow caught a shadowy figure **huddled** in the corner. Sarah held her breath and slowly stepped backward, her heart pounding. Just as she made it back to the barn door, she heard a young man's voice.

"Don't be afraid," the man said, limping barefoot out of the shadows. "I will do you no harm."

"Who are you?" Sarah asked. There was fear in her voice, but the sight of this poor soldier, half starved and hurt, had already lessened her alarm.

"My name is Charles Kent," he said. "I'm stationed with General Washington. The men are starving. Might you spare a little food?"

In recent weeks, word had spread that some of the soldiers had taken to begging. Not all of the farm families were **sympathetic** to their cause, however. Sarah's own father had told her he wasn't sure the soldiers could succeed in this conflict with the British. He didn't want anyone in his family to become **involved** in the war.

Text Evidence

❶ Comprehension
Character, Setting, Plot

Read the first paragraph. Underline the words that tell about Sarah's role in her family.

❷ Specific Vocabulary

Read the fourth paragraph. When people are huddled, they sit with their hands and legs close to their body. Why is the soldier huddled in the corner of the barn?

_____

_____

❸ Sentence Structure

Read the second sentence of the sixth paragraph. Circle the words that show a contrast or a change in how Sarah feels. How did Sarah's feelings change? Why?

_____

_____

31

Text Evidence

1. Sentence Structure

Read the second sentence of the first paragraph. Circle the word that connects two choices for Sarah. Underline her first choice. Draw a box around her second choice.

2. Comprehension
Character, Setting, Plot

Read the fourth paragraph through the seventh paragraph. How do John's feelings about the war change?

_____
_____
_____

3. Specific Vocabulary

Read the seventh paragraph. When something is erased, it is completely gone. What erased the anger from John's face? Draw a box around the phrase.

Sarah had a difficult decision to make. Should she obey her father, or should she help the soldiers? A moment later, Sarah spoke in a quiet voice. "I can see how hungry you are. Stay here. I'll try to smuggle out some of the salt beef we keep in our cellar for hard times." Sarah ran back to the house, and a short time later she returned to the barn with the food hidden under her cloak.

After that first night, Charles came back to the barn many times. Sarah would bring him beef or bread when she went out to do her evening chores.

One evening, Sarah had time to sit with Charles while he ate. He began to reminisce about his family back home. He spoke about life in the army and why he felt this fight for freedom was a worthy one.

Suddenly, they heard a creak. It was the barn door. Sarah jumped to her feet as her 18-year-old brother John walked in. She saw surprise and then anger cross his face. Before he could say a word, Sarah swiftly introduced her new friend.

"But Sarah, you know Father doesn't want us involved in this war," John scolded. Then, a bit uncertainly, he added, "This fight is none of our business."

"I know that's how Father feels," she answered. "But I believe the war is important. These men are fighting for us, for our freedom. We can't just stand by while they suffer from hunger and disease. How is it fair that soldiers fighting for such a just cause should have these harsh conditions inflicted on them?"

Sarah's brave words erased the anger from her brother's face. John hesitated a moment and then sat down with Sarah and Charles. He listened eagerly to the soldier's tales of battles against the British. Later that night, John brought Charles a pair of old shoes to wear.

Soon, the harsh winter melted away into spring, and Sarah noticed that the army encampment seemed increasingly busy with activity. The troops, who had been held prisoners by the cold, were breaking free from the confinement of their winter quarters. Were they getting ready to fight the British again?

Sarah knew John was sneaking away to speak with the soldiers, and she was sure he had formed an alliance with Charles and the others. Now, when Sarah and John knew their parents couldn't hear, they even spoke about their growing **loyalty** to the cause of independence.

One sunny morning in June, Sarah awoke to the steady thump of drumbeats echoing through the sleepy valley like a heartbeat. She dressed quickly and ran outside to join her parents. Just beyond the farm, General Washington's troops were marching out of Valley Forge. Though their uniforms were tattered, they all stood as straight as arrows. They had retrieved the **resolve** that had been tested during the long, difficult winter.

Sarah suddenly realized that her brother was missing. "Where is John?" she asked. Without answering, her mother stifled a sob and wiped tears from her eyes. A feeling of worry rose in Sarah's heart, but it was mixed with pride.

Just then, more soldiers strode by. In their ranks were John and Charles. When John waved, Sarah could see in his eyes that he was a true supporter of the cause. Now Sarah stood straight and tall. She waved to her brother as he marched away to the drumbeat of freedom.

Make Connections

Talk about the alliance that changes Sarah's understanding of the events unfolding near her home. **ESSENTIAL QUESTION**

Compare the alliance that Sarah forms to one you have formed in your own life. **TEXT TO SELF**

Text Evidence

1 Comprehension
Character, Setting, Plot

Read the second paragraph. How did the soldiers marching out of Valley Forge look? How did they feel? Underline the two sentences that tell you.

2 Sentence Structure

Read the third paragraph. Circle the subject of the third sentence. Then underline two things the subject of this sentence did.

3 Talk About It

Describe how Sarah feels when she sees that her brother John has joined General Washington's army. Justify your answer.

_____

_____

_____

33

Respond to the Text

Partner Discussion Work with a partner. Answer the questions. Discuss what you learned about "Drumbeat of Freedom." Write the page numbers where you found text evidence.

Why did Sarah form an alliance with Charles?	Text Evidence
One evening, Sarah saw _____.	Page(s): _____
That night, Sarah _____.	Page(s): _____
Another evening, Sarah _____.	Page(s): _____

Why did John form an alliance with Charles?	Text Evidence
At first, John _____.	Page(s): _____
But then John _____.	Page(s): _____
In the spring, John _____.	Page(s): _____

Group Discussion Present your answers to the group. Cite text evidence to justify your thinking. Listen to and discuss the group's opinions about your answers.

Write Review your notes about "Drumbeat of Freedom." Then write your answer to the Essential Question. Use text evidence to support your answer. Use vocabulary words from this week's reading in your writing.

Why did Sarah and John form an alliance with Charles?

Sarah became involved when _____.

Then she _____.

John changed his mind about the war after he _____.

Both Sarah and John grew to believe that _____.

Share Writing Present your writing to the class. Discuss their opinions. Think about what the class has to say. Did they justify their claims? Explain why you agree or disagree with their claims.

I agree that _____.

I disagree with _____ because _____.

35

Write to Sources

pages 30–33

Take Notes About the Text I took notes on the idea web to answer the question: *Is it wrong for the soldiers to beg for food from the farmers?*

Evidence
The men stationed with Washington are starving.

Evidence
Some men are begging for food.

Claim
It is not wrong for the soldiers to beg for food from the farmers.

Evidence
They are not stealing.

Evidence
The farmers can decide whether to help the soldiers.

Write About the Text I used notes from my idea web to write an argument about whether it is wrong for the soldiers to beg for food from the farmers.

Student Model: Argument

It is not wrong for the soldiers to beg for food from the farmers. The men stationed with General George Washington are starving. As a result, some of them are begging for food. They are not stealing food. In addition, the farmers can decide whether to help the soldiers. The soldiers are just asking for food to stay alive. That is not wrong.

TALK ABOUT IT

Text Evidence
Draw a box around the sentence with the word *starving*. Why does Miles use the word *starving* to justify his argument?

Grammar
Circle the noun phrase that begins the second sentence. Why does Miles use this phrase as the subject of the sentence?

Connect Ideas
Underline the last two sentences. How can you combine these two sentences to connect the ideas?

Your Turn

Was it wrong for Sarah to help Charles Kent? Use details from the story to support your argument.

>> *Go Digital!*
Write your response online. Use your editing checklist.

TALK ABOUT IT

Weekly Concept Environments

? Essential Question
How do life forms vary in different environments?

>> Go Digital

 **COLLABORATE** The photo shows the shady canopy layer in a rainforest. Describe what you see in this layer. Write words in the chart.

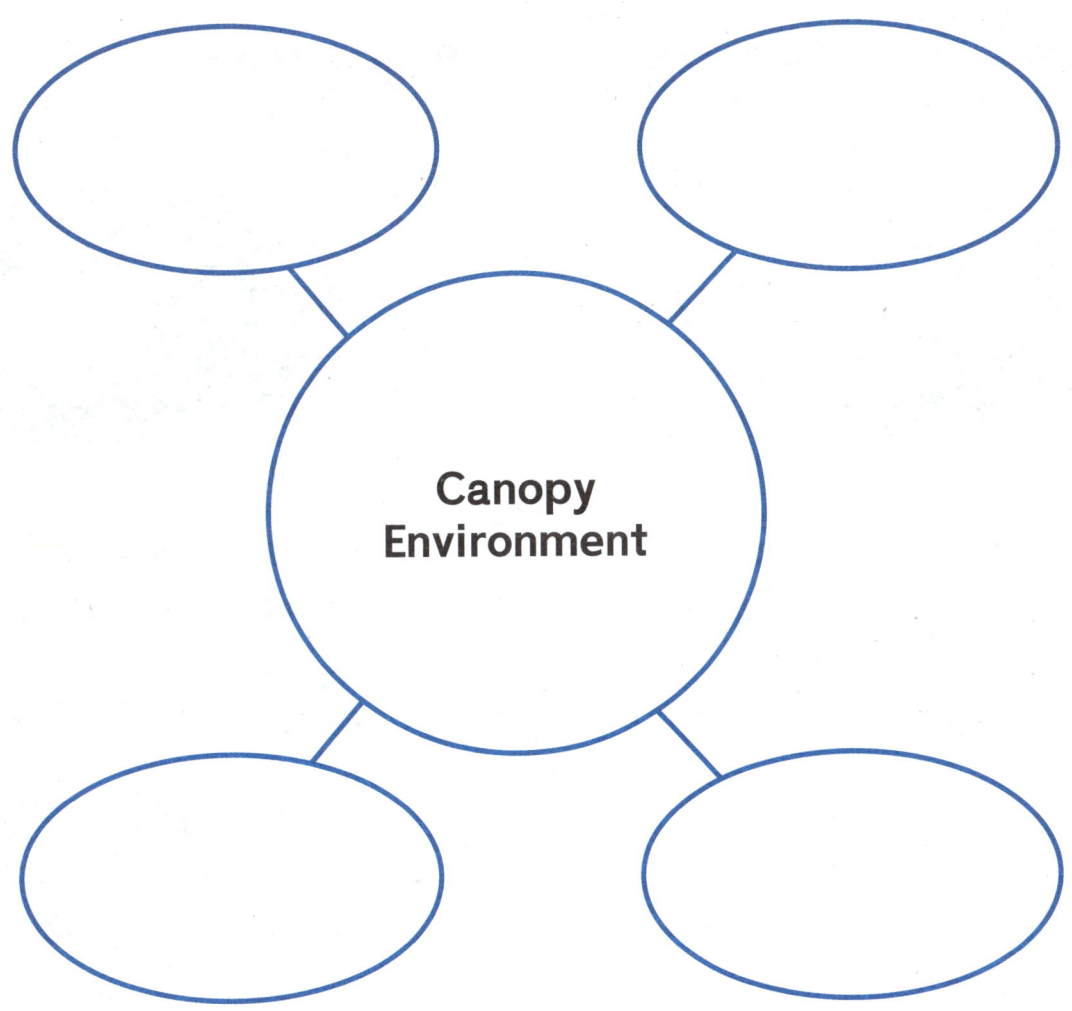

Discuss the frog and its environment. Use the words from the chart. You can say:

The canopy environment has _____. The frog

can live there because it _____.

More Vocabulary

 Look at the picture and read the word. Then read the sentences. Talk about the word with a partner. Write your own sentence.

detect

The animals can **detect** sounds far away.

I can *detect* _____

_____ with my eyes closed.

outermost

Neptune is the **outermost** planet.

From my town, the *outermost* place I have

visited is _____.

envelops

A fog **envelops** the city.

Another word for *envelops* is _____

_____.

protected

The castle is **protected** by a high wall.

My home is *protected* by _____

_____.

40

steep

He is skiing down the **steep** mountain.

After I climb *steep* places, I feel _____

_____.

vulnerable

These houses are **vulnerable** to flooding.

I _____ so that I am not *vulnerable*

to _____.

Words and Phrases
Comparative Adjectives

A comparative adjective compares two people, places, or things. We add *–er* to form the comparative adjective. We use the word *than* after a comparative adjective.

cool + *er* = **cooler**
Fall is cool.
Winter is <u>cooler</u> than fall.

deep + *er* = **deeper**
The river is deep.
The ocean is <u>deeper</u> than the river.

Read the sentences below. Underline the comparative adjective in each sentence.

Brazil is warmer than Canada.

A rabbit is faster than a turtle.

Write your own sentences using *cooler* and *deeper*.

_____

_____.

» Go Digital Add these comparative adjectives to your New Words notebook. Include your sentences.

Text Evidence

Shared Read Genre • Expository Text

1 Talk About It

Read the title. Talk about what you see. Write your ideas.

What does the title tell you about this text?

_____
_____
_____
_____

What does the photograph show?

_____
_____
_____
_____

Take notes as you read the text.

The Secret World of Caves

Essential Question

? How do life forms vary in different environments?

Read how plant and animal life varies in different parts of caves.

42

In the Mouth of the Cave

Stepping into a cave is like entering an entirely new world. The environment is suddenly cooler and damper. Though there is some light here, it is dimmer than the light outside. There is a sense of stillness and quiet. This **outermost** area is called the *entrance zone*. It is a hallway leading to the many secrets of life in a cave.

An animal that uses the entrance zone of a cave belongs to the classification known as *trogloxenes*. Creatures in this category may seek shelter in caves but don't spend their whole life cycles in them. They also spend time on the surface. Some entrance zone organisms are called *accidentals* because they often find their way in accidentally. These cave guests stay for a while but not for long.

Bats are among the most common trogloxenes. Hanging upside down from a cave's ceiling, they are **protected** and sleep undisturbed. Bats also hibernate this way during the coldest months. In warm months, bats search for food outside the cave.

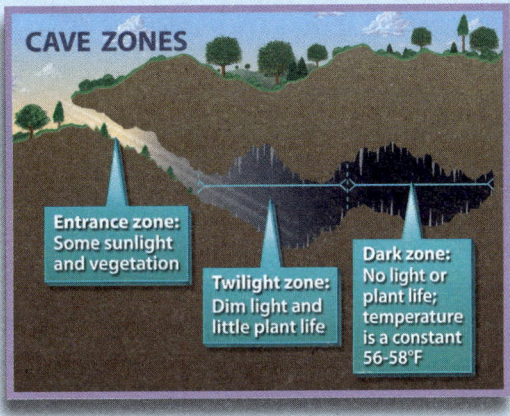

CAVE ZONES
- Entrance zone: Some sunlight and vegetation
- Twilight zone: Dim light and little plant life
- Dark zone: No light or plant life; temperature is a constant 56-58°F

Other species make use of the entrance zone for protection, too. Pack rats build nests using twigs and leaves from the outside. Their big eyes and long whiskers help in maneuvering through the dim light. Small gray birds called phoebes seek safety inside cave doorways. They make their nests in a compartment, or nook, in the cave walls. These small spaces hide the birds from animals that prey on them.

Text Evidence

❶ Comprehension
Main Idea and Details

Reread the first paragraph. Underline the details that describe the air, light, and sound in the entrance zone.

❷ Specific Vocabulary

Read the third paragraph. *Hibernate* means "to spend the winter sleeping." How do bats hibernate during the coldest months?

_____

_____

❸ Talk About It

Circle the names of three animals that live in the entrance zone. Explain how each animal is well adapted for the entrance zone. Then write your ideas.

_____

_____

_____

Text Evidence

1 Comprehension
Main Idea and Details

Read the first paragraph. How is the *twilight zone* different from the *entrance zone*? Underline the details that describe the light. Circle the details that describe the air.

2 Talk About It

Explain how animals in the *twilight zone* and animals in the *entrance zone* use caves in different ways. Then write your ideas.

_____

_____

3 Sentence Structure

Reread the first two sentences in the fourth paragraph. Circle the conjunction that signals surprising information. Then draw a box around the information that is surprising or unexpected.

Twilight Time

Deeper inside a cave, the walls and ceiling obscure most of the light from outside. This shadowy area is known as the twilight *zone*. The light in this zone is so dim that everything appears to be bathed in a bluish glow. This part of a cave feels even damper and cooler than the entrance zone.

Animals that rely on the environment of the twilight zone are called *troglophiles*. Their eyesight is often poor, and they usually have less colorful bodies than animals living outside of caves. These creatures spend their entire life cycles inside moist caves, but many can also survive in similar habitats outside of caves. Animals commonly found living in the twilight zones of caves are centipedes, fish, beetles, earthworms, and spiders.

Some twilight zone animals live submerged under water. This spring cavefish lives on microscopic organisms.

Totally in the Dark

Deeper still inside a cave, beyond the twilight zone, is the *dark zone*. Here passageways are flanked on either side by **steep** stone walls. There is no light at all. Darkness engulfs this place, and moist air **envelops** everything.

It is hard to believe that any animals could live their whole lives in total darkness. Yet many strange creatures live in the dark zones of caves. These animals, known as *troglobites*, include rare species of frogs, salamanders, spiders, worms, insects, and crabs. Cave biologists believe that these unusual creatures are distantly related to animals that once lived near caves. But they look only slightly similar to their surface relatives. Troglobites even need food that is unavailable outside of caves.

This salamander is sightless.

Troglobites are adapted to living with the absence of light. Most of them are completely sightless. So it is only logical that these unusual cave dwellers have heightened senses of smell and touch. For example, their bodies can **detect** the slightest vibrations. They can also sense changes in the air pressure around them. When something is moving nearby, these creatures can feel it. This special ability helps them catch food. It also helps them avoid becoming another animal's meal.

Most troglobites have ghostly white skin. Some even have skin you can see through. They don't need pigment in their skin to protect them from the sun's rays. And they don't need skin coloring to help them blend in with their surroundings for safety. These unusual adaptations mean that troglobites can never leave the dark zones of caves.

Scientists now know that cave animals are **vulnerable** to even minor changes in their environment. So their work includes protecting these least known and fascinating creatures.

This crayfish has see-through skin.

Make Connections

? Talk about how different life forms are well suited to living in each of the three cave zones.
ESSENTIAL QUESTION

What other animals have you seen or learned about that live in unusual habitats? **TEXT TO SELF**

Text Evidence

❶ Talk About It

Describe how creatures that live in the dark zone of a cave are adapted to living in a zone with no light. Then write your ideas.

_____

_____

❷ Specific Vocabulary

Reread the second paragraph. Underline the word that is a synonym for *pigment*. Then use phrases from the paragraph to describe what skin without pigment might look like.

_____

_____

❸ Sentence Structure

Read the first sentence of the last paragraph. Circle the part of the sentence that tells what scientists now know about animals that live in caves.

45

Respond to the Text

 **Partner Discussion** Work with a partner. Answer the questions. Discuss what you learned about "The Secret World of Caves." Write the page numbers where you found text evidence.

Describe the animals in the entrance zone of a cave.	Text Evidence
I read that these animals _____.	Page(s): _____
These animals use caves _____.	Page(s): _____

Describe the animals in the twilight zone of a cave.	Text Evidence
I read that these animals _____.	Page(s): _____
These animals spend _____.	Page(s): _____

Describe the animals in the dark zone of a cave.	Text Evidence
The text says these animals _____.	Page(s): _____
The author says these animals _____.	Page(s): _____

 **Group Discussion** Present your answers to the group. Cite text evidence to justify your thinking. Listen to and discuss the group's opinions about your answers.

Write Review your notes about "The Secret World of Caves." Then write your answer to the Essential Question. Use text evidence to support your answer. Use vocabulary words from this week's reading in your writing.

How are different animals well adapted to living in each of the three cave zones?

Animals in the entrance zone _____

_____.

Animals in the twilight zone _____

_____.

Animals in the dark zone _____

_____.

Share Writing Present your writing to the class. Discuss their opinions. Think about what the class has to say. Did they justify their claims? Explain why you agree or disagree with their claims.

I agree with _____ that _____.

I disagree with _____ because _____.

Write to Sources

Tyler

Take Notes About the Text I took notes on the idea web to answer the question: *How does the author help us understand what* trogloxenes *means?*

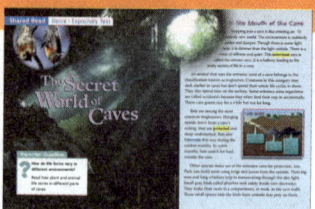

pages 42–45

Word
trogloxenes

Definition
Trogloxenes is "a classification of animals that use the entrance zone of caves."

Examples
Bats are among the most common; other species include pack rats and small gray birds called *phoebes*.

Explanation
The animals may seek shelter in caves but don't spend their whole life cycles in them. They also spend time on the surface.

Write About the Text I used notes from my idea web to write a paragraph about how the author helps us understand what *trogloxenes* means.

Student Model: *Informative Text*

The author uses three ways to help us understand what *trogloxenes* means. First, the author defines the word. The author defines *trogloxenes* as a "classification for animals that live in the entrance zone of caves." Then the author includes an explanation about the animals. The author explains that trogloxenes don't spend their whole life cycles in caves. They spend some time on the surface. Finally, the author gives examples of trogloxenes, including bats, pack rats, and small gray birds called *phoebes*.

TALK ABOUT IT

Text Evidence
Draw a box around a sentence that comes from the notes. Why did Tyler use the sentence as a supporting detail?

Grammar
Circle a present-tense verb. Why does Tyler use present-tense verbs to write about the author's text?

Condense Ideas
Underline the second and third sentences. How can you combine these sentences to condense the ideas?

Your Turn

How does the diagram of the Cave Zones help us understand the text better?

>> *Go Digital!*
Write your response online. Use your editing checklist.

TALK ABOUT IT

Weekly Concept Dynamic Earth

? Essential Question
How do natural forces affect Earth?

>> *Go Digital*

COLLABORATE What change in Earth's surface does the photo show? Why is this happening? Write words in the chart to describe what is happening.

```
   (         )          (         )
        \                  /
         \                /
          \              /
           (   Volcano   )
          /              \
         /                \
        /                  \
   (         )          (         )
```

Discuss how a volcano changes Earth's surface. Use the words from the chart. Complete the sentence.

A volcanic eruption changes Earth's surface when _____

_____.

More Vocabulary

Look at the picture and read the word. Then read the sentence. Talk about the word with a partner. Write your own sentence.

catastrophic

The damage from the hurricane was **catastrophic**.

Another example of a *catastrophic* event is

_____.

erupting

The volcano is **erupting**.

An *erupting* volcano causes _____

_____.

fascinated

The boy is **fascinated** by the small lizard.

I am *fascinated* by _____

_____.

increase

The store had an **increase** in customers during the sale.

I would like to see an *increase* in _____

_____.

probability

The **probability** of rain is high.

Today, the *probability* of _____

is _____.

terrifying

That was a **terrifying** scene in the movie.

Another word for *terrifying* is _____.

Words and Phrases
Suffix *-ion*

A suffix is a word part added to the end of a base word. The suffix *–ion* means "an act or process." Adding *–ion* to a verb changes the verb to a noun. Sometimes, there is a spelling change.

erupt + ion = eruption
The volcanic eruption caused damage.

evacuate + ion = evacuation
The evacuation of the building was quick.

Read the sentences below. Write the noun form of each underlined word.

We hope the volcano doesn't erupt.

We hope the volcano doesn't have an _____.

The mayor will evacuate the town because of the flood.

The town will have an _____ because of the flood.

» Go Digital Add these words to your New Words notebook. Write a sentence to show the meaning of each.

53

Text Evidence

Shared Read | Genre • Narrative Nonfiction

1 Talk About It

Read the title. Talk about what you see. Write your ideas.

What does the title tell you?

_____
_____
_____

What does the photograph show?

_____
_____
_____

Take notes as you read the text.

The MONSTER in the MOUNTAIN

Essential Question

? How do natural forces affect Earth?

Read how a scientist studies forces that cause volcanic activity at Mount Vesuvius.

54

Meet Marta Ramírez

As a young girl during World War II, Marta Ramírez saw newsreels that showed B-25 airplanes flying near the smoky plume of a volcanic eruption. The year was 1944, and Mount Vesuvius in Italy was erupting! Blankets of burning ash were seen smothering the airplanes. Shards of volcanic rock came plummeting from the sky. Soldiers on the ground ran for cover. Each glowing splinter of rock was like a deadly bullet.

Those images never left Marta. She has been fascinated by volcanoes ever since. When she got older, Marta earned degrees in geology and volcanology. Though she has studied many of the world's volcanoes, she returns again and again to Mount Vesuvius. Marta has climbed down into its smoking crater many times. In the following memoir, she describes one of her visits and why this volcano still inspires her work.

At the Monster's Mouth

I recently went to see this dynamic volcano again. I decided to climb its slope along with the dozens of curious tourists visiting that day. As we walked, our shoes crunched on cinders that had been dropped there long ago. Finally reaching the rim, we gazed at the spectacular view. We stared 800 feet down into the crater. It was quiet for now, but I knew it was only sleeping. Frequent tremors and small earthquakes prove that this monster is not dead. Did the others standing there with me know about the danger beneath their feet?

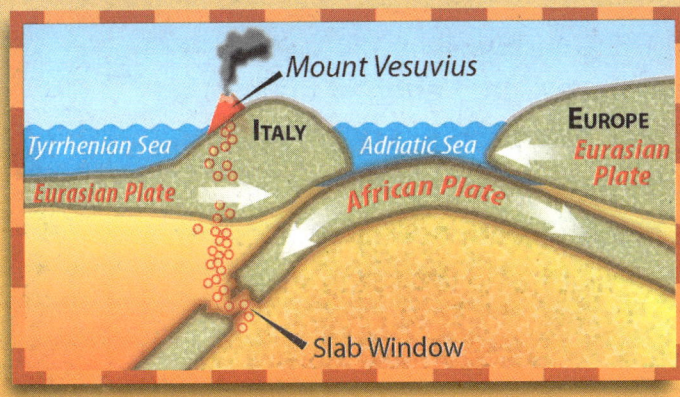

This model shows how Mount Vesuvius formed where one plate of Earth's crust pushes against another. Molten rock at this collision point exerts pressure upward until lava explodes from the volcano.

Text Evidence

❶ Sentence Structure ⒶⒸⓉ

Read the first sentence. Circle the comma. Underline the two prepositional phrases before the comma. Draw a box around the name of the "young girl" in this sentence.

❷ Specific Vocabulary ⒶⒸⓉ

Reread the second paragraph. A *crater* is a "round opening at the top of a volcano." Why did Marta climb down into the smoking crater?

_____

_____

❸ Comprehension
Main Idea and Key Details

Read the third paragraph. How does Marta know that Mount Vesuvius is only "sleeping" and "not dead"? Underline two details that tell you.

Text Evidence

1. Sentence Structure

Read the last two sentences in the first paragraph. Underline the noun phrase that the pronoun *it* refers to.

2. Talk About It

Explain how Mount Vesuvius has affected nearby cities in the past. Then write about it.

_____

_____

3. Specific Vocabulary

Reread the third paragraph. Circle the word *seismographs*. Underline the sentence that helps you understand what seismographs are and what they do.

Every time I see this volcano up close, I think about how it had roared like a lion back in 1944. The trembling earth shook buildings for miles around, and streams of scalding lava flowed down the sides. Like glowing red fingers, they stretched out to crush defenseless homes below. It must have been **terrifying** to witness in person. Today, the lava that once cascaded down the mountain is hard and dry. It looks a bit like the skin of an elephant.

When the Monster Awakens

There is a lot of documentation of Vesuvius's past. Geologists have gathered this evidence of earlier eruptions by studying the rocks that were formed. Before 1944, the most **catastrophic** eruption occurred in 79 A.D. A Roman writer named Pliny the Younger described it in detail in his letters. On the morning of that tragic day, no one guessed that an enormous volcanic explosion was about to pulverize tons of rock and send it raining down on the city. People couldn't know that thick, dark ash and fiery lava would completely destroy the nearby cities of Pompeii and Herculaneum. By evening, few people had survived.

Many smaller eruptions have occurred since then, including the one in 1944. Volcanologists believe that another major eruption could occur at any time. The **probability** grows with each passing year. To watch for geological changes within Vesuvius, we have set up **seismographs** on the slopes of its cone. These instruments measure the slightest shifts in the rock beneath the mountain.

During one dangerous but exciting mission, I climbed down into the crater itself. My crew and I worked on mapping what was going on underground. We also measured the gases leaking from small vents. Any sudden increase in carbon dioxide and other gases might signal an eruption.

Looking Ahead

I don't go into the crater anymore, but I often think about how Vesuvius threatens the environment around it. Today, the city of Naples lies at the foot of Mount Vesuvius. If an eruption occurred tomorrow, the city would not be ready. Tons of ash and rock would once more be hurled into the air. This volcanic debris would keep cars, planes, and trains from operating. People would try escaping on foot. Sadly, no one can outrun such an eruption.

The only sure way to protect people who live near this volcano is to give them enough warning. The city of Naples has detailed evacuation plans. For the plans to work, however, officials need to be warned seven days before an eruption occurs. I hope the work that volcanologists do will help to give people the warning they need. Until then, I'll be watching this sleeping monster, just in case it starts to wake up.

Behind Vesuvius are the remains of Mount Somma, a volcano that erupted 25,000 years ago. Vesuvius formed inside Somma's crater.

Make Connections

 Talk about how Earth's natural forces affect the environment around Mount Vesuvius. **ESSENTIAL QUESTION**

What natural occurrences have you experienced that could pose a danger to people? **TEXT TO SELF**

Text Evidence

❶ Specific Vocabulary

Read the last sentence in the first paragraph. The verb *signal* means "to show that something is going to happen." What do scientists look for that might signal an eruption?

_____

_____

❷ Sentence Structure

Read the third sentence in the second paragraph. Circle the comma that breaks the sentence into two parts. Read each part. Underline what would happen if an eruption occurred tomorrow.

❸ Comprehension
Main Idea and Key Details

Read the last paragraph. If there were an eruption, what is the only sure way to protect people who live near Mount Vesuvius? Underline the sentence that tells you.

Respond to the Text

 **Partner Discussion** Work with a partner. Answer the questions. Discuss what you learned about "The Monster in the Mountain." Write the page numbers where you found text evidence.

How did Mount Vesuvius affect Earth when it erupted in 1944?

I read that volcanic rock and scalding lava _____ _____.   Page(s): _____

The trembling earth _____.   Page(s): _____

How did Mount Vesuvius affect Earth when it erupted in 79 A.D.?

I learned that the volcanic explosion caused _____ _____.   Page(s): _____

Based on the text, dark ash and fiery lava _____ _____.   Page(s): _____

I read that few people _____.   Page(s): _____

 **Group Discussion** Present your answers to the group. Cite text evidence to justify your thinking. Listen to and discuss the group's opinions about your answers.

Write Review your notes about "The Monster in the Mountain." Then write your answer to the Essential Question. Use text evidence to support your answer. Use vocabulary words from this week's reading in your writing.

How do volcanoes affect Earth?

When a volcano erupts, it causes the earth _____.

Volcanic rock _____,

and ash and lava _____.

Based on the text, _____ affect Earth because _____.

Share Writing Present your writing to the class. Discuss their opinions. Think about what the class has to say. Did they justify their claims? Explain why you agree or disagree with their claims.

I agree with _____.

I disagree with _____ because _____.

Write to Sources

Abby

Take Notes About the Text I took notes on the idea web to answer the question: *What were the effects of the eruption of Mount Vesuvius in 1944?*

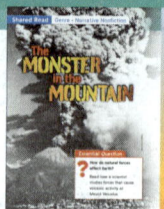
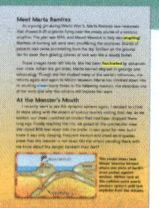

pages 54–57

Effect
The erupting volcano threw burning ash and volcanic rock into the air.

Effect
The ash smothered planes; soldiers ran from the volcanic rock.

Cause
Mount Vesuvius in Italy erupted in 1944.

Effect
The trembling earth shook buildings.

Effect
The lava flowed down the mountain and destroyed homes.

60

Write About the Text I used notes from my idea web to write a paragraph about the effects of the eruption of Mount Vesuvius in 1944.

Student Model: *Informative Text*

The effects of the eruption of Mount Vesuvius in Italy in 1944 were devastating. The erupting volcano threw burning ash and volcanic rock into the air. The burning ash smothered planes; soldiers on the ground ran from the volcanic rock. The trembling earth shook buildings for miles around. The scalding lava flowed down the sides of the mountain and destroyed homes.

TALK ABOUT IT

Text Evidence

Draw a box around a sentence that comes from the notes. Does Abby use the sentence as the main idea or a supporting detail? Why?

Grammar

Circle the verb in the first sentence. Why does Abby use the plural form of the verb?

Connect Ideas

Underline the last two sentences. How can you combine these sentences to connect the ideas?

Your Turn

How does the use of text features in "The Monster in the Mountain" add to your understanding of the text? Use text evidence in your writing.

>> *Go Digital!*
Write your response online. Use your editing checklist.

TALK ABOUT IT

Weekly Concept Using Money

? Essential Question
What factors influence how people use money?

>> Go Digital

 What is the man in the photo doing? What things should the man think about to shop wisely? Write your ideas in the chart.

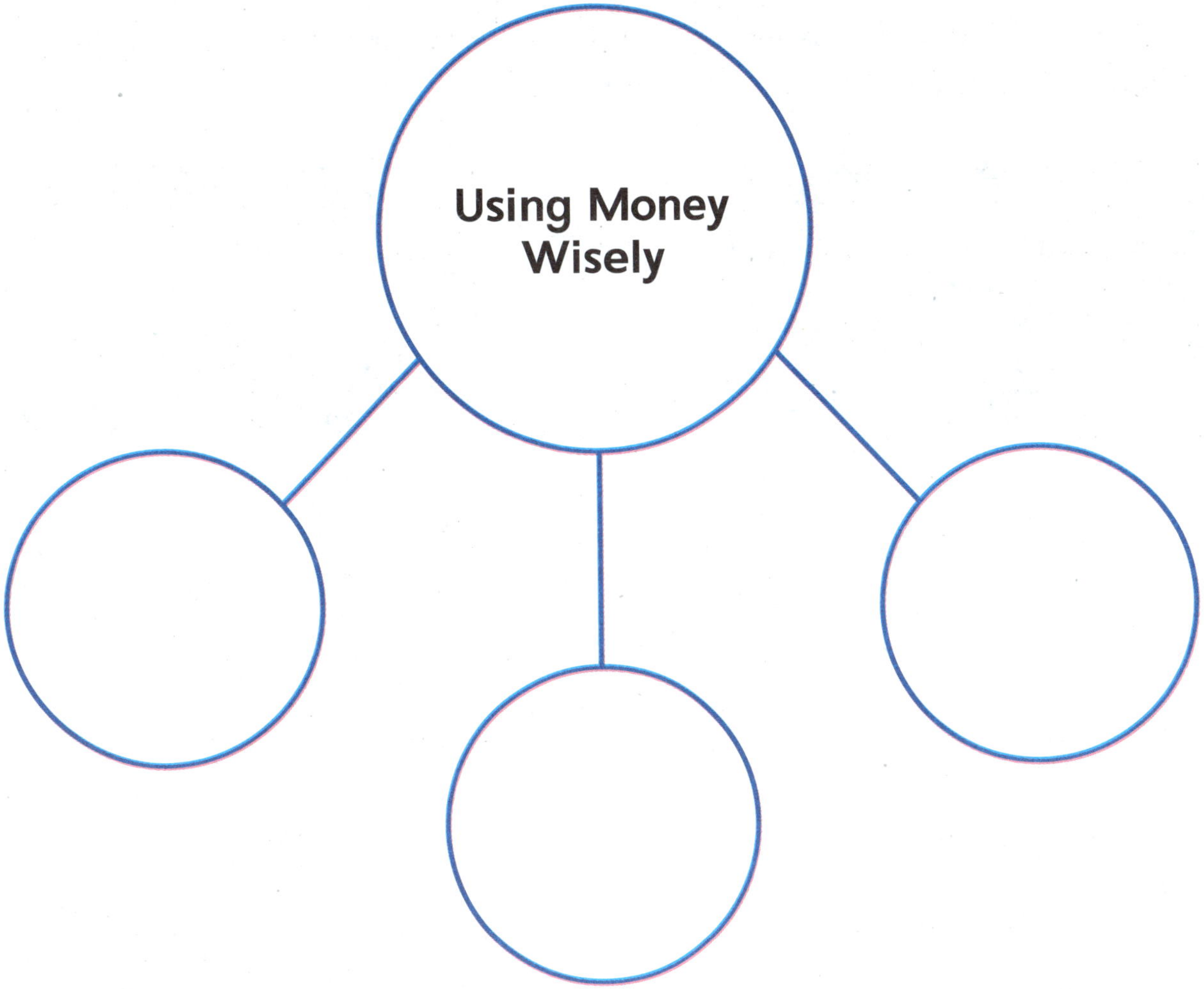

Using Money Wisely

Discuss how the man can shop wisely. Use words from the chart. You can say:

The man can shop wisely by _____

_____.

More Vocabulary

 Look at the picture and read the word. Then read the sentences. Talk about the word with a partner. Write your own sentence.

advantage

The tall player has an **advantage** over the short player.

I have an *advantage* over _____

because _____.

exchanging

They enjoy **exchanging** their lunches.

I like *exchanging* _____

with friends because _____.

recent

The **recent** graduate takes a photo of himself and his sister.

A *recent* event that made me happy was

_____.

represent

The colors **represent** different states on the map.

Some items that *represent* good luck are

_____.

64

resemble

The sisters **resemble** each other.

I think _____ *resembles*

_____.

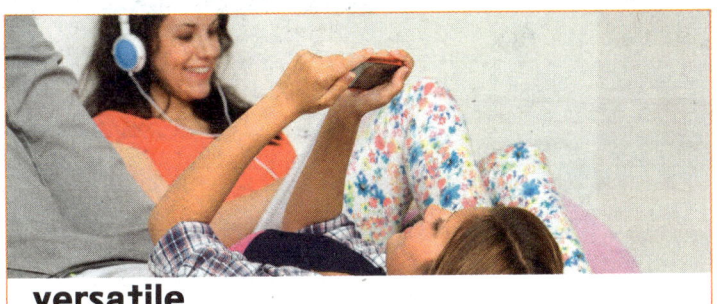
versatile

A cell phone is a **versatile** tool.

I think _____ is a *versatile*

tool because _____.

Words and Phrases
Superlative Adjectives

A superlative adjective compares three or more people, places, or things. We add *–est* to form the superlative adjective. Sometimes, there are spelling changes. We use the word *the* before a superlative adjective.

high + *est* = **highest**
That is the <u>highest</u> building in the city.

rare + *est* = **rarest**
This is the <u>rarest</u> coin in the world.

Read the sentences below. Underline the superlative adjective.

The Gobi bear is the rarest bear in the world.

Mt. Everest is the highest mountain in the world.

Write your own sentences using *highest* and *rarest*.

_____

_____.

» Go Digital Add these superlative adjectives to your New Words notebook. Include your sentences.

Text Evidence

Shared Read Genre • Informational Article

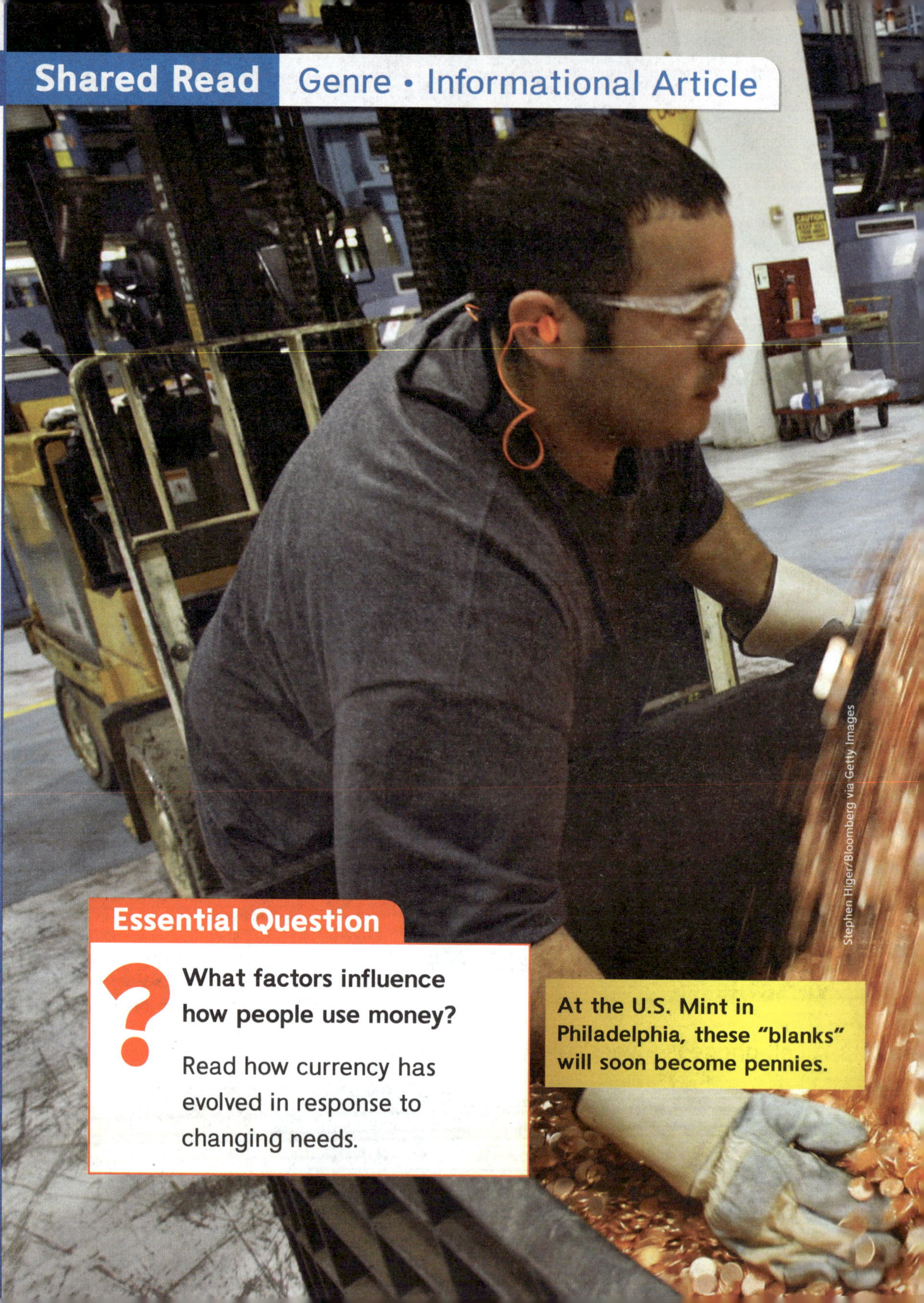

1 Talk About It

Read the title. Talk about what you see. Write your ideas.

What does the title tell you?

_____

_____

_____

_____

What is the man in the photograph doing?

_____

_____

_____

_____

Take notes as you read the text.

Essential Question

What factors influence how people use money?

Read how currency has evolved in response to changing needs.

At the U.S. Mint in Philadelphia, these "blanks" will soon become pennies.

MAKING MONEY
A STORY OF CHANGE

What do cows, sacks of grain, seashells, strings of beads, and swaths of deerskin have in common? They have all been used as money. Currency in the form of coins and bills is a fairly **recent** development. And before there was any currency at all, there was barter.

Let's Make a Deal

Barter is basically a cashless system for **exchanging** goods or services. People likely bartered from the earliest days of human society. Maybe someone was good at making tools but needed help hunting for food. Another person was a good hunter but needed an axe to build a shelter. When they bartered, the toolmaker got help hunting, and the hunter got a new axe. Today, the give-and-take of bartering with a neighbor can be a useful formula for exchanges of goods and services, but most of us use money to buy what we need.

How Many Cows Does That Cost?

About 9000 B.C., humans developed agriculture and started living in communities. They grew crops and raised animals for food. So the first form of currency was probably livestock. People could pay for goods and services with cattle, sheep, goats, pigs, or camels. Grain and other crops served as money, too. As societies developed, however, ships and caravans made a growing inventory of goods available for trade over great distances. Suddenly, big live cows and huge sacks of grain were no longer **practical** to use as currency. People needed money that would not die or spoil after a short time.

Shopping with Shells

About 1200 B.C., the Chinese began using cowrie shells as money. Cowries are animals that live along many coastlines, so people in Africa

Text Evidence

❶ Sentence Structure ACT

Reread the first paragraph. Then circle the commas in the first sentence. Underline each item listed in the sentence. What do these items have in common? Box the sentence that tells you.

❷ Comprehension
Author's Point of View

Read the second paragraph. What is the author's point of view about bartering with a neighbor for goods and services today? Underline the sentence that tells you.

❸ Specific Vocabulary ACT

Read the seventh sentence in the third paragraph. The word *practical* means "useful or suitable for a particular purpose." Why were animals and grains no longer a practical currency?

_____

_____

67

Text Evidence

1. Specific Vocabulary

Read the fourth sentence in the first paragraph under "Metal Money." The expression *before long* means "soon." What type of currency did Asia Minor, Greece, and Rome start using before long?

Before long, _____.

2. Talk About It

Discuss the advantages of metal money. Then write about it.

_____

_____

3. Specific Vocabulary

Read the first sentence in the first paragraph under "Paying with Paper." The verb *developed* means "designed or made a new idea or product." What form of money did the Chinese develop about 100 B.C.?

They developed _____.

and India used this more convenient form of currency, too. On the other side of the world, Native Americans made money by stringing beads carved from clamshells. They called their currency *wampum*.

Wampum is made from quahog clams.

Metal Money

The Chinese were the first to use metal for making currency. At first, they cast bronze or copper into shapes that **resembled** cowrie shells or small tools. These manufactured "coins" later became flat and, eventually, -round. Before long, the use of round metal coins was adopted in other parts of the world, including Asia Minor, Greece, and Rome. Many early coins were stamped with images of animals, deities, or kings.

A number of factors gave metal coins an **advantage** over earlier forms of currency. They lasted a long time, were easily recognized and counted, and had values based on the metals

Examples of coins from the ancient world

from which they were made. The rarest metals, such as silver and gold, had the highest values.

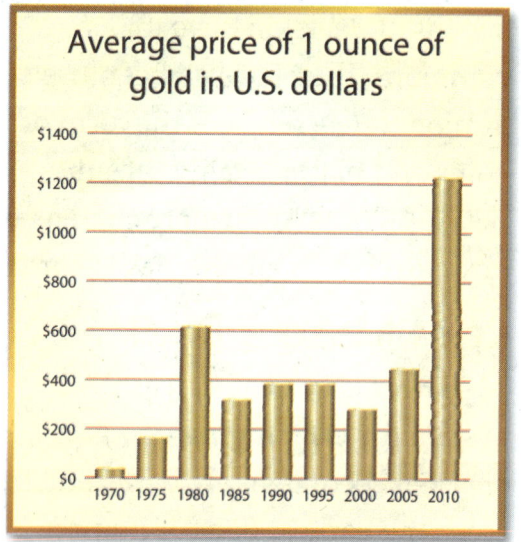

Paying with Paper

The Chinese developed yet another form of money about 100 B.C. It was flat, like today's paper money, but each "bill" was actually made of deerskin. In the seventh century A.D., the Chinese even started printing the very first paper money. Its popularity in China didn't last, but the idea really caught on in Europe by the eighteenth century.

Money Now

The key idea about money today is that it is issued by governments. In the U.S., your one-dollar bill is worth the same as anyone else's. The same is true for the South African *rand*, the Chinese *yuan*, the Brazilian *real*, and the *euro* of the European Union. However, the value of one nation's currency in relation to others can fluctuate daily.

Today's money is far more **versatile** than ancient varieties. In addition to exchanging actual coins and bills, we can write checks that **represent** the money we have in the bank. We also use the least physical form of money: electronic, or computer-based, currency. When employers deposit salaries directly into their workers' bank accounts, or when we charge an online purchase to a debit or credit card, the exchange is made entirely in the digital realm.

Barter or Bucks?

Barter Is Better by Jonah M.

I've learned how to get things I need without spending a dime! Officially, it's called "bartering," but it's as simple as trading what I don't need anymore for something I want. Last week I traded my in-line skates for my friend Robert's guitar. It's a lot like recycling: things you were going to throw away will be used by somebody else. Another way to barter is to trade your time and some work for something you want.

The Case for Cash
by Haylee D.

Cash lets me choose exactly what I want to buy. I can also compare prices of similar items at different stores. I don't always spend my money right away. My mom helped me open a savings account when I was 7 years old. Whenever I receive some cash, I go straight to the bank to deposit at least half of it. Over time, the money I save, and any interest it earns, will help me buy things I wouldn't be able to afford otherwise.

Make Connections

 Talk about how people's changing needs caused them to develop various currencies. **ESSENTIAL QUESTION**

What are some of the different forms of currency you have used to pay for goods and services? **TEXT TO SELF**

Text Evidence

1 Comprehension
Author's Point of View

Read the second paragraph. What is the author's point of view about today's money? Underline the sentence that tells you.

2 Sentence Structure

Read the fourth sentence in the second paragraph. Circle the word that connects the two examples of exchanging money in the digital realm. Underline the examples.

3 Talk About It

Reread "Barter or Bucks?" Describe one benefit of bartering and one benefit of using cash. Then write about it.

When you barter, you can _____

_____.

When you use cash, you can _____

_____.

Respond to the Text

Partner Discussion Work with a partner. Answer the questions. Discuss what you learned about "Making Money: A Story of Change." Write the page numbers where you found text evidence.

How has currency changed?

I read that the first form of currency was probably _____. Page(s): _____

Thousands of years later, the Chinese developed _____ Page(s): _____
_____.

In addition to using coins and bills, people can now _____. Page(s): _____

What factors caused currency to change?

People stopped using animals and grain as money because _____ Page(s): _____
_____.

Metal coins replaced shells and beads because _____. Page(s): _____

Compared to ancient money, today's money is _____. Page(s): _____

Group Discussion Present your answers to the group. Cite text evidence to justify your thinking. Listen to and discuss the group's opinions about your answers.

Write Review your notes about "Making Money: A Story of Change." Then write your answer to the Essential Question. Use text evidence to support your answer. Use vocabulary words from this week's reading in your writing.

What factors influence new forms of currency?

People started using shells and beads because _____
_____.

Metal coins replaced shells and beads because _____
_____.

Therefore, new forms of currency develop when _____
_____.

Share Writing Present your writing to the class. Discuss their opinions. Think about what the class has to say. Did they justify their claims? Explain why you agree or disagree with their claims.

I agree with _____.

I disagree with _____ because _____.

Write to Sources

Victor

pages 66–69

Take Notes About the Text I took notes on the idea web to answer the question: *Is bartering sometimes better than using cash?*

Claim
Sometimes, bartering is better than using cash, especially for kids.

Evidence
Kids don't have a lot of money to buy things.

Evidence
We can trade something we don't need for something we want.

Evidence
We can trade our time for something we want.

Evidence
When we barter, we are helping our environment. Bartering is like recycling.

Write About the Text I used notes from my idea web to write an argument about how bartering is sometimes better than using cash.

Student Model: *Argument*

Sometimes, bartering is better than using cash, especially for kids. First, kids don't have a lot of money. Second, we can trade something we don't need for something we want. For example, we can trade an old skateboard for a friend's ice skates. Third, we can also trade our time for something we need. For example, we can help a friend with homework in exchange for help with hitting a baseball. Last, when we barter, we are helping the environment. Bartering is like recycling.

TALK ABOUT IT

Text Evidence
Draw a box around a sentence that comes from the notes. Does Victor use this sentence as the main idea or a supporting detail? Why?

Grammar
Circle the phrase *for example* in the fourth sentence. Why does Victor use this phrase to begin the sentence?

Connect Ideas
Underline the last two sentences. How can you combine these sentences to connect the ideas?

Your Turn

What is the easiest form of money to use and why? Support your argument with evidence and clear reasons.

>> Go Digital!
Write your response online. Use your editing checklist.

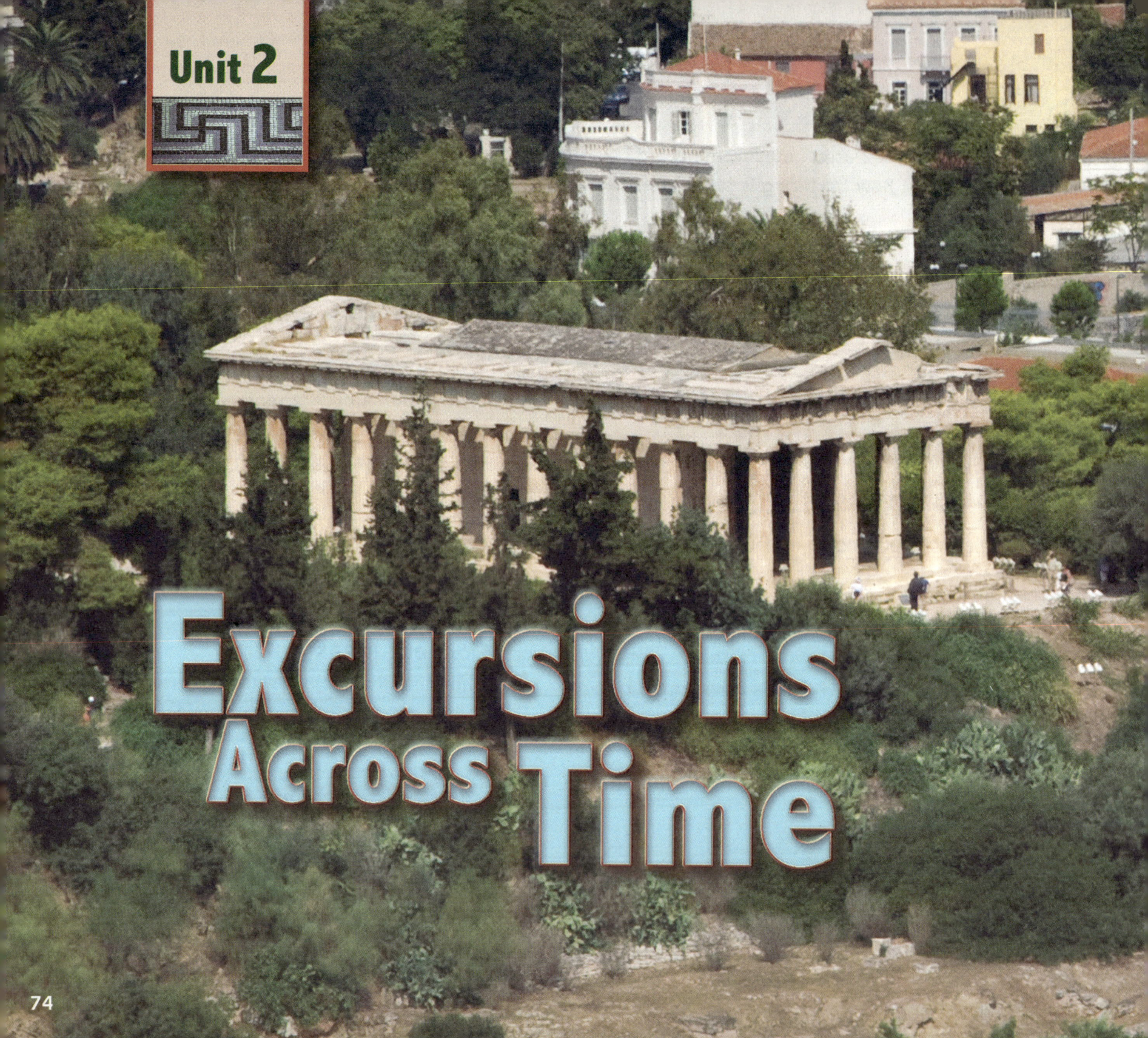

Unit 2

Excursions Across Time

The Big Idea

What can we gain from reading about past civilizations?

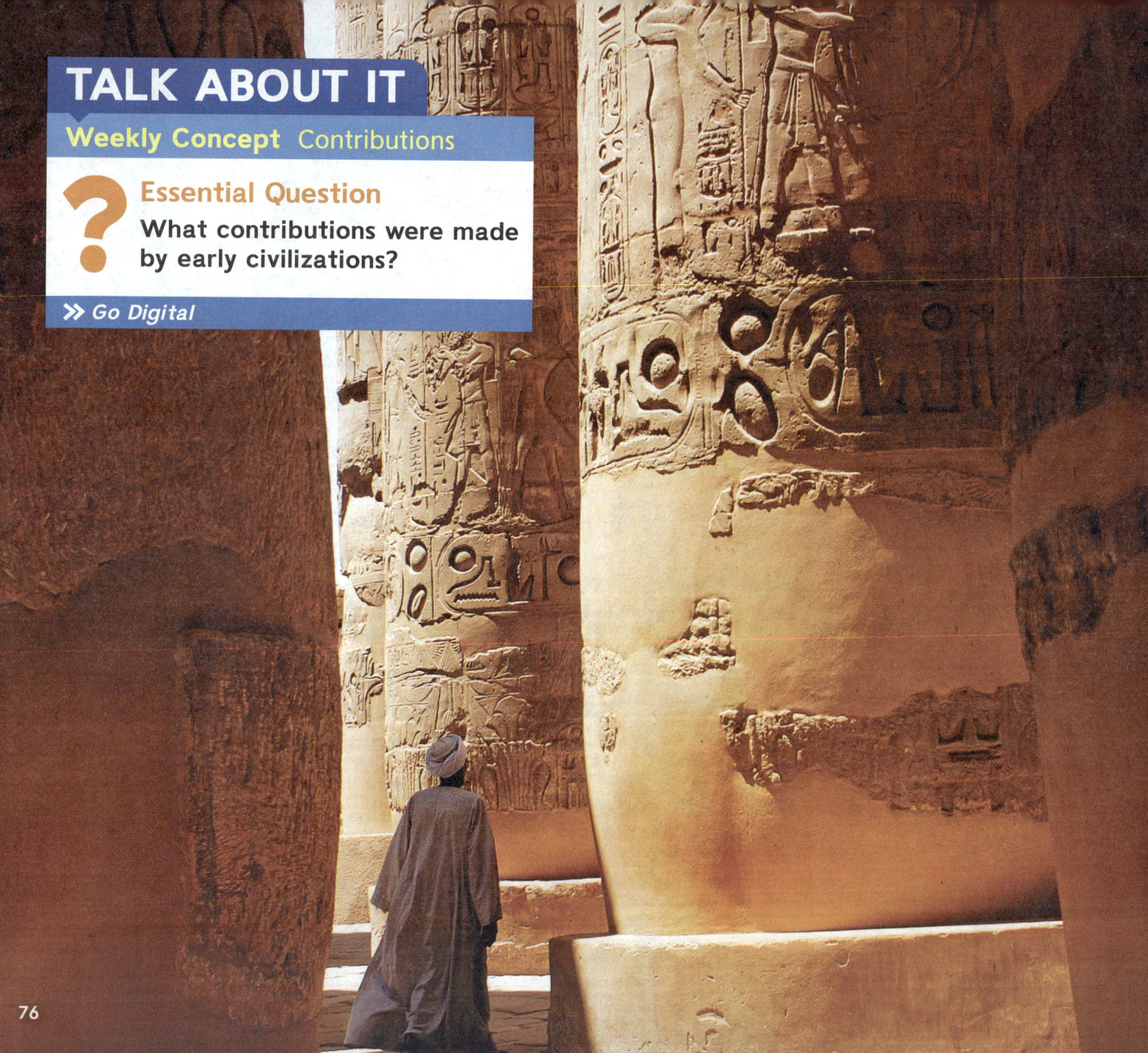

TALK ABOUT IT

Weekly Concept Contributions

? Essential Question
What contributions were made by early civilizations?

›› *Go Digital*

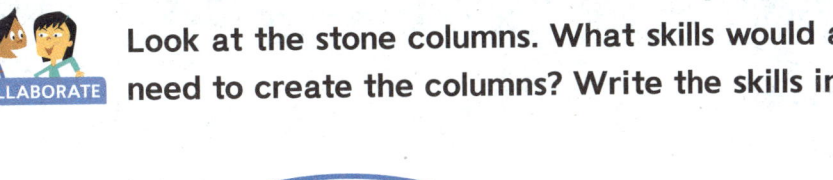

Look at the stone columns. What skills would an ancient builder need to create the columns? Write the skills in the chart.

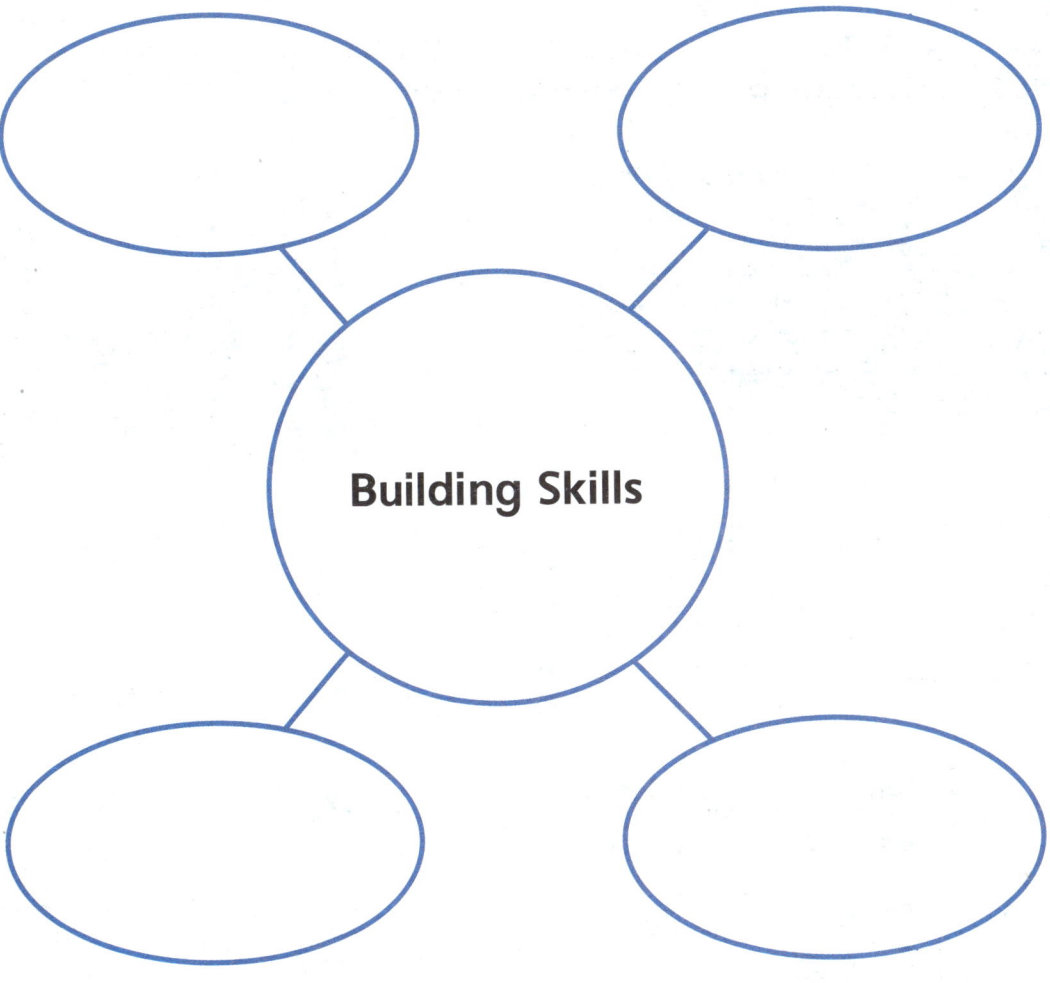

Discuss why the ancient builders needed skills to create the columns. Use words from the chart. You can say:

First, the builders had to _____. Then they had to

_____ and _____.

More Vocabulary

 Look at the picture and read the word. Then read the sentence. Talk about the word with a partner. Write your own sentence.

adopted

The students **adopted** a new way to do math.

I *adopted* a new way to _____

because _____.

flourish

The new park will **flourish** in the city.

I think _____ will *flourish* in my city.

constructed

Marcus and his father designed and **constructed** a tree house.

When I was younger, I *constructed* _____
_____.

remarkable

Jacob's grade is **remarkable**.

I think _____ is *remarkable* because _____.

78

system

The doctors have a **system** for filing papers.

I have a good *system* for _____

_____.

thrive

These plants **thrive** in a warm, wet climate.

Some plants can *thrive* in _____

_____.

Words and Phrases
Multiple-Meaning Words

The noun *records* means "copies of something."
We learn about the past from historical records.

The verb *records* means "writes something down."
She records the important information at her group's meeting.

Read the sentences below. Circle the correct meaning of the boldfaced word.

Julia always **records** notes when her group meets.
copies of something   writes something down

My school **records** include my name and address.
copies of something   writes something down

» Go Digital Add these words to your New Words notebook. Write a sentence to show the meaning of each.

Text Evidence

Shared Read | Genre • Expository Text

1 Talk About It

Read the title. Talk about what you see. Write your ideas.

What does the title tell you?

_____
_____
_____

What does the photograph show you?

_____
_____
_____

Take notes as you read the text.

Empire of the Sea

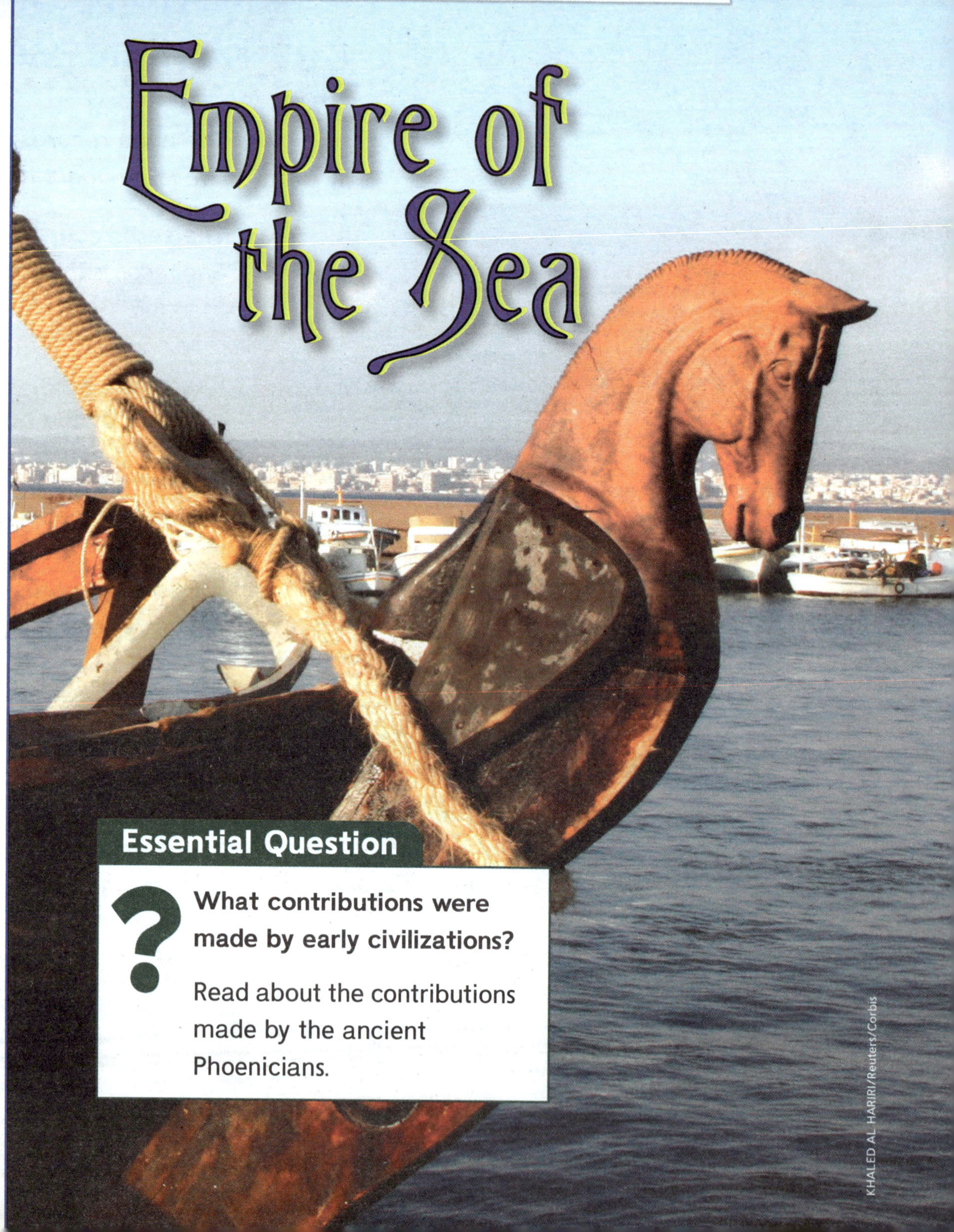

Essential Question

? What contributions were made by early civilizations?

Read about the contributions made by the ancient Phoenicians.

Between the Mountains and the Sea

Around 1500 B.C., a **remarkable** civilization began to develop. Squeezed between tree-covered mountains to the east and the Mediterranean Sea to the west, tiny Phoenicia would **flourish** for more than 1,000 years. During that millennium, the Phoenicians would explore far beyond their homeland and establish a trading empire. It was their clever solutions to key problems that enabled them to **thrive**.

Resource Rich

Imagine what it was like to live in Phoenicia. Although your country is not big in size, it is rich in resources. Cedar trees cover the hills. Farmers grow many crops, including large yields of grapes, olives, and wheat. There are more than enough resources for your own people. How will you profit from what you don't use?

To benefit from their resources, the Phoenicians began producing various goods. For example, they cut cedar trees to use as timber for building. They used the shells from a type of snail called the murex to make a highly prized purple dye. And as more than one ancient artifact shows, they also made beautiful objects of glass. The Phoenicians believed they could find buyers for all of these goods.

From Cedar Trees to Cargo Ships

Because of Phoenicia's location, your neighbors include Greeks, Egyptians, Hebrews, and other groups. These people are all possible trading partners. The most practical way of reaching them is to cross the Mediterranean. But your merchants have access only to small boats, which cannot hold much cargo. How will you transport your goods to the people who want them?

Text Evidence

❶ Sentence Structure

Read the second sentence. Circle the subject of the sentence. What would Phoenicia do for more than 1,000 years? Underline the verb phrase that tells you.

❷ Specific Vocabulary

Read the second paragraph. Resources are natural things, such as trees, that a country can use to increase its wealth. List two resources in Phoenicia that would contribute to its success.

_____

_____

❸ Comprehension
Problem and Solution

Read the third paragraph. The Phoenicians needed to benefit from their extra resources. How did they solve this problem? Underline the sentence that tells you.

81

Text Evidence

1 Talk About It

Explain how the Phoenicians constructed their ships. Discuss what their ships could do. Then write your ideas.

_____

_____

_____

2 Specific Vocabulary

Read the second paragraph. Draw a box around the word *navigators*. Underline the sentences that help you figure out the meaning of *navigators*.

3 Comprehension
Problem and Solution

Read the fourth paragraph. How did the Phoenicians solve the problem of having few trade routes? Underline the sentence that tells you.

◀ Modern shipbuilders reproduce the designs of Phoenician ships.

Archaeologists have been able to utilize written records from other civilizations to learn about the Phoenicians. From those records, they have derived evidence that the Phoenicians **constructed** enormous cargo ships from cedar wood. They used a method called "keeling the hull." The keel was a large wooden beam forming the central spine of the ship. The ship's curved hull, or frame, was built around the keel. This technique kept the ship strong and stable in the water. As a result, Phoenician ships could safely carry large, heavy loads.

The Phoenicians also became skilled navigators. In earlier times, traders had sailed only during the daytime. They stayed close to the coast for fear of losing their way. But the Phoenicians learned how to find their way using the stars. They could chart a course and steer their ships by locating the North Star, which soon became known as the "Phoenician star."

Trade Routes and Trading Posts

Your work as a Phoenician merchant includes exporting timber, dyed fabrics, glassware, and some foods. You also want to import copper, tin, silk, spices, horses, and papyrus for making stationery to write on. How will you create a **system** *of trade routes for buying and selling these goods?*

At first, there were few set trade routes for the Phoenicians to follow. So they developed their own. They traveled west and south around Africa and north to Europe. Phoenician routes helped other people trade, too. As Phoenician merchants sailed from place to place, they exchanged goods, ideas, and customs among people in many cultures. Their routine ports even developed into cities. Carthage in northern Africa provided a safe harbor for Phoenician merchants over many years.

Timeline of Phoenician History

- **1300 B.C.** Phoenicians establish treaties with Egypt.
- **810 B.C.** The port city of Carthage is founded.
- **600 B.C.** Phoenicians sail as far as present-day Great Britain.
- **332 B.C.** The Greek army conquers the key Phoenician city of Tyre.

From Aleph to Zayin

With trade going well, you need to keep accurate records of sales. But writing systems were complicated. Egyptian writing involved making an inscription, or carving, of symbols called hieroglyphs. Mesopotamian writing, called cuneiform, grouped wedge-like shapes to represent ideas and numbers. What simpler, communal system of writing could you use to help everyone understand your records?

The Phoenicians found a solution: an alphabet. This new system of writing used combinations of the same letters to represent different sounds. Beginning with the letter *aleph*, their alphabet included 22 consonants. Because of its simplicity, it was soon widely **adopted** in many places. It also became the basis for alphabets used in many modern languages, including ours.

By 300 B.C., the Phoenician trading civilization had fallen into decline. But the Phoenicians' alphabet, navigational methods, and shipbuilding designs lived on. Thousands of years later, the contributions of ancient Phoenicia continue to enrich our world.

▲ The Phoenician alphabet used letters to represent sounds.

Make Connections

❓ Talk about the important contributions of the Phoenicians. **ESSENTIAL QUESTION**

Describe how one Phoenician innovation affects your everyday life. **TEXT TO SELF**

Text Evidence

❶ Comprehension
Problem and Solution

Read the first two paragraphs. What problem did the Phoenicians face? Underline the two sentences in the first paragraph that tell you. What solution did the Phoenicians find? Circle the sentence in the second paragraph that tells you.

❷ Sentence Structure 🅐🅒🅣

Read the fourth sentence of the second paragraph. What noun phrase in the third sentence does the pronoun *it* refer to? Underline the noun phrase.

❸ Specific Vocabulary 🅐🅒🅣

Read the third paragraph. Circle the verb *enrich*. *Enrich* means "to improve something by adding something to it." List three Phoenician inventions that enriched the world.

_____

Respond to the Text

Partner Discussion Work with a partner. Answer the questions. Discuss what you learned about "Empire of the Sea." Write the page numbers where you found text evidence.

How did the Phoenicians improve ships?

Before the Phoenicians, _____.

According to the text, the Phoenicians _____.

Text Evidence

Page(s): _____

Page(s): _____

How did the Phoenicians improve navigation?

Before the Phoenicians, _____.

According to the text, the Phoenicians _____.

Text Evidence

Page(s): _____

Page(s): _____

How did the Phoenicians improve writing?

Before the Phoenicians, _____.

According to the text, the Phoenicians _____.

Text Evidence

Page(s): _____

Page(s): _____

Group Discussion Present your answers to the group. Cite text evidence to justify your thinking. Listen to and discuss the group's opinions about your answers.

Write Review your notes about "Empire of the Sea." Then write your answer to the Essential Question. Use text evidence to support your answer. Use vocabulary words from this week's reading in your writing.

What contributions did the Phoenicians make?

The Phoenicians improved shipbuilding by _____
_____.

The Phoenicians improved navigation by _____
_____.

The Phoenicians improved writing by _____
_____.

Share Writing Present your writing to the class. Discuss their opinions. Think about what the class has to say. Did they justify their claims? Explain why you agree or disagree with their claims.

I agree that _____.

I disagree with _____ because _____.

Write to Sources

Isabel

Take Notes About the Text I took notes on the idea web to answer the prompt: *Describe a typical day in Carthage during the time of the Phoenicians. Use sensory details.*

pages 80–83

Topic
Typical Day in Carthage

Detail
Phoenician ships with timber, dyed fabrics, glassware, and foods were in the port.

Detail
Phoenician merchants were on land selling their goods to the merchants of Carthage.

Detail
The merchants of Carthage were selling their goods to the merchants of Phoenicia.

Detail
The two groups were exchanging ideas and discussing local customs.

Write About the Text I used notes from my idea web to write an informative paragraph about Carthage.

Student Model: *Informative Text*

It was a busy trading day in Carthage in 800 B.C. The large Phoenician ships with timber, dyed fabrics, glassware, and foods were safe in the port. The Phoenician merchants were on land selling these goods to the merchants of Carthage. In addition, the merchants of Carthage were selling their goods to the Phoenician merchants. Besides exchanging goods, the two groups shared ideas. They also discussed their local customs. The loud talk and laughter could be heard all around the lively harbor.

TALK ABOUT IT

Text Evidence
Draw a box around a sentence that comes from the notes. How does this detail help Isabel describe a typical day in Carthage in 800 B.C.?

Grammar
Circle the verb *were* in the second sentence. Underline the verb phrase *were selling* in the fourth sentence. Why does Isabel use the past tense and the past progressive form?

Condense Ideas
Underline the fifth and sixth sentences. How can you combine the sentences to condense the ideas?

Your Turn

How does the author use reasons and evidence to support the claim that the Phoenician civilization was remarkable?

>> Go Digital
Write your response online. Use your editing checklist.

TALK ABOUT IT

Weekly Concept Democracy

? Essential Question
How did democracy develop?

>> Go Digital

 What does the photo show? Why was this building important to the government of Priene? Write words in the chart to describe the government of Priene.

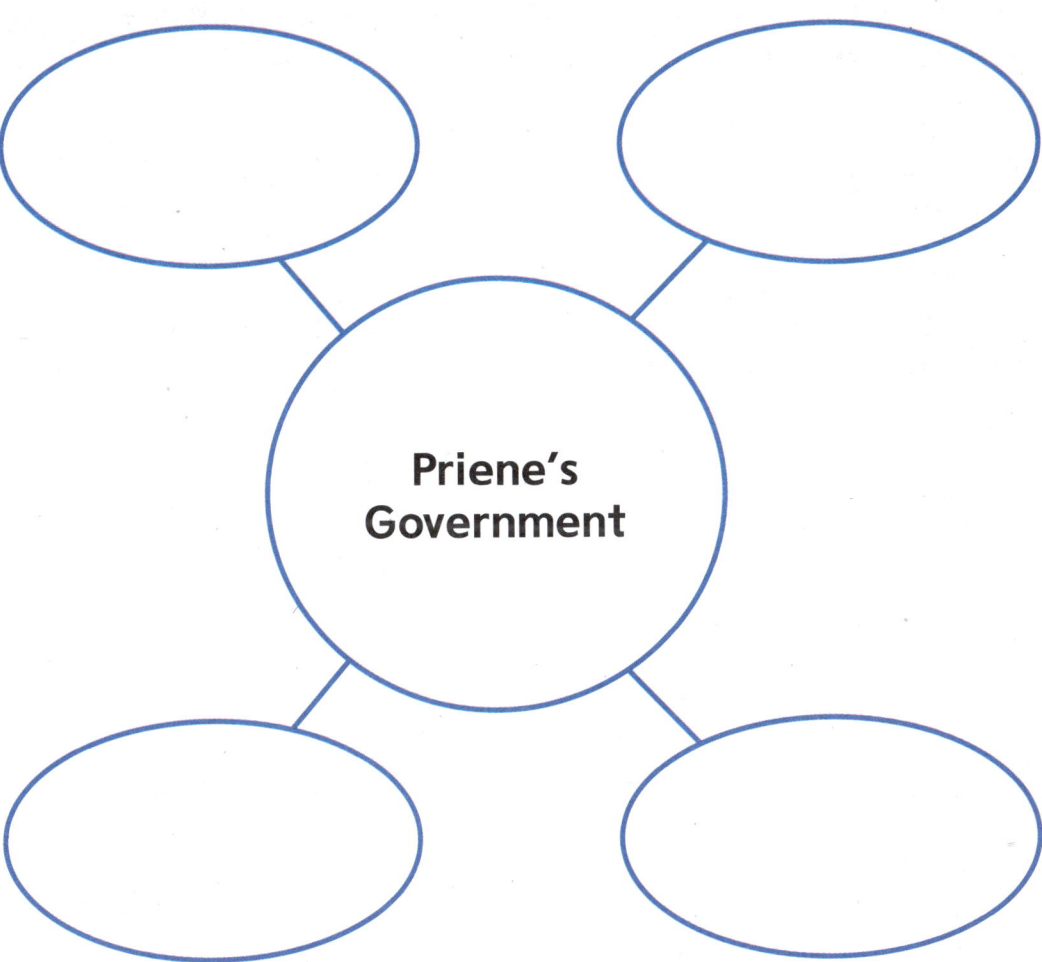

Discuss what the government was like in Priene. Use words from the chart. You can say:

The government in Priene was a _____ because

_____.

More Vocabulary

Look at the picture and read the word. Then read the sentence. Talk about the word with a partner. Write your own sentence.

balance

This meal has a **balance** of healthy foods.

My school has a good *balance* of _____ _____.

debated

Madison and Anthony **debated** the benefits of longer school days.

Recently, our class *debated* _____ _____.

critics

The mayor's plan has many **critics**.

Critics can help a community by _____ _____.

endorsed

The students **endorsed** the teacher's plan to clean the playground.

My class *endorsed* my idea to _____ _____.

governing

The president had the responsibility of **governing** the country for eight years.

I would like the responsibility of *governing* _____.

urged

The lifeguard **urged** the people to get out of the water.

My _____ *urged* me to _____ _____.

Words and Phrases
Phrasal Verbs

pick up = **learn easily by observing other people**
Mark can pick up a new language after hearing people speak it.

breaks down = **stops working**
My old bicycle often breaks down.

Read the sentences below. Write the phrasal verb that means the same thing as the underlined words.

An old computer slowly stops working.

An old computer slowly _____.

Elena can easily learn new computer skills.

Elena can _____ new computer skills.

>> *Go Digital*   Add these phrasal verbs to your New Words notebook. Write a sentence to show the meaning of each.

Text Evidence

1 Talk About It

Read the title. Talk about what you see. Write your ideas.

What does the title tell you?

_____

_____

_____

Describe the structures shown in the photograph.

_____

_____

_____

Take notes as you read the text.

Shared Read Genre • Expository Text

The Democracy DEBATE

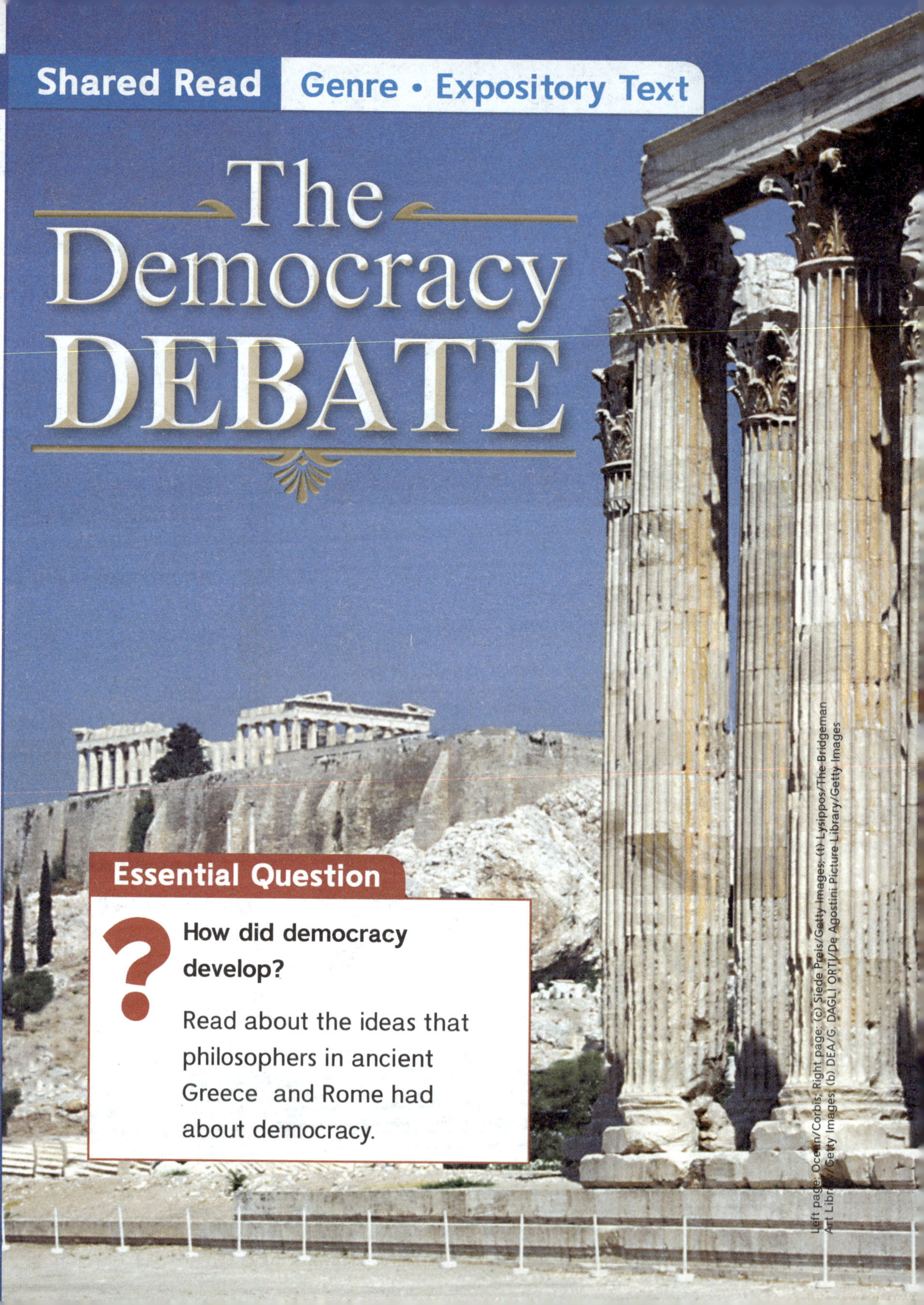

Essential Question

How did democracy develop?

Read about the ideas that philosophers in ancient Greece and Rome had about democracy.

Born and Raised in Greece

Have you ever heard the phrase "government by the people?" That is the meaning of the word *democracy*. The United States is a democratic republic, as are many countries around the world. But where did democracy come from? Some of the earliest ideas about democracy arose in the city of Athens in ancient Greece. But how should democracy be put into practice? The answer to that question has been strongly **debated** for centuries.

Even when democracy was a new idea, people argued about how it should work. How should power be shared? Should *all* people be allowed to vote and make important decisions? Among the first people to think about these key issues were the ancient Greek philosophers.

Great Minds

The word *philosopher* means "lover of wisdom," a person who seeks knowledge and is able to make good and fair decisions. One of the best-known Greek philosophers, Socrates, lived nearly 2,500 years ago. He valued wisdom highly, and he thought deeply about democracy. Socrates was one of the principal **critics** of government run by the people. He felt that only fair and wise individuals should be allowed to decide things.

The ideas that Socrates had about democracy were considered dangerous to the existing democracy in Athens. The current Athenian leaders did not want some other "fair and wise" people aspiring to run their city. Socrates was a famous teacher. And speculation among the city's leaders included worries that he would encourage young students to pick up his **radical** ideas. So they chose to execute him.

Students of Philosophy

The philosopher Plato had studied with Socrates. He also thought seriously about democracy. In 380 B.C., Plato shared his ideas about government in his book *The Republic*. He agreed with Socrates that rule by the people would bring

Text Evidence

❶ Comprehension
Compare and Contrast

Read the third and fourth paragraphs. Socrates believed that only fair and wise individuals should run the government. What did the current Athenian leaders believe? Underline the sentence that tells you.

❷ Sentence Structure 🅐🅒🅣

Read the second sentence of the third paragraph. Draw a box around *Socrates*. Underline the phrase that tells more about Socrates.

❸ Specific Vocabulary 🅐🅒🅣

Reread the fourth paragraph. Underline the sentence that helps you understand the meaning of *radical*. Why did the city's leaders worry about Socrates and his radical ideas?

_____

_____

93

Text Evidence

1 Talk About It

According to Aristotle, what problems might happen in a government run by a few educated men and in a government run by common people?

_____

_____

2 Sentence Structure ACT

Read the second sentence in the first full paragraph. Circle the comma. Underline the independent clause before the comma. Draw a box around the dependent clause that gives more information about Aristotle.

3 Specific Vocabulary ACT

Read the first paragraph under "Changes in Rome." The word *influence* means "the power to affect someone or something." How did the influence of Greek thinking affect Cicero?

Like Aristotle, Cicero _____.

---

about poor decisions and a weak government. But, unlike his teacher, he believed that three different groups of people could share the responsibility of **governing**. The "highest" group would be philosopher-kings guided only by what is best for the state. The second group would be soldiers who protected the state. The last group would be common people who provided goods and services.

Around 388 B.C., Plato formed a school called the Academy. A star pupil there was the philosopher Aristotle, who believed in **balance** and moderation. About 350 B.C., Aristotle wrote in his book *Politics* that a government that tries to restrict power to a few educated men would not work. It would benefit only the rich. A democracy run by common people would not work either, because such people might not make wise decisions. Aristotle's solution was combining the two. This would give people from all parts of society a voice.

Changes in Rome

About 400 years after Aristotle, the **influence** of Greek thinking was still felt by philosophers in Rome. Cicero is the best known Roman philosopher. Like Aristotle, he believed a balance of power brought peace and prosperity. That was because different types of people took part in government.

Cicero believed that the Roman republic was the best model for government because it was mixed. It combined features of a monarchy, an aristocracy, and a democracy. Cicero saw that the Roman republic was breaking down, mostly because the aristocracy had gained too much power. In his book, *On the Republic*, he **urged** a return to a more balanced government.

Philosopher Kings
Soldiers
Producers of Goods and Services

Philosopher	Place	Time Period	Ideas About Democracy
Socrates	Greece	469–399 B.C.	Only wise and just people should govern.
Plato	Greece	427–347 B.C.	Rule should be shared by philosopher-kings, soldiers, and providers of goods.
Aristotle	Greece	384–322 B.C.	Educated and common people should each have a role in government.
Cicero	Rome	106–43 B.C.	The Roman republic—a monarch, an aristocracy, and the people—is best.

The Debate Continues

The founders of the United States also thought about how a democracy should be organized. They studied governments that had preceded ours and believed that the foundation of any new government should revisit Greek and Roman ideas. For example, Thomas Paine wrote booklets to promote the idea that people should govern themselves. James Madison admired Aristotle's and Cicero's beliefs in balancing power among different groups.

In 1787, Madison helped Alexander Hamilton write a set of essays called *The Federalist* to encourage states to ratify the Constitution. They made the case for having *a pair* of law-making groups. The smaller Senate would be similar to Rome's senate, while the House of Representatives would give more people a voice. They also **endorsed** having one president and a system of courts to interpret the laws.

Today, people are still debating what the meaning of *democracy* is and how our government should be organized. The U.S. Constitution has been **amended** more than 25 times to reflect changing ideas. Yet it is important to remember that our government has roots in ideas from ancient times. Democracy has withstood the test of time.

Make Connections

Talk about how the philosophers' ideas influenced our democracy. **ESSENTIAL QUESTION**

How does your understanding of democracy compare to the ideas the philosophers had? **TEXT TO SELF**

Text Evidence

1 Sentence Structure A C T

Read the third sentence of the second paragraph. The word *while* tells us that two things would happen at the same time. Circle the two things that would happen at the same time.

2 Specific Vocabulary A C T

Look at the last paragraph. The verb *amended* means "changed and made something better." How many times has the United States Constitution been amended? Why?

_____

_____

3 Talk About It

Explain how the United States government has its roots in the ideas from ancient times. Justify your response.

_____

_____

Respond to the Text

Partner Discussion Work with a partner. Answer the questions. Discuss what you learned about "The Democracy Debate." Write the page numbers where you found text evidence.

How did the ancient Greeks develop democracy?

Socrates believed _____. Page(s): _____

Aristotle believed _____. Page(s): _____

Text Evidence

How did the ancient Romans develop democracy?

Cicero believed _____. Page(s): _____

Text Evidence

How did the founders of the United States develop democracy?

The Senate _____. Page(s): _____

The House of Representatives _____. Page(s): _____

The Constitution of the United States _____. Page(s): _____

Text Evidence

Group Discussion Present your answers to the group. Cite text evidence to justify your thinking. Listen to and discuss the group's opinions about your answers.

Write Review your notes about "The Democracy Debate." Then write your answer to the Essential Question. Use text evidence to support your answer. Use vocabulary words from this week's reading in your writing.

How did democracy develop?

Plato believed that a democracy _____.

Cicero believed that a democracy _____.

The founders of the United States believed that a democracy _____
_____.

Share Writing Present your writing to the class. Discuss their opinions. Think about what the class has to say. Did they justify their claims? Explain why you agree or disagree with their claims.

I agree that _____.

I disagree with _____ because _____.

97

Write to Sources

Kevin

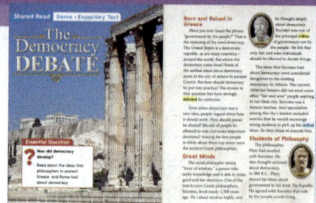

pages 92–95

Take Notes About the Text I took notes on this idea web to answer the prompt: *Pretend you are Plato. Tell why your ideas about democracy are the best. Support your argument with details from the text.*

Main Idea
Three groups should share the responsibility of governing Greece.

Details
The highest group would be philosopher-kings, guided only by what is best for the state.

Details
The second group would be soldiers. They would protect the state.

Details
The last group would be common people. They would provide goods and services.

Write About the Text I used notes from my idea web to write an argument.

Student Model: *Argument*

My ideas about democracy are the best. There are three important groups of people to Greece. These three groups should share the responsibility of governing Greece. Philosopher-kings would be the highest group. They are wise and would do what is best for the state. Soldiers would be the second group. They would protect everyone. Common people would be the third group. They would provide goods and services. These three important groups to Greece would share the responsibility of governing Greece well.

TALK ABOUT IT

Text Evidence
Underline a detail that comes from the notes. How does this detail support Kevin's argument?

Grammar
Draw a box around the verb phrase *should share*. Why does Kevin use the helping verb *should* in his argument?

Condense Ideas
Underline the second and third sentences in the argument. How can you combine the sentences to condense ideas?

Your Turn

Pretend you are one of the forefathers of the United States. Write an argument about why the proposed democracy is better than Greek and Roman democracy.

>> *Go Digital*
Write your response online. Use your editing checklist.

TALK ABOUT IT

Weekly Concept Ancient Societies

? **Essential Question**
What was life like for people in ancient cultures?

>> *Go Digital*

 This wall painting is from ancient Rome. What can you tell about the woman from the painting? Write details in the chart.

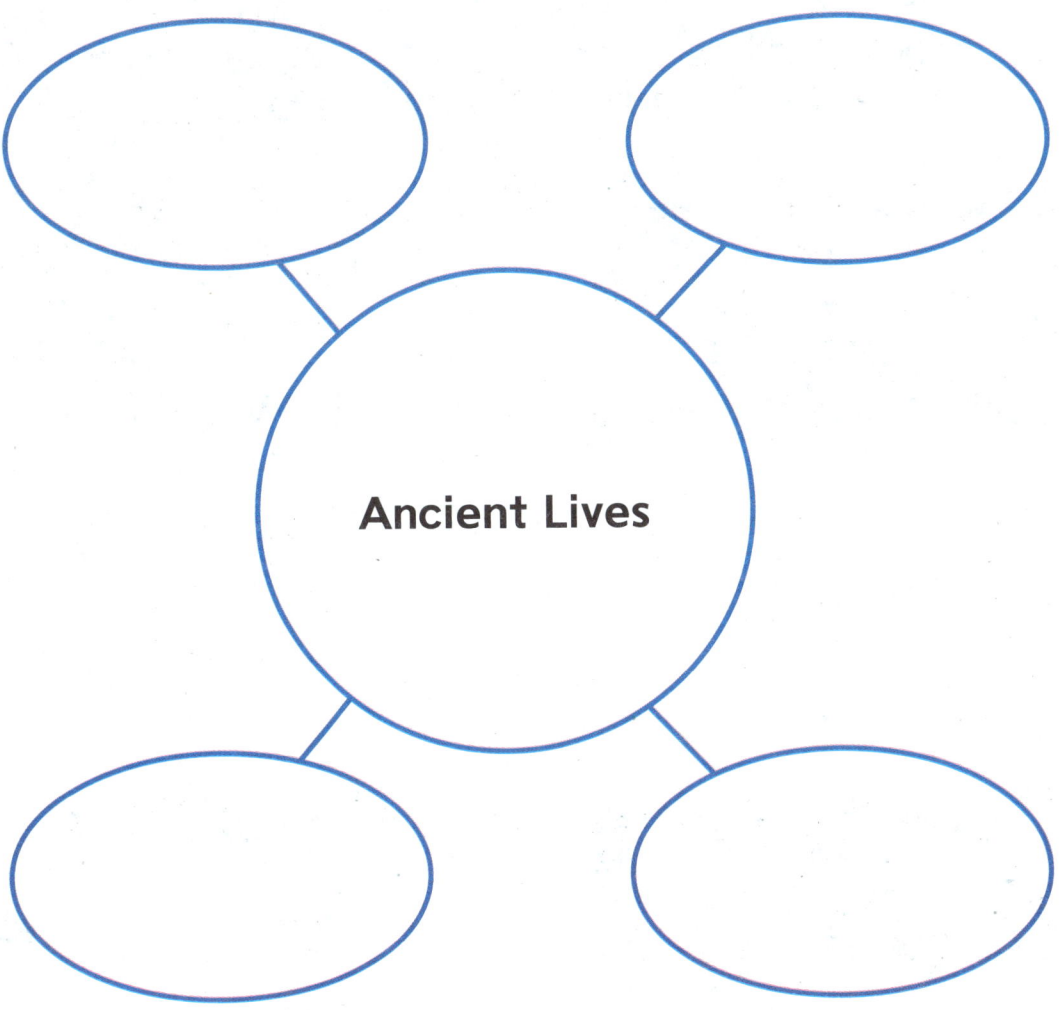

Ancient Lives

Discuss what the painting tells you about the woman's life. Use words from the chart. You can say:

I think the woman liked to _____ because _____.

I think she was rich because _____.

More Vocabulary

 Look at the picture and read the word. Then read the sentence. Talk about the word with a partner. Write your own sentence.

ancient

These pyramids were built in **ancient** Egypt.

Ancient Greece was interesting because _____.

eager

The friends are **eager** to eat the delicious meal.

Another word for *eager* is _____.

convince

The lawyer has to **convince** the jury that the man is innocent.

I have to *convince* _____ that _____.

impressed

Mr. Smith is **impressed** by Angela's work.

I am *impressed* by _____ because _____.

obtain

April is trying to **obtain** her driver license.

I need to *obtain* _____ to

_____.

possess

The students **possess** the knowledge to answer the question.

I would like to *possess* the skills to _____

_____.

Words and Phrases
Suffix *-ly*

The suffix *-ly* means "in a certain way." You can often add *-ly* to an adjective to change it into an adverb. Sometimes, there is a spelling change.

nervous + *-ly* = nervously
nervously = in a nervous way
They entered the dark house <u>nervously</u>.

gentle + *-ly* = gently
gently = in a gentle way
She held the baby <u>gently</u>.

Read the sentences below. Write the adverb for each underlined phrase.

The farmer watched the weather report <u>in a nervous way</u>.

The farmer watched the weather report _____.

The baker took the cake out of the oven <u>in a gentle way</u>.

The baker took the cake out of the oven _____.

» Go Digital Add these adverbs to your New Words notebook. Write a sentence to show the meaning of each.

Text Evidence

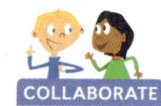

1 Talk About It

Read the title. Talk about what you see. Write your ideas.

What does the title tell you?

____

____

____

What does the illustration show?

____

____

____

Take notes as you read the story.

Shared Read Genre • Historical Fiction

Yaskul's Mighty Trade

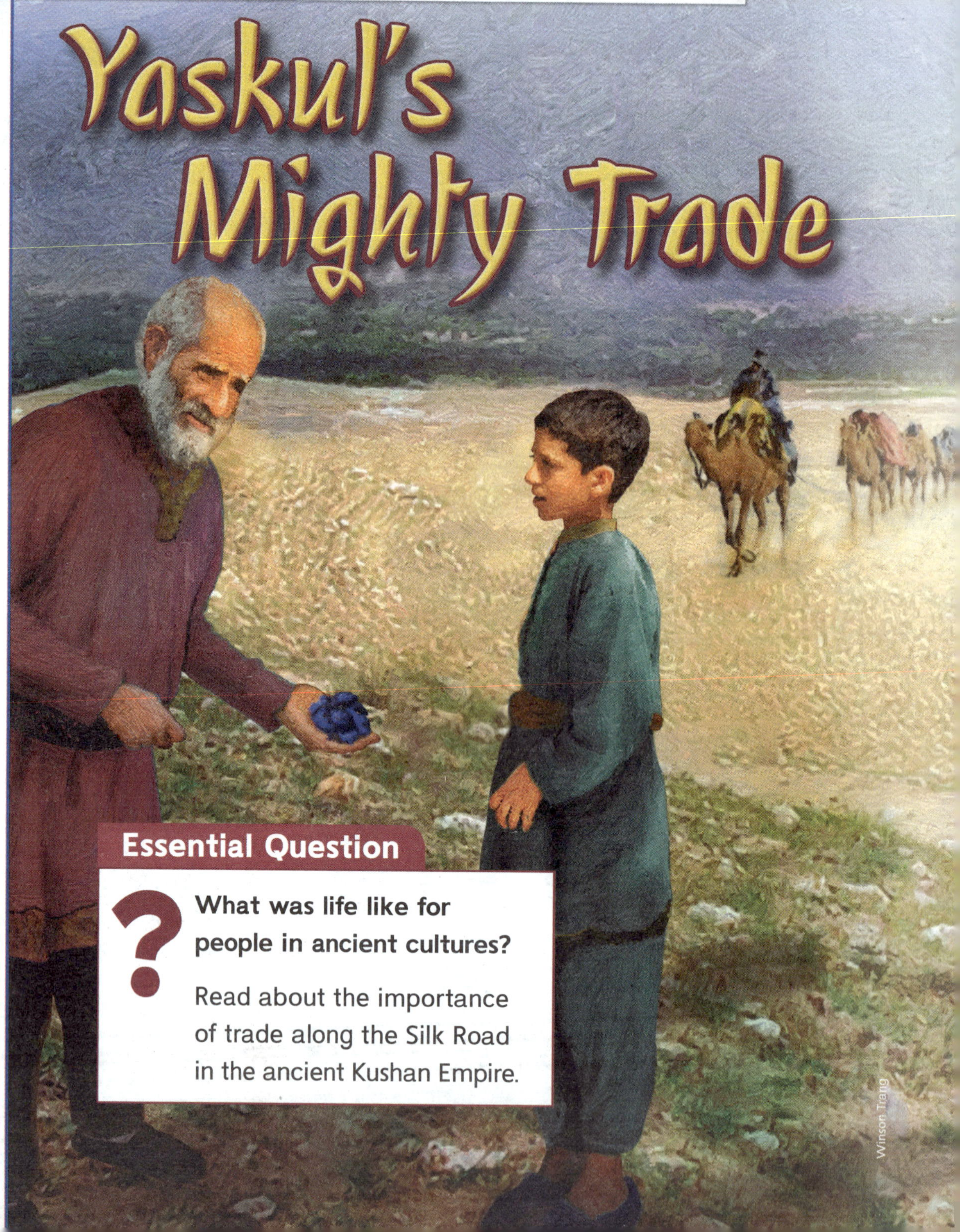

Essential Question

What was life like for people in ancient cultures?

Read about the importance of trade along the Silk Road in the ancient Kushan Empire.

Winson Trang

Located in what is now Afghanistan, the ancient city of Bactra in the Kushan Empire was a key market for merchants traveling the Silk Road trade route. In A.D. 110, lively commerce attracted merchants from east and west to the famous market in Bactra. In the following, Yaskul, the 12-year-old son of a Bactrian merchant, is eager to make his first official trade.

I Make Plans

It is early, but I am awake. Though we are only in the month of *Hyperberetaios*, it is a cold autumn day. As I quickly dress, I think about how the Chinese caravan arrived last night. If winter comes early, we may not see another caravan for months, as snow will close the passes. My family must have success at the market tomorrow.

Tomorrow I become a trader, I think. Father says I will be there only to watch and learn, but Grandfather says that Father is too cautious. He says Father makes timid trades and does not obtain the best prices, especially for lapis lazuli.

Lapis lazuli! How I love the brilliant blue stone that comes from the mines up north. Grandfather says that even the Egyptians prized this stone. He has awarded me some beads of my own and is instructing me on how to price them. "You listen, and you learn from me. Always watch the eyes of the man you bargain with. The eyes say when he is willing to pay more and when he will walk away."

Thieves!

When Grandfather and I reach our storage room today, Father is already there. "Thieves!" he cries. "They took everything!" Grandfather surveys the room and says it is not everything. I too spot yarn and metal cups tossed on the floor.

Text Evidence

❶ Comprehension
Point of View

Read the Introduction and the first paragraph. Who is speaking in the first sentence of the first paragraph? Circle the name in the Introduction.

❷ Sentence Structure

Read the fourth sentence in the first paragraph. Circle the commas. What will happen if winter comes early? Underline the part of the sentence that tells you. Draw a box around the part of the sentence that tells you why.

❸ Specific Vocabulary

Read the last paragraph. The word *surveys* means "looks at carefully in order to form an opinion." What does Grandfather survey? What does Grandfather determine?

_____

_____

Text Evidence

1 Talk About It

Discuss why Yaskul's stones are the family's only hope for a successful trade. Then write about it.

_____

_____

2 Sentence Structure ACT

Read the second sentence of the third paragraph. The word *and* connects two actions that Grandfather takes. Circle the first action. Draw a box around the second action.

3 Specific Vocabulary ACT

Read the first sentence in the fourth paragraph. The phrase *slip away* means "go away quietly or in secret." Why does Yaskul slip away that evening?

_____

_____.

Father points to a small alcove, a shelf we have carved in the wall. "The thieves missed our wool rugs and sacks of salt. But all our lazuli stones are gone!" I comprehend how little is left for the market tomorrow. What remains are domestic items, and common home goods will not fetch many *drachm* coins. The merchants from China will likely dismiss our wares. Quickly, I remind Father that I still have my lazuli beads.

Grandfather peers at me, thinking. "Yes," he says, nodding. "Your stones are now of the utmost importance, our only hope for a successful trade. You must <mark>convince</mark> the Chinese that your stones are of the highest quality, or we will not get the best price."

I swallow hard. Grandfather smiles and puts his hand on my shoulder. "Don't fret, Yaskul. You <mark>possess</mark> the skill to make this trade a mighty one."

I Make a Friend

In the evening, I <mark>slip away</mark> to observe the Chinese traders before we meet them at market. I feel my eyes widen when the traders draw close to their fire's light. Their exotic robes truly glow with color. They are so much finer than my clothes.

Suddenly, one man of perhaps 19 years walks toward me. I jump back, but he smiles and waves at me. "Do not be frightened." His voice is friendly. "Is Bactra your home?" I am amazed that he is so fluent in my language. This young man has traveled much already, I think. "Are you a trader?" he asks me.

"I am Yaskul," I say. "My family are traders." He introduces himself as Zhang. "I have heard that name," I answer. "Did not a great man named Zhang come to Bactra long ago?"

Zhang nods. "Zhang Qian was sent to find allies for us. But he found instead your marvelous marketplace. He called your people 'shrewd

traders.'" We smile. I tell him of the upheaval caused today by the theft of our goods. "Your luck was hard. Even so, you will trade well," Zhang says. I hope he is right.

Market Day

I have strung my beads as a necklace, which shows the stones well. Father has guarded our remaining merchandise all night. With Grandfather, we transport it to the marketplace. Today's bright sun will make the stalls grow hot and stifling.

I am amazed by all the goods for sale: tea, almonds, elegant ceramics, carved ivory and jade, and the finest Chinese silk. We reach our stall as the Chinese traders arrive. Zhang nods to me as Father begins bartering with the oldest Chinese merchant, but this elder does not seem **impressed** by our offerings.

Then Zhang speaks. "Do you have any of the vivid blue stones your people are known for?" Grandfather gently pushes me forward. Nervously, I hold out my necklace. I notice the oldest merchant's **eyes light up**, and I hear myself tell him how particularly fine these beads are. The trading grows lively, and before I realize it, we agree on a high price. I hand him the necklace, and Father collects a handful of *drachms*.

Zhang winks at me, but says not a word. After the Chinese traders depart, Grandfather embraces me, and even Father thumps me on the back. Now I can truly call myself a trader!

Make Connections

Talk about the importance of trade in the lives of people living in the ancient city of Bactra. **ESSENTIAL QUESTION**

Describe a time when you overcame nervousness to succeed at something important to you. **TEXT TO SELF**

Text Evidence

❶ Comprehension
Point of View

Read the second paragraph. Circle the pronouns that tell you this story is written from the first-person point of view.

❷ Specific Vocabulary

Read the fifth sentence in the third paragraph. The idiom *eyes light up* means "eyes look happy or excited." Why do the oldest merchant's eyes light up?

_____

_____

❸ Talk About It

How does Zhang help Yaskul at the end of the story? Justify your answer.

_____

_____

Respond to the Text

 **Partner Discussion** Work with a partner. Answer the questions. Discuss what you learned about "Yaskul's Mighty Trade." Write the page numbers where you found text evidence.

Where did Yaskul and his family live?

Yaskul and his family lived _____. Page(s): _____

I read that Bactra was a key market on _____. Page(s): _____

In A.D. 110, Bactra _____. Page(s): _____

What did Yaskul and his family trade?

Yaskul's family traded _____. Page(s): _____

I read that common home goods _____. Page(s): _____

Yaskul's stones were important because _____
_____. Page(s): _____

 **Group Discussion** Present your answers to the group. Cite text evidence to justify your thinking. Listen to and discuss the group's opinions about your answers.

Write Review your notes about "Yaskul's Mighty Trade." Then write your answer to the Essential Question. Use text evidence to support your answer. Use vocabulary words from this week's reading in your writing.

Why was trade important to Yaskul and his family?

In A.D. 110, Bactra _____.

Yaskul's family traded _____.

Trade was important to _____ because

_____.

Share Writing Present your writing to the class. Discuss their opinions. Think about what the class has to say. Did they justify their claims? Explain why you agree or disagree with their claims.

I agree that _____.

I disagree with _____ because _____.

Write to Sources

Paige

Take Notes About the Text I took notes on this idea web to answer the prompt: *Add an event to the story. Write a scene in which Yaskul sells a rug to a merchant and gets a good price for it. Use the first-person point of view and include dialogue.*

pages 104–107

First
Yaskul strings his beads to show the stones well.

Next
Yaskul shows the oldest merchant his necklace.

Then
They agree on a high price.

Last
Yaskul says he can truly call himself a trader.

Write About the Text I used notes from my idea web to extend the story.

Student Model: Narrative Text

Several merchants walk up to our stall. They look at the rugs we have for sale. I point to our finest rug. I notice that one of the merchants looks interested.

"Do you want to take a closer look at this fine rug?" I ask.

"It is very beautiful," he says.

While he examines the rug, I tell him that he will not find another like it. It is of the highest quality, too. We begin to discuss price. I can tell he really wants the rug. I try for a higher price. To my surprise, he agrees. I have made my second successful trade!

TALK ABOUT IT

Text Evidence
Underline a sentence that comes from the notes. Why is this event likely to happen, based on what happened in the story?

Grammar
Draw a box around an adjective that describes the rug. Why does Paige use this adjective in the story?

Connect Ideas
Underline the sentences about price. How can you combine the sentences to connect ideas?

Your Turn

Add an event to the story in which Yaskul and Zhang talk to each other after Yaskul sells the beads. Use details from the story.

>> *Go Digital*
Write your response online. Use your editing checklist.

TALK ABOUT IT

Weekly Concept Influences

? Essential Question
What influences the development of a culture?

›› *Go Digital*

 What does the photo show about farming on Longji Mountain? Write words in the chart about what you see.

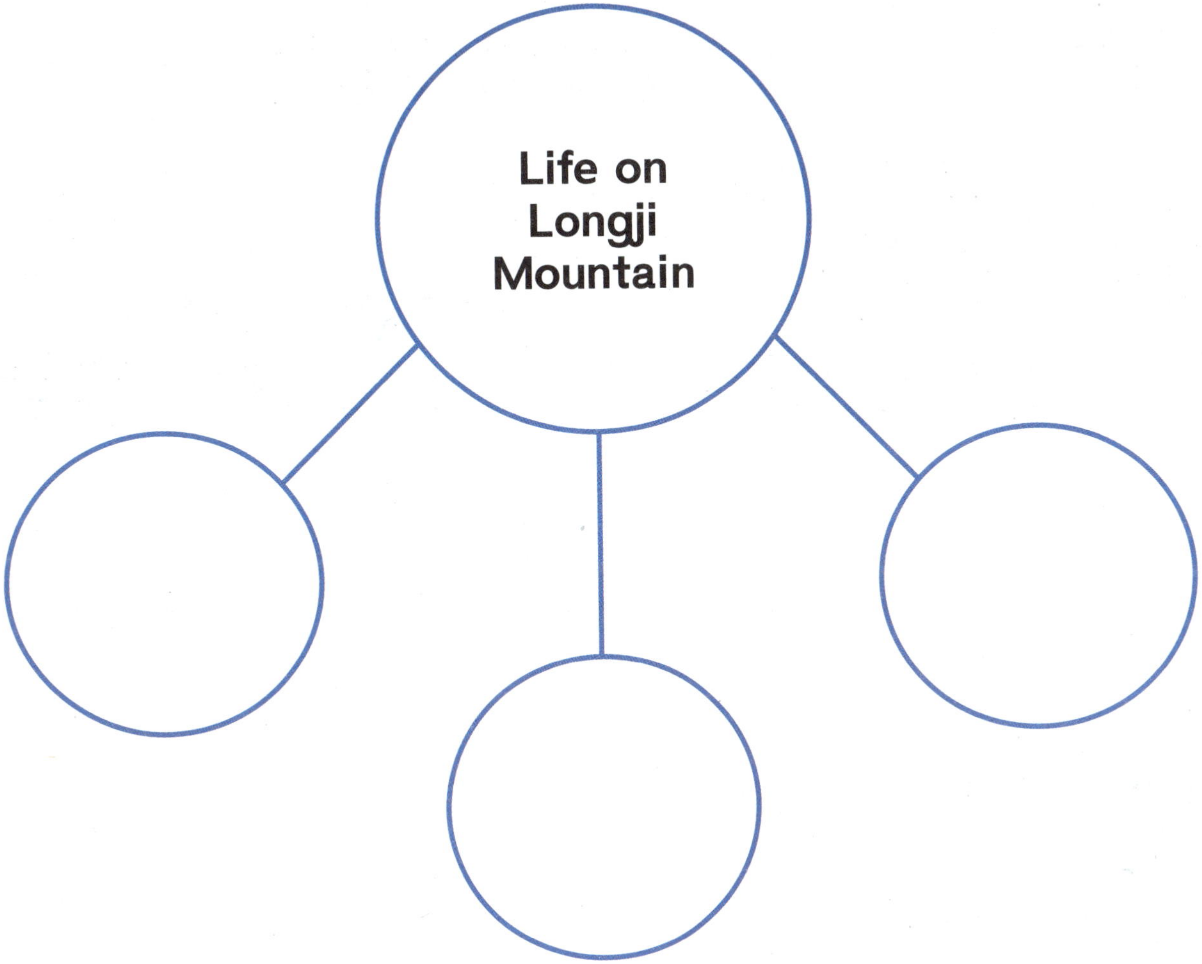

Life on Longji Mountain

Discuss how the land influences the farming culture on Longji Mountain. Use words from the chart. You can say:

The people of Longji Mountain farm by _____. They farm this way because _____.

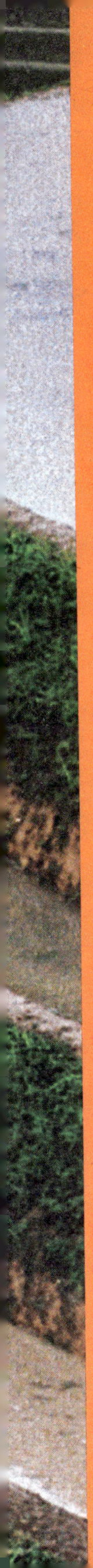

More Vocabulary

 Look at the picture and read the word. Then read the sentence. Talk about the word with a partner. Write your own sentence.

amazement

The girls looked in **amazement** as the insect crawled by.

I looked in *amazement* when _____

_____.

display

The sports fans often **display** their excitement.

I *display* my excitement when _____

_____.

longingly

Claudio looked **longingly** at the new bicycle.

I once looked *longingly* at _____

_____.

optimism

The farmer showed **optimism** even when there was no rain.

Another word for *optimism* is _____.

patiently

The students waited **patiently** for their lunches.

I wait *patiently* to buy _____.

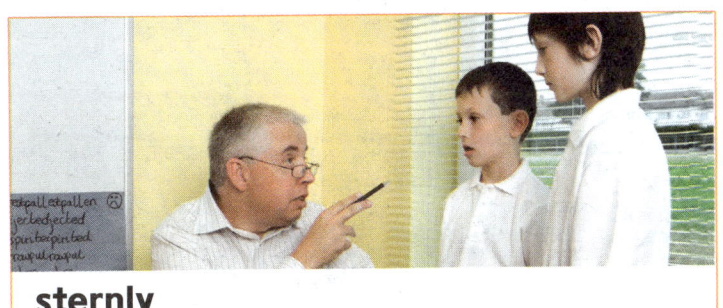

sternly

The principal talked to the students **sternly** when they brought their cell phones to class.

My teacher talked to me **sternly** when

_____.

Words and Phrases
Phrasal Verbs

show off = show something proudly
My brothers often <u>show off</u> their basketball skills.

lit up = showed excitement
My face <u>lit up</u> when I received an A for my report.

Read the sentences below. Write the phrasal verb that means the same thing as the underlined words.

The students <u>proudly show</u> their paintings at the school fair.

The students _____ their paintings at the school fair.

My friend's face <u>showed excitement</u> when she received a new watch.

My friend's face _____ when she received a new watch.

» Go Digital Add these phrasal verbs to your New Words notebook. Write a sentence to show the meaning of each.

Text Evidence

Shared Read | Genre • Historical Fiction

1 Talk About It

Read the title. Talk about what you see. Write your ideas.

What does the title tell you?

_____

_____

_____

What does the illustration show?

_____

_____

_____

Take notes as you read the story.

Cusi's Secret

Essential Question

? What influences the development of a culture?

Read about how an Incan girl's skill with weaving helps her learn about her culture.

116

Beautiful textiles had great value to the Inca, whose empire arose in what is now Peru. The year is 1430, and 11-year-old Cusi is an Incan girl with a special talent for weaving. Although few girls were allowed to receive an education in Inca society, Cusi dreams of going to school.

A Family Tradition

As they did most mornings, Cusi and her mother were working at their handheld looms. A curious girl, Cusi asked, "Tell me again, Mama: How is it that our family became such fine weavers?"

"When I was a girl, your grandmother taught me to shear wool from the alpaca in our herds and then to weave with it," Cusi's mother **patiently** responded. "It was *her* mother—your great grandmother—who had passed our family's legacy on to her."

When the sun grew warm, Cusi took her loom to the shadows beneath the eaves of their house. Alone now, she gazed over at the girls' schoolhouse gleaming on a nearby hill. "How I wish I could go there," she said **longingly**. "I do not understand why there are schools for all the boys but so few girls have a chance to learn. It is not fair!"

A Special Invitation

As Cusi was voicing her thoughts, she spied one of the school's *mamaconas*, or teachers, walking along a nearby path. Cusi fell silent as the woman stopped to watch her weave. Pretending not to see the teacher, she did her very best to show off her skills.

Cusi began working a vibrant pattern into the perimeter of the cloth. Her hands deftly glided over the woolen strands, darting as quickly as a hummingbird flies. The teacher watched in **amazement**, impressed by the loveliness and symmetry of Cusi's design.

Then Cusi's **concentration was broken** by a knocking sound. She looked up to see her parents greeting Mamacona at the door. Humbly, the teacher said to them, "I watched your daughter working at her loom. She is young to have such expertise. Will you allow her to become one of my students?"

ILLUSTRATIONS: Janet Broxon

Text Evidence

❶ Sentence Structure

Read the first sentence of the first paragraph. Circle the pronoun *they*. Underline the nouns that the pronoun *they* refers to. Who worked on looms most mornings?

_____

_____

❷ Comprehension
Point of View

Read the third paragraph. Circle the pronouns that tell you the story is written from the third-person point of view.

❸ Specific Vocabulary

Read the last paragraph. The idiom *concentration was broken* means "thinking was interrupted by someone or something." Why is Cusi's concentration broken?

_____

_____

_____

117

Text Evidence

1. Specific Vocabulary

Read the second sentence in the fourth paragraph. The word *relished* means "got great pleasure or satisfaction from something." What does Cusi relish learning in weaving class?

_____

_____

2. Sentence Structure

Read the first sentence of the fifth paragraph. The word *while* tells you that two things happen at the same time. When did Cusi begin to daydream? Draw a box around the part of the sentence that tells you.

3. Talk About It

Discuss why the man shouts at Cusi when she asks how to use the *quipu*. Then write about it.

_____

_____

Hearing this, Cusi wanted to rush forward and shout for joy, but she knew Incan girls should not **display** such impudence. So she remained still. After what seemed like hours, Cusi's father spoke. "We will miss her, but yes, we would be honored to have Cusi attend school. An education will be of great benefit to her."

That night, Cusi's parents made the arrangements for her to begin school. She would leave them in just one week. Cusi felt such **optimism**, but she was nervous, too.

Much to Learn

Cusi found living at the school so different from being at home. She had to memorize the essentials of Incan history and beliefs, and she also learned to prepare foods, including *chicha morada*, a special drink made from purple corn.

But the highlight of Cusi's new life was weaving class. She **relished** learning to spin yarn from the precious wool of *vicuñas*. Cusi had glimpsed the tiny camels roaming distant hills, and once on market day she had even secretly stroked a garment made from their silky wool. She knew only royal people could wear such robes. "It is a privilege just to touch fibers as fine as these," she sighed contentedly.

One afternoon, while the other girls were practicing techniques she had already mastered, Cusi began to daydream. Her thoughts drifted back to a day when she had seen a village elder using a *quipu* to count and record the number of alpacas in the herds. The counting tool, made by knotting strands of wool, had fascinated her.

"Excuse me, sir," she had said to the man. "Will you please show me how to use the counting threads?"

With a sneer of derision, the man had shouted angrily at Cusi. "Foolish girl! Has no one told you only men may use the *quipu*? Never speak such nonsense again!"

Cusi had run away as fast as her legs would take her, yet she never forgot about the *quipu*. Even now, as she recalled that long ago scene, her fingers worked at tying knots in a wool cord. She was convinced the secrets of this forbidden tool were the key to great knowledge.

Suddenly, a classmate's shout startled Cusi from her thoughts. "Cusi has fallen asleep!" The girls broke into laughter and, blushing, Cusi hid the knots in her lap.

"Enough!" the teacher said to quiet the class. "Cusi, please step outside."

A Secret to Treasure

When they were alone, Mamacona gestured toward the knotted wool that Cusi held behind her back. "Show me what you have made," she said **sternly**. When Cusi gave her the knots, the woman's eyes widened in alarm. "Is this a *quipu*? Women should not possess these things. You take great risk!"

"But if I knew how to use the *quipu*," Cusi pleaded, "I could keep school records, and the royal merchants could no longer cheat us when buying our *vicuña* robes."

Mamacona struggled with her thoughts. She knew well the ban against women using the *quipu*, but she herself had possessed this thirst for knowledge when she was a girl. She recalled how her brother had secretly taught her to keep accounts with the *quipu*. In the end, she was won over by Cusi's hopeful plea.

"I will teach you to make a *quipu* properly," she whispered. Cusi's face lit up. "*But*…you must promise never to tell anyone!"

Cusi hugged her teacher. "Thank you, Mamacona. I promise. I will not disappoint you. I will learn, and I will forever keep our secret!"

Make Connections

? Talk about the importance of wool and weaving in the Inca culture. ESSENTIAL QUESTION

Describe a time when you learned something you had wanted to know for a long time. TEXT TO SELF

Text Evidence

❶ Comprehension
Point of View

Read the first paragraph. Circle the nouns and pronouns that tell you the story is written from the third-person point of view.

❷ Sentence Structure ACT

Read the first sentence in the third paragraph. Draw a box around the prepositional phrase that indicates the location of the knotted wool.

❸ Specific Vocabulary ACT

Read the last sentence of the fifth paragraph. The idiom "was won over" means "was persuaded." Write the sentence that tells you what won over Mamacona.

_____

_____

Respond to the Text

Partner Discussion Work with a partner. Answer the questions. Discuss what you learned about "Cusi's Secret." Write the page numbers where you found text evidence.

Why is Cusi invited to attend school?	Text Evidence
A teacher from the girls' school watches _____.	Page(s): _____
So Cusi _____.	Page(s): _____
The teacher is impressed and _____.	Page(s): _____

What does Cusi learn about her culture?	Text Evidence
At school, Cusi learns _____ _____.	Page(s): _____
Cusi wants to learn _____, but _____.	Page(s): _____
Mamacona agrees _____.	Page(s): _____

Group Discussion Present your answers to the group. Cite text evidence to justify your thinking. Listen to and discuss the group's opinions about your answers.

Write Review your notes about "Cusi's Secret." Then write your answer to the Essential Question. Use text evidence to support your answer. Use vocabulary words from this week's reading in your writing.

How does Cusi learn about her culture?

A teacher from the girls' school watches _____

and _____.

At school, Cusi learns about _____

_____.

Therefore, Cusi is able to learn more about _____ because

_____.

Share Writing Present your writing to the class. Discuss their opinions. Think about what the class has to say. Did they justify their claims? Explain why you agree or disagree with their claims.

I agree that _____.

I disagree with _____ because _____.

Write to Sources

Take Notes About the Text I took notes on this idea web to answer the prompt: *Write a paragraph from Mamacona's point of view. Tell how she feels about teaching Cusi how to make and use a quipu. Use details from the text.*

pages 116–119

Nicolás

Detail
Mamacona struggled with her thoughts. She knew about the ban against women using a quipu.

Detail
Mamacona had also possessed a thirst for knowledge when she was a girl.

Topic
Mamacona

Detail
Her brother had secretly taught her to keep accounts with the quipu.

Detail
In the end, Mamacona was won over by Cusi's hopeful plea.

Write About the Text I used notes from my idea web to write a paragraph from Mamacona's point of view.

Student Model: *Narrative Text*

At first, I didn't know whether I should teach Cusi how to make and use a quipu. It is a great risk because of the ban against women using a quipu. But then I thought about my own childhood. I had also possessed a thirst for knowledge when I was a young girl. My brother had secretly taught me how to use the quipu. Knowing how to use the quipu is important knowledge. It has helped me in my life. It has helped me in my work. I want to help Cusi learn these skills, too. She is very hopeful about learning and using them.

TALK ABOUT IT

Text Evidence
Draw a box around a sentence that comes from the notes. Why does Nicolás use this detail in his paragraph?

Grammar
Circle the verb phrase in the seventh sentence. Why does Nicolás use the present perfect form of the verb in this sentence?

Condense Ideas
Underline sentences 6-8. How can you combine the sentences to condense ideas?

Your Turn

Write a paragraph from Cusi's point of view. Describe what she will do the next time she sells her vicuña robes to the royal merchants. Use text evidence for support.

» Go Digital
Write your response online. Use your editing checklist.

123

TALK ABOUT IT

Weekly Concept Past and Present

? Essential Question
What can the past teach us?

>> *Go Digital*

 What are the people in the photo looking at? What questions might they have about what they see? Write the questions in the chart.

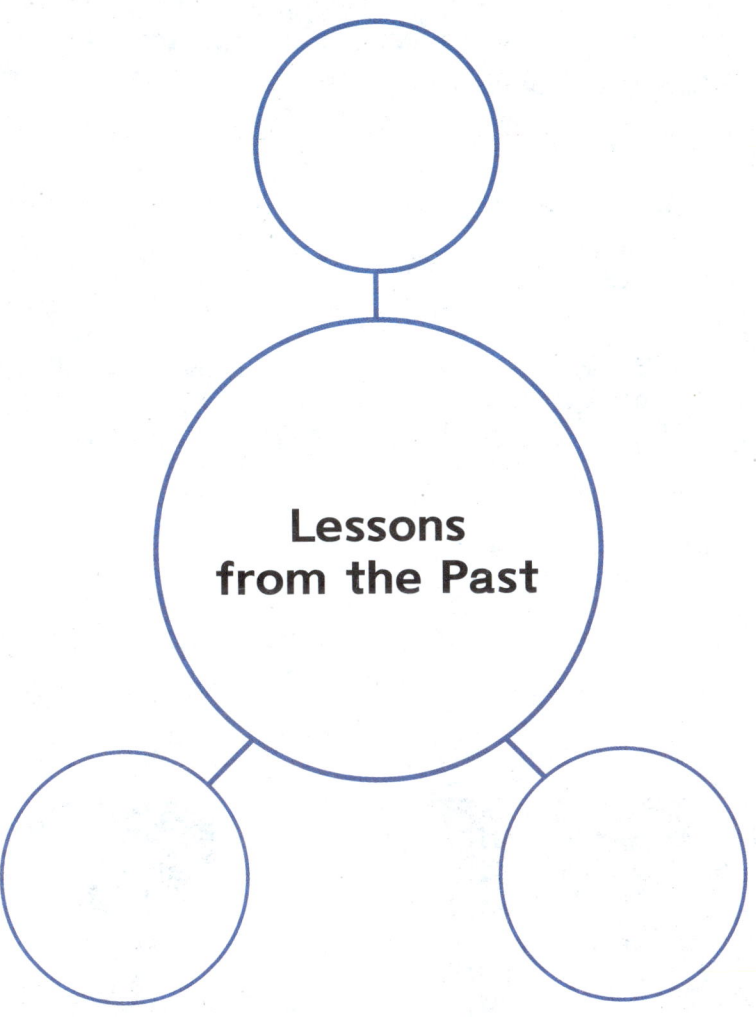

Discuss how thinking about the ruins connects the past and the present. Use words from the chart. You can say:

The ruins connect the past and the present by making us think about _____.

More Vocabulary

 Read the sentence. Look at the picture. Talk about the word with a partner. Answer the questions.

create

The students **create** posters for their class play.

What do you like to create?

_____

gloom

The class was filled with **gloom** when their field trip was cancelled.

When was your class filled with gloom?

_____

shun

Margaret chooses to **shun** unhealthy food to stay healthy.

What do you shun to stay healthy?

_____

view

In the girls' **view**, the party is very exciting.

In your view, what thing is exciting?

_____

Poetry Terms

rhyme scheme

Some poems have rhyming words at the end of lines. This is called a **rhyme scheme**. Rhyme schemes can have different patterns.

Cats and kittens express their views
With hisses, purrs, and little mews.
Instead of taking baths like me,
They use their tongues quite handily.

The pattern of rhyme in this poem is *aabb*. The letters show which lines rhyme.

aa = views and mews

bb = me and handily

personification

When a writer uses **personification**, the writer gives a human ability—such as laughing—to something that is not human—such as an animal.

Hey diddle, diddle
The cat and the fiddle
The cow jumped over the moon;
The little dog laughed
To see such sport
And the dish ran away with the spoon.

COLLABORATE

Work with a partner.
Read the poem together.
Then complete each sentence.
Underline the correct answer.

When danger is very near,
The shy turtle doesn't fear.
He pulls in his head and feet
And he's gone. How very neat!

The rhyme scheme is _____.

The use of the word _____ shows personification.

Text Evidence

Shared Read | Genre • Poetry

1. Talk About It

Look at the photograph. Talk about what you see. Write your ideas.

The photograph shows _____

_____

_____.

2. Specific Vocabulary

Read the first line. The word *antique* refers to something from many years ago. Rewrite the first line of the poem using a synonym for the word *antique*.

_____

_____

3. Literary Element
Rhyme Scheme

Look at the first five lines of the poem. Draw boxes around the words that rhyme with *land*. Draw a circle around the word that almost rhymes with *stone*.

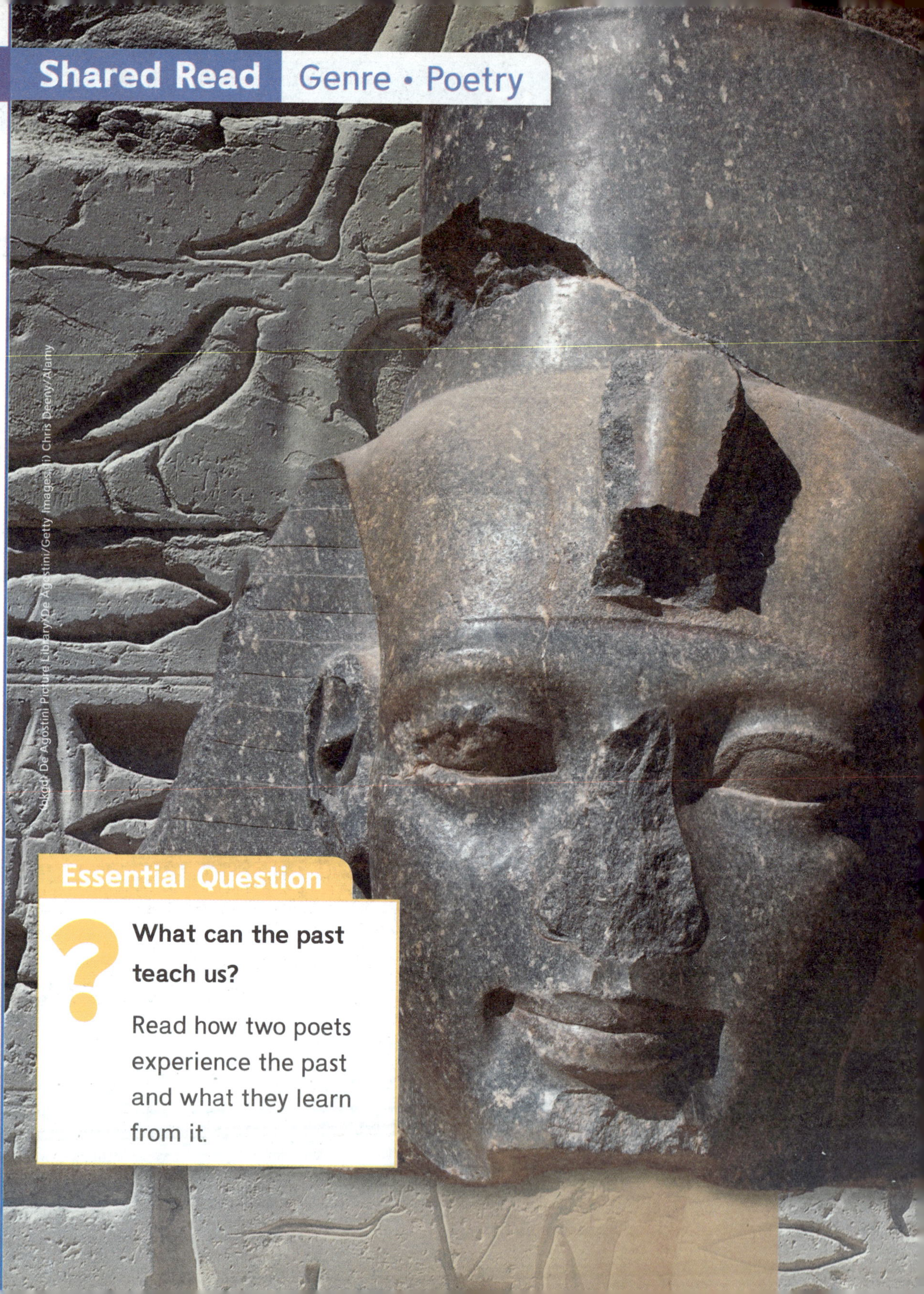

Essential Question

What can the past teach us?

Read how two poets experience the past and what they learn from it.

128

Ozymandias

I met a traveler from an antique land

Who said: "Two vast and trunkless legs of stone

Stand in the desert . . . Near them, on the sand,

Half sunk, a shattered visage lies, whose frown,

And wrinkled lip, and sneer of cold command,

Tell that its sculptor well those passions read

Which yet survive, stamped on these lifeless things,

The hand that mocked them, and the heart that fed:

And on the pedestal these words appear:

'My name is Ozymandias, king of kings:

Look on my works, ye Mighty, and despair!'

Nothing beside remains. Round the decay

Of that colossal wreck, boundless and bare

The lone and level sands stretch far away."

—Percy Bysshe Shelley

Text Evidence

❶ Specific Vocabulary

Read lines 4 and 5. Underline the context clues for *visage*. What word is a synonym for *visage*?

_____ is a synonym for *visage*.

❷ Talk About It

Explain who Ozymandias is. Then write about it.

_____

_____

❸ Comprehension
Theme

Circle the words that tell you what the traveler sees beside the sculpture's remains. What is the poet's message?

_____

_____

_____

Text Evidence

1. Literary Element
Rhyme Scheme

Read the first stanza. Which words rhyme? Write the words.

_____

_____

2. Talk About It

Reread the first and second stanzas. Where did the speaker work as a boy? What did he learn to make there?

_____

_____

3. Specific Vocabulary

Read the third stanza. The word *majestic* means "grand or impressive." What two things does the speaker describe as majestic? Write the words.

_____

Lifelong Friends

When I was but a lad of ten,
I joined the world of working men,
Apprentice was the name I took,
I learned the way to print a book.

The print shop had an air of **gloom**,
And sunlight seemed to **shun** the room,
My master was a man I feared,
He raged at me and pulled his beard.

The printing press was friend to me,
Majestic as a mighty tree,
And so I grew to love that place,
My heart would sing, my pulse would race.

Each time I worked with type and ink,
I always trembled just to think
That all those many rows of words
Would soon fly up and out like birds.

Those books were tutors glad to share
Their words with people everywhere,
So many books for eager hands,
For rich and poor in many lands.

Though now my youth has passed away,
And near the hearth I spend my day,
When I'm forlorn, I contemplate
The many books I helped create.

As I commemorate my past,
One view of mine will always last:
Each book a lifelong friend might be
To someone, yes, but most to me.

—Constance Andrea Keremes

Make Connections

Talk about the way in which the past affects the speaker in each poem. **ESSENTIAL QUESTION**

Explain how reflecting on the past could have an influence on you in the present. **TEXT TO SELF**

Text Evidence

❶ Literary Element
Personification

Read the first two lines of the second stanza. Who or what shared "their words"?

_____

_____ shared their words.

❷ Talk About It

Discuss the meaning of the third stanza. Then write about it.

When the speaker is _____,

he _____

_____.

❸ Comprehension
Theme

Read the last stanza. A theme of the poem is to take pride in your work. Underline the words that support this idea.

Respond to the Text

 **Partner Discussion** Work with a partner. Answer the questions. Discuss what you learned about "Ozymandias" and "Lifelong Friends." Write the page numbers where you found text evidence.

What does the speaker in "Ozymandias" learn from the past?

In the past, _____.

In the present, _____.

The speaker learns _____.

Text Evidence

Page(s): _____

Page(s): _____

Page(s): _____

What does the speaker in "Lifelong Friends" learn from the past?

As a boy, the speaker _____.

As an adult, the speaker _____
_____.

The speaker learns _____.

Text Evidence

Page(s): _____

Page(s): _____

Page(s): _____

 **Group Discussion** Present your answers to the group. Cite text evidence to justify your thinking. Listen to and discuss the group's opinions about your answers.

 **Write** Review your notes about "Ozymandias" and "Lifelong Friends." Then write your answer to the Essential Question. Use text evidence to support your answer. Use vocabulary words from this week's reading in your writing.

What do the two speakers learn from the past?

The speaker in "Ozymandias" learns _____
_____.

The speaker in "Lifetime Friends" learns _____
_____.

Both speakers _____, but they
_____.

Share Writing Present your writing to the class. Discuss their opinions. Think about what the class has to say. Did they justify their claims? Explain why you agree or disagree with their claims.

I agree that _____.

I disagree with _____ because _____.

133

Write to Sources

Take Notes About the Text I took notes on this idea web to answer the question: *How does the poet of "Lifelong Friends" use personification to describe ordinary objects in new ways?*

pages 128–131

Brianna

Topic
Personification in "Lifelong Friends"

Evidence
"The print shop had an air of gloom,"

Evidence
"The printing press was friend to me,"

Evidence
"And sunlight seemed to shun the room,"

Write About the Text I used notes from my idea web to write an informative paragraph about personification in "Lifelong Friends."

Student Model: *Informative Text*

The poet of "Lifelong Friends" uses personification to describe ordinary things in new ways. First, the poet writes, "The print shop had an air of gloom." This image helps the reader experience the shop as a person filled with gloom. Next, the poet writes, "And sunlight seemed to shun the room." This image helps the reader experience sunlight as a person who is avoiding the room. By using personification, the poet helps the reader experience the objects in new ways. The poet also helps the reader experience the objects in exciting ways.

TALK ABOUT IT

Text Evidence
Underline a sentence that comes from the notes. Why does Brianna use this detail in her paragraph?

Grammar
Circle the phrase "in new ways" in the first sentence. What is the purpose of this phrase?

Condense Ideas
Underline the last two sentences. How can you combine the sentences to condense the ideas?

Your Turn

Write a paragraph that tells how the poet of "Lifelong Friends" uses personification to describe the printing press and books.

>> *Go Digital*
Write your response online. Use your editing checklist.

Unit 3
Accomplishments

The Big Idea

What does it take to accomplish a goal?

TALK ABOUT IT

Weekly Concept Common Ground

? Essential Question
What happens when people share ideas?

» *Go Digital*

 **COLLABORATE** What are the girls in the photo doing? How did they find common ground to create the design? Write the ways in the chart.

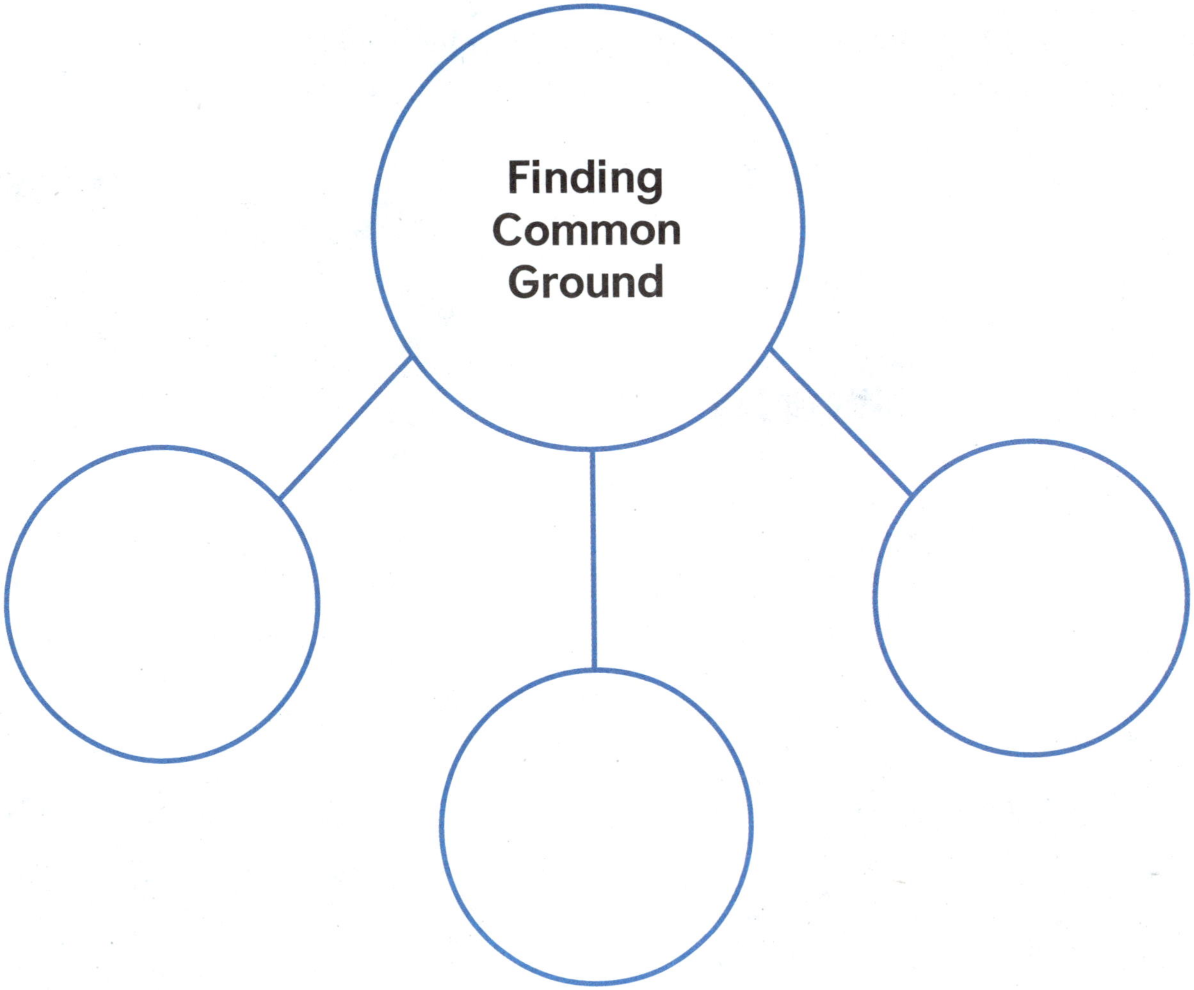

Finding Common Ground

Discuss how the girls found common ground. Use words from the chart. You can say:

The girls found common ground by _____

_____.

More Vocabulary

 Look at the picture and read the word. Then read the sentence. Talk about the word with a partner. Write your own sentence.

applauded

The class **applauded** Margaret after she read her poem aloud.

I *applauded* _____

after _____.

discussion

The class had a thoughtful **discussion** about the assignment.

I would like to have a *discussion* with my

classmates about _____.

awed

The girls were **awed** by the video on the computer.

I was *awed* by _____

because _____.

incredible

The weightlifter has **incredible** strength.

People might think something is *incredible*

because _____

_____.

opposing

The **opposing** teams line up before the game starts.

Opposing teams are teams that _____

_____.

routine

Tim's **routine** after school includes putting the trash in the trash bin.

My *routine* after school includes _____

_____.

Words and Phrases
Verbs with Prepositions

soaked through = completely wet
After walking in the rain all morning, the children were <u>soaked through</u>.

slip through = slide past or through something
They saw the fish <u>slip through</u> the fisher's hands and go back into the water.

Read the sentences below. Write the verb and preposition that mean the same thing as the underlined words.

I fell into the pool, so my clothes were <u>completely wet</u>.
I fell into the pool, so my clothes were _____.

The teams saw the ball <u>slide through</u> the player's hand.
The teams saw the ball _____ the player's hand.

» Go Digital Add these verbs with prepositions to your New Words notebook. Write a sentence to show the meaning of each.

Text Evidence

Shared Read | Genre • Realistic Fiction

1 Talk About It

Read the title. Look at the picture. Talk about what you see. Write your ideas.

What does the title tell you?

_____
_____
_____
_____

What is the girl doing?

_____
_____
_____
_____

Take notes as you read the story.

The Rockers Build a Soccer Field

Essential Question

? What happens when people share ideas?

Read how all members of a team contribute toward reaching their goal.

A Dream to Share

"Buenos días, Mariana," Mr. Sanchez greeted his daughter at the breakfast table. *"¿Dormiste bien?"*

"I slept very well, Papa. I had a dream that I scored the winning goal on a brand new soccer field!"

Mr. Sanchez smiled and said, "Your dream could be a sign that River Edge will finally get a regulation soccer field. Maybe you have special insight into what will happen at tonight's Town Council meeting. Remember, we must get the whole team there to convince them we need a better field."

That night, Mariana and her father arrived at the meeting hall to find it filled to capacity. They sat with the other River Edge Rockers, their community soccer team. Councilwoman Maloof opened the discussion, and Mr. Boyd, the Rockers' manager, spoke first. "Our team currently practices in a tiny school yard, and only when it's not already booked." The team nodded briskly.

Mrs. Yamagata, owner of Something Sushi, walked to the podium. "I believe the town owns an empty lot next to my restaurant," she said. "Couldn't that be a soccer field?" The Rockers applauded.

"A soccer field would be a good use for that lot," Councilwoman Maloof said. "But the town simply doesn't have the money to build and maintain one."

"The Rockers can do it!" Jamil spoke up.

"Jamil's right," Mr. Sanchez said. He began to negotiate with the Council. "If the town lets the Rockers use the vacant lot, *we* will turn it into a soccer field." After some discussion, the Council reached a decision. "We hereby approve using the vacant lot adjacent to Something Sushi for a community soccer field!" Mariana looked nervously at her cheering teammates, then at her father. Mr. Sanchez winked at her, as if to say, "Didn't you have a dream?"

Text Evidence

❶ Specific Vocabulary

Read the second paragraph. The phrase *brand new* means "new and unused." Underline the name of the thing that is brand new in Mariana's dream.

❷ Sentence Structure

Read the first sentence of the fourth paragraph. Underline the compound subject. Circle the word that connects the two subjects in the compound subject. Who arrived at the meeting hall? Write the two subjects.

_____

_____

❸ Comprehension
Theme

Read the fifth paragraph. At the Town Council meeting, what does Mrs. Yamagata suggest to help solve the soccer team's problem?

_____

_____

Text Evidence

1 Sentence Structure

Read the first sentence. Circle the commas. Write the phrase that tells where the team got together.

_____
_____
_____

2 Comprehension
Theme

Read the fifth paragraph. What great idea about raising money does Benny share with the group? Underline Benny's idea.

3 Specific Vocabulary

Read the last sentence of the last paragraph. The word *ecstatic* means "very happy." Why were the Rockers ecstatic?

_____
_____
_____

Dirty Dogs Raise Funds

The following day, at Something Sushi, the team got together to share ideas for raising money. "A karaoke night would be fun," said Mariana.

"Cool!" Jamil shouted. "I'll get to show off my **incredible** voice."

"Next idea—*please*!" the team's goalie, Benny Chan, joked.

"What about a car wash?" suggested Mr. Boyd.

"That's good," Benny said, "except the Environment Club is already having one." Then suddenly he shouted, "Hey, let's have a DOG wash!" Everyone thought it was a great idea—until they met the dirty dogs.

On the day of the dog wash, dog owners lined up in the middle school parking lot, where six wading pools had been set up. Mariana began washing a large shaggy dog, shielding herself from the suds that flew each time the dog shook himself off.

Suddenly, a poodle Jamil was washing jumped out of the pool to chase a dachshund. Then several others took off, barking and tangling their leashes.

Mr. Boyd was not amused. "Owners, control your dogs!" After this near disaster, things settled into a **routine**. By the end of the day, the Rockers were soaked through but **ecstatic** about raising $750.

144

This Lot Rocks!

A week later, the team gathered at the lot, carrying tools purchased with their earnings. Staring at the fallow field of dirt, rubble, and weeds, Mariana thought, "This bears no resemblance to the soccer field in my dream." But she kicked into action with the others, scooping up debris and depositing it in a rented dumpster.

Then Mariana bent down to pick up a rock. She grunted when it wouldn't budge. Jamil helped her shovel around it until they saw it was a huge boulder. Mr. Sanchez studied it. *"Esta roca es enorme.* We need a bigger tool." All were **awed** when he returned a while later with a **backhoe**.

After the boulder had been extracted, they all looked into the gaping hole. "Let's haul in dirt from the perimeter," Jamil proposed. It took a while, but with everyone working together they moved enough soil from the field's edges to fill the hole. In the next few weeks, the Rockers even enlisted neighbors to donate materials for a drainage system, sod for grass, and bleachers.

Opening day attracted a huge crowd of soccer fans, all enthralled by the new field. Before the game, the Rockers huddled together. "We did it. Together we turned an unseemly lot into our 'field of dreams,'" Mr. Boyd said. "Now let's get out there!"

Later, as the clock was running out on the 0-0 score, Mariana kicked the ball hard. When she saw it slip through the **opposing** goalie's hands, she realized that her dream had actually come true!

Make Connections

 Tell how sharing ideas helps build the soccer field. **ESSENTIAL QUESTION**

When has working with others helped you accomplish a goal? **TEXT TO SELF**

Text Evidence

1 Talk About It

Read the first paragraph. Compare the soccer field in Mariana's dreams to the vacant lot. What does each field look like? Then write about it.

_____

_____

2 Specific Vocabulary

Read the last sentence of the second paragraph. A backhoe is a large digging machine. Why do you think the kids are awed when they see the backhoe?

_____

_____

3 Comprehension
Theme

Read the fourth paragraph. What does Mr. Boyd say that points to the theme of the story? Underline the sentence.

145

Respond to the Text

 **Partner Discussion** Work with a partner. Answer the questions. Discuss what you learned about "The Rockers Build a Soccer Field." Write the page numbers where you found text evidence.

What ideas do people share at the Town Council meeting?

First, Mr. Boyd _____. Page(s): _____

Then Mrs. Yamagata _____. Page(s): _____

Finally, Jamil _____. Page(s): _____

Text Evidence

What ideas does the team share with each other?

The day after the meeting the team _____. Page(s): _____

When Mariana and Jamil find a boulder, _____. Page(s): _____

When the boulder leaves a gaping hole, _____. Page(s): _____

Text Evidence

 **Group Discussion** Present your answers to the group. Cite text evidence to justify your thinking. Listen to and discuss the group's opinions about your answers.

Write Review your notes about "The Rockers Build a Soccer Field." Then write your answer to the Essential Question. Use text evidence to support your answer. Use vocabulary words from this week's reading in your writing.

How does sharing ideas help the Rockers build a soccer field?

At the Town Council meeting, Mrs. Yamagata, Jamil, and Mr. Sanchez _____ _____.

After sharing ideas, the team decides to raise money by _____.

After sharing ideas, the team uses the money to _____.

Sharing ideas helps the Rockers because_____ _____.

Share Writing Present your writing to the class. Discuss their opinions. Think about what the class has to say. Did they justify their claims? Explain why you agree or disagree with their claims.

I agree with _____ that _____.

I disagree with _____ because _____.

147

Write to Sources

Michael

Take Notes About the Text I took notes on the main idea and details chart to respond to the prompt: *Add a scene to the story about Mariana asking a neighbor to donate paint for the bleachers. Use details from the story in your new scene.*

pages 142–145

Detail
At the Town Council meeting, Mrs. Yamagata suggested that the city should let the Rockers use an empty lot for their soccer field; the Council agreed.

Detail
Mr. Boyd, the Rockers' coach, helped the team run a charity dog wash to raise money for their soccer field.

Detail
Mr. Sanchez used a backhoe to move a giant rock, and other neighbors donated materials to help the Rockers complete their field.

Main Idea
The people of River Edge cheerfully pitched in to help make Mariana's dream come true and help the Rockers get their soccer field.

Write About the Text I used the notes from my main idea and details chart to help me add a scene to the story.

Student Model: *Narrative Text*

After the soccer game, Mariana saw Mrs. Lopez, her next-door neighbor, working in her flower garden.

"Hi, Mrs. Lopez," Mariana said. "I'm sorry to bother you, but I wanted to ask if you could help our soccer team. We cleared the vacant lot next to Something Sushi and created a soccer field. We're almost finished. But we still need to paint the bleachers. Would you be able to donate some paint?"

"Oh, Mariana, I am happy to help. You kids did a wonderful thing," Mrs. Lopez answered.

TALK ABOUT IT

Text Evidence
Draw a box around the sentence where Mariana asks Mrs. Lopez for help. Use your notes to answer this question: Why would Mariana expect that Mrs. Lopez would help her?

Grammar
Circle the two action verbs in the third sentence of the second paragraph. What action verbs mean about the same as the verbs you circled?

Connect Ideas
Underline the two sentences in the last paragraph. Then combine them using a connecting word.

Your Turn

Add a scene that uses foreshadowing at the end of the story. Include details from the story.

>> *Go Digital!*
Write your response online. Use your editing checklist.

149

TALK ABOUT IT

Weekly Concept Transformations

? Essential Question
What kind of challenges transform people?

>> Go Digital

 **Think about the challenges of rock climbing. Why might rock climbing be a transforming experience for the man? Write the reasons in the chart.**

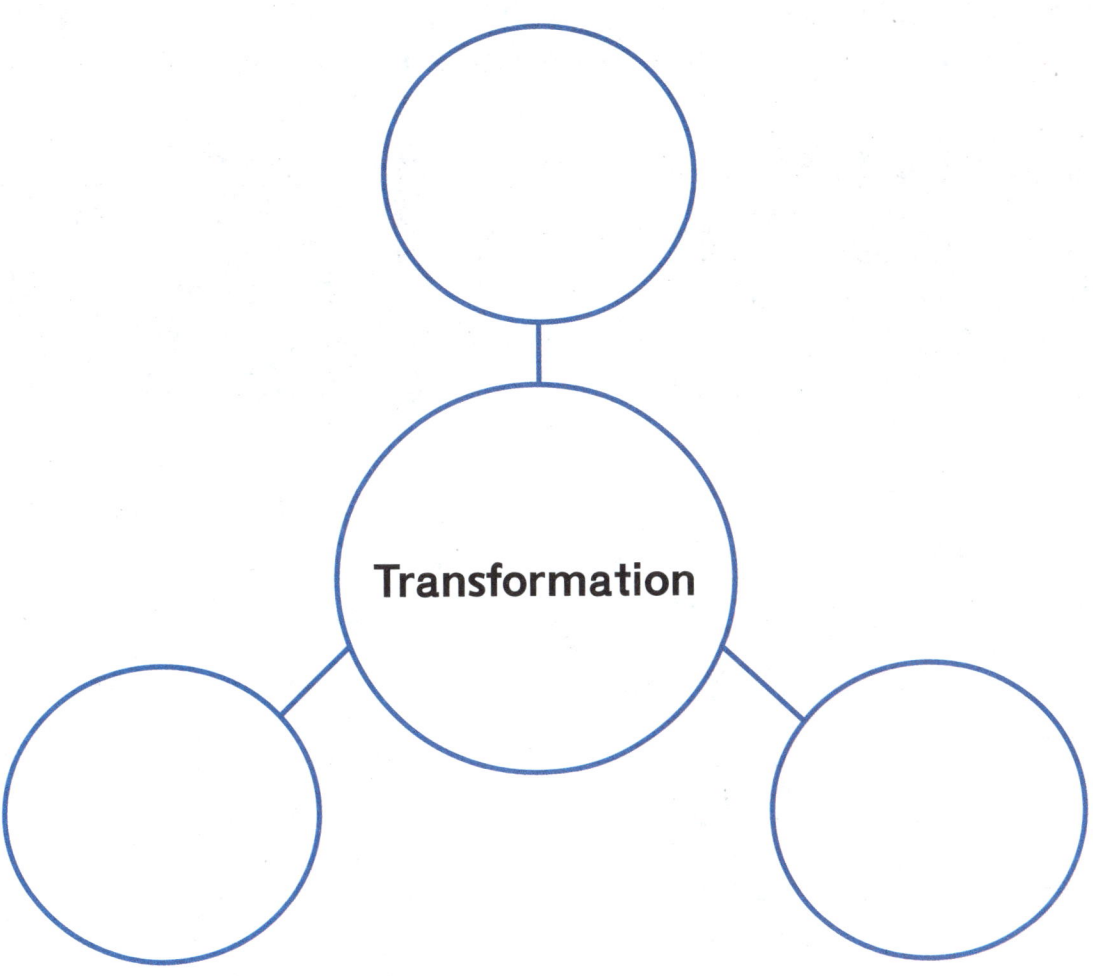

Transformation

Discuss why learning to rock climb might transform the man. Use words from the chart. You can say:

Rock climbing might transform the man because _____

_____.

More Vocabulary

Look at the picture and read the word. Then read the sentence. Talk about the word with a partner. Write your own sentence.

considering

After **considering** the menu, Rico chose a cheese sandwich for lunch.

Before *considering* a topic for my report, I will _____.

foresight

Erika had the **foresight** to take an umbrella with her today.

An example of having *foresight* is _____.

conviction

Amber spoke to her class with **conviction** about her ideas.

To speak with *conviction* means _____.

subside

Jake is waiting for the rain to **subside** so he can play outside.

Sometimes, while I am waiting for the rain to *subside*, I _____.

unnerved

Sara was **unnerved** by the thunder and lightning.

I sometimes become *unnerved* when

_____.

volunteer

Magda is a **volunteer** at an animal shelter.

I would like to be a *volunteer* at _____

_____.

Words and Phrases
Idioms

the quiet was shattered = something loud disturbed a quiet place
At the library, <u>the quiet was shattered</u> by a man coughing.

a worried expression crossed his face = his face suddenly showed that he was worried
When the ship's captain saw the giant wave, <u>a worried expression crossed his face</u>.

Read the sentences below. Write the idiom that means the same thing as the underlined words.

While we took the test, <u>something loud disturbed us</u>, and we all looked up.
While we took the test, _____, and and we all looked up.

When our teacher saw a dog run into the school, <u>his face suddenly showed that he was worried</u>.
When our teacher saw a dog run into the school, _____.

» Go Digital Add these idioms to your New Words notebook. Write a sentence to show the meaning of each.

Text Evidence

1. **Talk About It**

Read the title. Look at the illustration. Talk about what you see. Write your ideas.

What does the title tell you?

_____

_____

What do you notice about the setting of the story?

_____

_____

What do you notice about the two girls in the illustration?

_____

_____

Take notes as you read the story.

Shared Read | **Genre • Realistic Fiction**

Facing the STORM

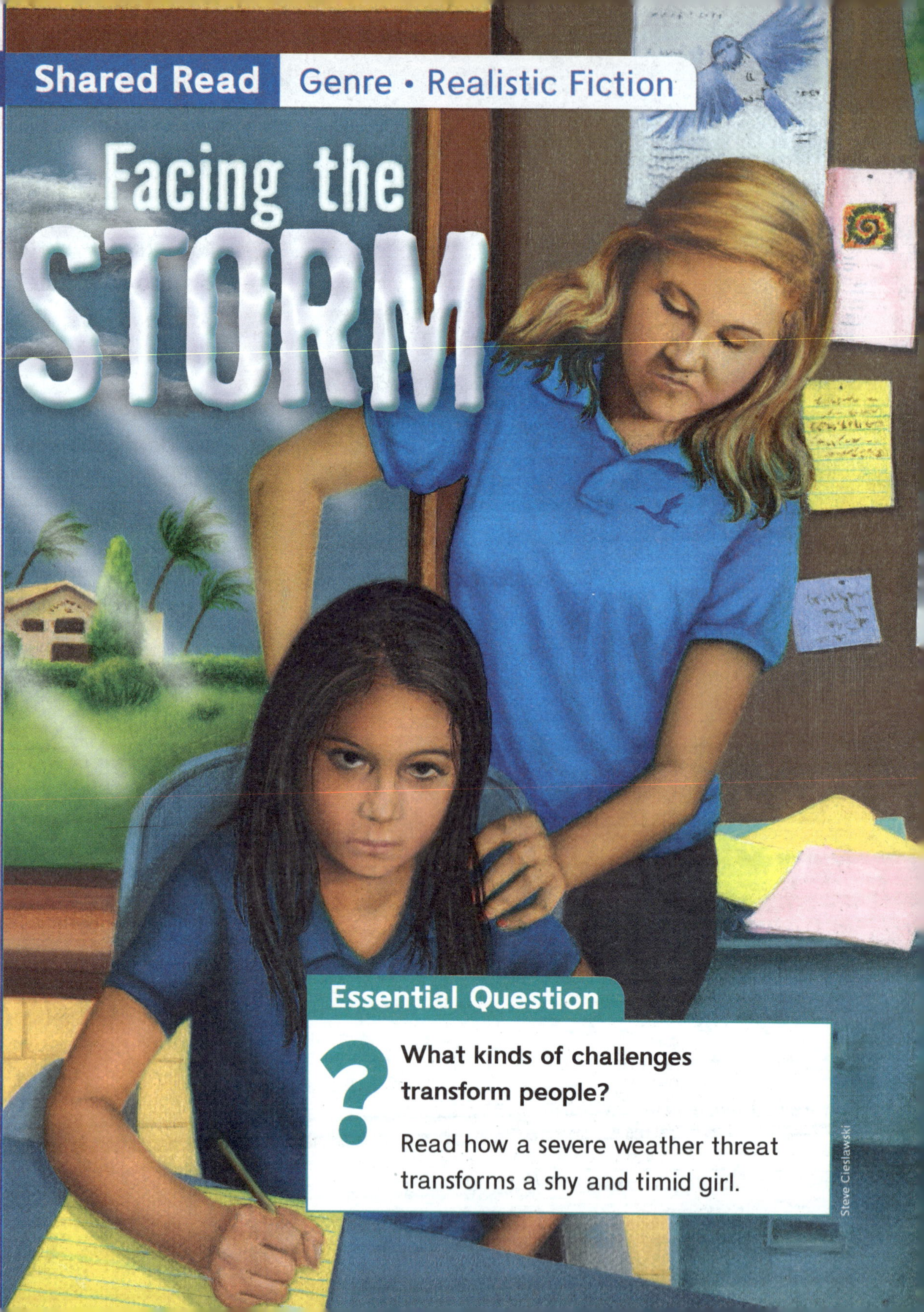

Essential Question

? What kinds of challenges transform people?

Read how a severe weather threat transforms a shy and timid girl.

154

Isabel Moreno sat carefully inserting papers into a folder. She had been at the Gateway Nature Center's office all morning and was weary of filing. She wanted desperately to work with the animals, especially the injured birds that the center rehabilitated. But her mom, who was the assistant director of the center, said Isabel was too young and there was no time to supervise her.

"I've been a weekend volunteer this whole school year," Isabel thought. "I know more about birds than almost anyone here," she said to herself with **conviction**, recalling as evidence the extensive research she had done reading books and web sites on natural history. Then she sighed. She had never been good at speaking up for herself, and who would listen to a shy seventh grader anyway?

Suddenly, the quiet was shattered by Amy Jensen bursting in and letting the door slam. Isabel felt herself shrink. Amy, who had been a **volunteer** a bit longer than Isabel, was 16 and strutted around like she owned the place. "Hey, Isabel, I've got a job for you," she barked, planting a hand on Isabel's shoulder.

Isabel recoiled from Amy's touch, but she willed herself to remain still. "Don't make trouble," she reminded herself, though she would have loved to brush Amy's hand off. "I have to finish this filing," she squeaked feebly.

Just then, Isabel's mother rushed into the room with Mr. Garza, the custodian. "The hurricane forecast for Miami has skewed to the south and is entering the Gulf," Mrs. Moreno reported. "We should be okay up here in the inlet, but we'll likely get some fierce and persistent winds. I've sent the other volunteers home, but I need you girls to help Mr. Garza get the storm shutters down in here and in the **aviary**. Then I'll take you home." Isabel leaped to her feet, excited to have an opportunity to help the birds.

Text Evidence

❶ Comprehension
Theme

Read the fourth paragraph. What would Isabel have loved to do after Amy planted her hand on Isabel's shoulder? Underline the words that tell you. Why didn't Isabel do that?

_____

_____

❷ Sentence Structure ACT

Read the second sentence of the fifth paragraph. What is entering the Gulf? Underline the word that tells you.

❸ Specific Vocabulary ACT

Reread the last paragraph. An aviary is a caged area where birds are kept. Underline the sentence in the paragraph that helps you understand the meaning of *aviary*. Why is Isabel excited about helping Mr. Garza in the aviary?

_____

_____

Text Evidence

1 Talk About It

Explain what Amy means when she says she is "in charge." Also, explain why Isabel groans inwardly, but says nothing. Then write about it.

_____

_____

2 Specific Vocabulary

Reread the last sentence in the second paragraph. The phrase *we're in for* means "we're going to get." Circle the reason Mr. Garza thinks they are going to have some flooding.

3 Sentence Structure

Read the third sentence in the fourth paragraph. Circle the pronoun *she*. Whom does this pronoun refer to? Draw a box around the name of the person.

Mrs. Moreno's cell phone jangled, and she answered it at once, listening intently. "Change of plans," she announced as she hung up. "The winds are worse than expected along the coastline, so the Gulf Shore Preserve needs help preparing for the storm. I've got to go down there with the staff. We'll take the inlet bridge, so we shouldn't be gone long. Stay inside with Mr. Garza after you get the storm shutters down. And call me on my cell if there are any problems," she directed as she dashed out.

Amy crowed that she was now "in charge." Isabel groaned inwardly, but said nothing. Mr. Garza and the girls worked quickly and were soon back inside, listening to the wind batter and rattle the shutters. When Mr. Garza found an emergency weather report on the computer, a worried expression crossed his face. "A storm surge is heading our way, right up the inlet," he announced. "We're in for some flooding."

Authoritative as ever, Amy called Isabel's mother to tell her the news, but she sounded flustered when she hung up. "The surge has flooded the bridge, and they're stuck there!" she gasped. "What do we do?"

Isabel was **unnerved** that both Mr. Garza and Amy seemed so panicked, but after silently **considering** the dilemma for a few seconds, she roused herself and said calmly, "We should move the birds to the reptile house. It's on higher ground." As she strode out of the building with Mr. Garza and Amy following, she caught a glimpse of the satellite image on the computer. The vastness of the storm nearly filled the entire Gulf now.

Once inside the aviary, Isabel watched Amy lunge from cage to cage, agitating the birds. "Don't jump around so much!" Isabel instructed. "They're scared enough as it is, and your sudden movements aren't helping." Amy meekly calmed down, but she was shaking.

"Just think about the birds," Isabel said as they carried each cage up to the reptile house. The hawks screeched and beat their wings when they felt the wind. Isabel spoke soothingly to them, and they soon grew calmer. Amy watched in awe and tried to mimic Isabel's tone. Just as the water in the bird house had risen to their shins, they finished relocating the birds and waited inside the reptile house for the storm to subside.

After several hours, the water had receded, and Mrs. Moreno was able to return to the center. She expressed concern that she'd left them alone for so long, but Mr. Garza reassured her that Isabel's foresight and cool thinking had saved the birds.

Mrs. Moreno gazed at her daughter admiringly. "How did you summon such confidence and courage?" she asked Isabel.

"I'm not sure," Isabel admitted. "All I could think about was how scared the birds must have felt in their cages, and I just took charge."

"I'm proud of you, Isabel," said Mrs. Moreno.

Isabel paused a second. "I guess I'm proud of myself, Mom!"

Make Connections

? Talk about how Isabel was transformed during the hurricane. **ESSENTIAL QUESTION**

Describe a time when you showed unexpected courage. **TEXT TO SELF**

Text Evidence

1 Specific Vocabulary ACT

Read the first sentence of the first paragraph. The word *agitating* means "upsetting." How was Amy agitating the birds?

Amy was agitating the birds by

_____

2 Talk About It

Reread the first and second paragraphs. How has Isabel changed from the beginning of the story? Justify your answer.

_____

_____

_____

3 Comprehension
Theme

Reread the last four paragraphs. What helped Isabel take charge during the storm? Underline the sentence that tells you. Is she proud of herself? Circle the sentence that tells you.

157

Respond to the Text

 **Partner Discussion** Work with a partner. Answer the questions. Discuss what you learned about "Facing the Storm." Write the page numbers where you found text evidence.

Describe Isabel's actions at the beginning of the story.

At the beginning of the story, Isabel _____. Page(s): _____

When Amy tells her what to do, Isabel _____. Page(s): _____

Text Evidence

Describe Isabel's actions in the middle of the story.

When she hears about the storm, Isabel _____. Page(s): _____

As the flooding begins, Isabel _____. Page(s): _____

Text Evidence

Describe Isabel's actions at the end of the story.

As the storm continues, Isabel _____. Page(s): _____

At the end of the story, Isabel _____. Page(s): _____

Text Evidence

 **Group Discussion** Present your answers to the group. Cite text evidence to justify your thinking. Listen to and discuss the group's opinions about your answers.

Write Review your notes about "Facing the Storm." Then write your answer to the Essential Question. Use text evidence to support your answer. Use vocabulary words from this week's reading in your writing.

How was Isabel transformed during the story?

At the beginning of the story, Isabel _____.

In the middle of the story, Isabel _____.

At the end of the story, Isabel _____.

Share Writing Present your writing to the class. Discuss their opinions. Think about what the class has to say. Did they justify their claims? Explain why you agree or disagree with their claims.

I agree with _____ that _____.

I disagree with _____ because _____.

Write to Sources

Evelyn

Take Notes About the Text I took notes on this chart to help me respond to the prompt: *Add descriptive details and dialogue to the scene when Isabel's mother returns to the nature center after the storm. Include details from the story.*

pages 154–157

Character's Thoughts	Character's Actions
-Isabel wanted to work with birds, but her mom said she was too young. -Isabel was weary of filing. -Isabel thought she knew more about birds than anyone else there.	-Isabel stayed calm and took charge of the situation. -Isabel thought of the idea to move the birds to higher ground. -Isabel kept the birds safe. -Isabel showed Amy how to move the birds.

Write About the Text I used the notes from my chart to help me add descriptive details and dialogue to the end of the story.

Student Model: Narrative Text

Suddenly, Isabel realized this was her big chance. "I think I proved something, Mom," Isabel added. "I showed that I'm *not* too young to work with the birds. During this emergency, I stayed calm. I kept the birds safe. It was my idea to move the birds to higher ground. I also showed Amy how to move the birds without scaring them. I think I'm ready for training."

Isabel's mother paused for a moment, and then said with a smile, "You're right, Isabel. We'll start your training tomorrow. You earned it!"

TALK ABOUT IT

Text Evidence
Underline the three actions Isabel took to help the birds. Why does she point these things out to her mother?

Grammar
Draw a box around two past-tense verbs in the dialogue. Why did Evelyn use the past tense?

Connect Ideas
Circle the fourth and fifth sentences in the first paragraph. How can you combine the sentences to connect the ideas?

Your Turn

Add a scene in which Amy and Mr. Garza explain to Isabel's mother what Isabel did during the storm. Include details from the story.

>> *Go Digital!*
Write your response online. Use your editing checklist.

TALK ABOUT IT

Weekly Concept Inspiration

? Essential Question
What can people accomplish by working together?

›› *Go Digital*

 What are the people in the photo doing? How does working together help them accomplish their goal? Write your ideas in the chart.

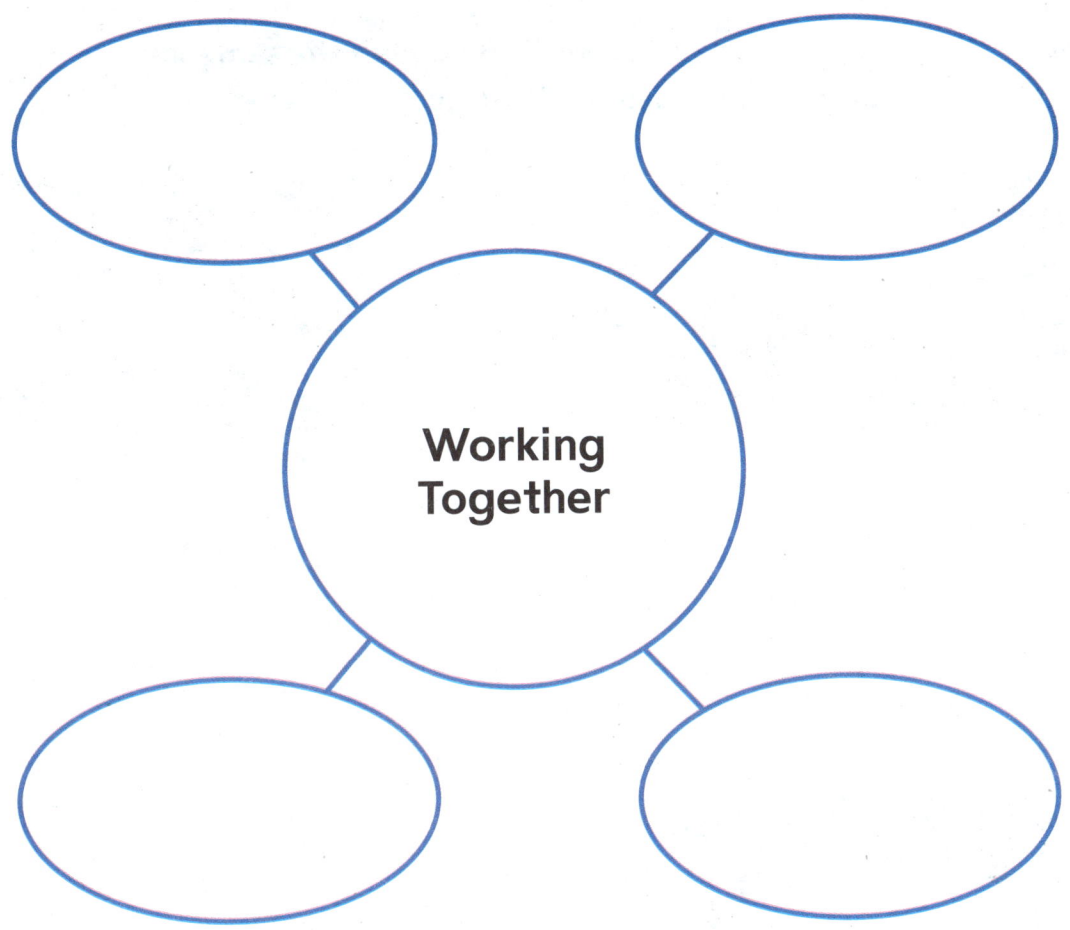

Discuss how working together helps the people build the house. Use words from the chart. You can say:

When people work together, they can _____

and _____. This helps them

_____ and _____.

More Vocabulary

Look at the picture and read the word. Then read the sentence. Talk about the word with a partner. Write your own sentence.

cultivated

Rodney **cultivated** his strawberry plants.

If I had a garden, I would want to *cultivate* _____.

discarded

Lucia **discarded** her water bottle in the recycling bin.

I *discarded* _____ in the trash.

declined

The number of people attending movie theaters has **declined**.

In my town, the number of _____ has *declined*.

experience

Traveling to Paris was an incredible **experience** for Lin.

_____ would be an incredible *experience* for me.

harvested

Using machinery, the farmer **harvested** his crop of wheat.

When something is *harvested*, it is _____ _____.

replenish

The waiter will **replenish** our water.

I try to *replenish* _____ whenever _____.

Words and Phrases
Suffixes -less and -ful

The suffix –less means "without something."
limit*less* = without limit
Some scientists believe that the universe is <u>limitless</u>.

The suffix –ful means "full of."
success*ful* = full of success
Tom is a <u>successful</u> *writer.*

Read the sentences below. Write the word with the suffix -less or -ful that means the same thing as the underlined words.

The number of sentences we can make is <u>without limit</u>.

The number of sentences we can make is _____.

That actress is <u>full of success</u>.

That actress is _____ .

» Go Digital Add these words to your New Words notebook. Write a sentence to show the meaning of each.

Text Evidence

1 Talk About It

Read the title. Look at the photographs on these pages. Talk about what you see. Write your ideas.

What does the title tell you?

_____

_____

_____

What are the women in the photograph doing?

_____

_____

_____

_____

Take notes as you read the text.

Shared Read — Genre • Narrative Nonfiction

Jewels from the Sea

Essential Question

? What can people accomplish by working together?

Read about the way one group of women improved their lives and their community.

A Life by the Sea

On their windswept island off the coast of eastern Africa, the women of Zanzibar were living much as their ancestors had. They cared for their children and cultivated their gardens. They farmed seaweed from the ocean and gathered shells to sell to tourists who visited their beautiful homeland. Some of the women worked long hours breaking rocks into gravel. Life on the Fumba Peninsula had often been hard for them. They made very little money, and some would say the women were impoverished. But they had always managed to feed their families. The ocean had provided for them, supplying abundant fish and oysters for food, and colorful shells to sell.

However, gifts from the ocean were not limitless. In the early 2000s, the women began to notice that oysters were not as plentiful as they once had been. In fact, Zanzibar's oysters were being harvested faster than they could replenish themselves. In ten short years, the number of oysters had declined dramatically. The women worried about the uncertain future.

A Fresh Approach

The women began to look beyond the solitude of their isolated coastal villages for help. To start, they welcomed the interest of scientists who were studying marine life in the waters surrounding Zanzibar. With guidance from the scientists, the women would work together to manage the way oysters were harvested. They soon discovered they had the power to bring oyster populations back to healthy levels.

The lustrous interior of an oyster shell.

Text Evidence

1 Sentence Structure ACT

Read the last sentence in the first paragraph. Circle the verb phrase *had provided*. Does this action take place in the past, the present or the future?

_____

2 Comprehension
Sequence

Read the second paragraph. What did the women do after they noticed that the number of oysters had declined? Underline the sentence that tells you.

3 Specific Vocabulary ACT

Read the second sentence in the last paragraph. *Marine* means "relating to the sea." Write a word or phrase from the sentence that helps you understand the meaning of *marine*.

_____

_____

167

Text Evidence

1 Talk About It

Read the first paragraph. Explain the important new idea the women of Zanzibar learned. Then write about it.

_____

_____

_____

_____

2 Specific Vocabulary

Read the sixth sentence in the first paragraph. Underline the words that help you understand the meaning of *income*.

3 Comprehension Sequence

Read the second paragraph. What happens after the oyster coats the bead or other irritant with nacre? Underline the sentence that tells you.

The women's search for solutions also unearthed another new idea. The women had always **discarded** the oysters' shells after removing the flesh. But visiting experts, who help communities sustain their resources, pointed out that the shells could be valuable, too. They offered to teach the women the skills needed for polishing the shells and turning them into jewelry. Before long, local residents and tourists were buying earrings, necklaces, and bracelets that the women made from shells. The income the women earned from selling jewelry was more than they had ever made before. It occurred to them that, with a little ingenuity, they had actually become businesswomen.

Building on Their Success

The women believed they could do even more. They wanted to have control of their business, not to be like a sharecropper who owns no land and so keeps only a part of the harvest. It was suggested that they join forces to cultivate *mabe* (MAH-bay) pearls, also known as "half-pearls." These pearls are created when a bead or other irritant is placed inside a living oyster. The oyster coats the irritation with layers of a shiny substance called *nacre* (NAY-ker). The nacre later hardens into a shimmering pearl, perfectly suited for jewelry.

This new project would also work well with the plans to restore the oyster beds. Four "no-take" zones were soon established for the oysters that would produce mabe pearls. There was only one problem. The pearls had to be cultivated underwater. Even though the women had lived all their lives by the sea, they did not know how to swim! So the next step for these strong-willed women was to learn to swim. Others in the village were impressed by the women's determination. Many joined

The women are harvesting oysters.

them to help see the project through. The first harvest of mabe pearls in 2008 was so successful that professional jewelers quickly bought up the gleaming harvest to make expensive jewelry.

Toward New Horizons

The women wanted to learn still more ways to improve their business. To do so, they would have to travel thousands of miles across the ocean. Just as learning to swim had been a first, leaving Zanzibar would be a new **experience**. But together they would go. In 2009, a small group flew to Newport, Rhode Island, in the U.S. to learn about designing and marketing jewelry. They met a master jeweler, who taught them how to wrap strands of fine silver wire into delicate designs around the mabe pearls. They also met people who shared tips on expanding small businesses into large ones. The women absorbed all this and brought it home with them.

The women of Zanzibar still live on their beautiful island. But today there is a difference. By working together, the women have become powerful caretakers of local natural resources and created prosperity in their community. Their hard-earned productivity will continue when they teach the next generation of young women how to accomplish great things.

One of the women polishes a *mabe* shell.

Make Connections

 Explain the steps that the women of Zanzibar took together to accomplish their goal. **ESSENTIAL QUESTION**

Talk about a time when you worked together with others to accomplish a common goal. **TEXT TO SELF**

Text Evidence

❶ Specific Vocabulary

Read the last sentence in the first paragraph. In this sentence, *absorbed* means "learned." Underline two things the women of Zanzibar absorbed while they were in Rhode Island.

❷ Sentence Structure

Read the first sentence of the second paragraph. Circle the pronoun *their*. Whom does the pronoun refer to? Underline the noun phrase that tells you.

❸ Talk About It

Name three ways the women of Zanzibar have helped their communities. Write your ideas.

_____

_____

_____

_____

Respond to the Text

 **Partner Discussion** Work with a partner. Answer the questions. Discuss what you learned about "Jewels from the Sea." Write the page numbers where you found text evidence.

Tell what problem the women of Zanzibar faced.

The women noticed _____

_____.

This was a problem because they worried _____

_____.

Text Evidence

Page(s): _____

Page(s): _____

Tell what the women did to solve the problem.

First, the women _____.

Next, the women _____.

Then the women _____.

Finally, the women _____.

Text Evidence

Page(s): _____

Page(s): _____

Page(s): _____

Page(s): _____

 **Group Discussion** Present your answers to the group. Cite text evidence to justify your thinking. Listen to and discuss the group's opinions about your answers.

Write Review your notes about "Jewels from the Sea." Then write your answer to the Essential Question. Use text evidence to support your answer. Use vocabulary words from this week's reading in your writing.

What did the women of Zanzibar accomplish by working together?

The women saved the oysters by _____
_____.

The women helped their community by _____
_____.

The women can now help the next generation of women by _____
_____.

Share Writing Present your writing to the class. Discuss their opinions. Think about what the class has to say. Did they justify their claims? Explain why you agree or disagree with their claims.

I agree with _____ that _____.

I disagree with _____ because _____.

171

Write to Sources

Dena

Take Notes About the Text I took notes in the chart to answer the question: *What steps did the women of Zanzibar take to improve their community and lives?*

pages 166–169

First
The women leaned how to bring oyster populations back to a healthy level.

↓

Next
They learned how to turn oyster shells into jewelry.

↓

Then
They worked together to cultivate and sell *mabe* pearls.

↓

Finally
They visited the United States and learned to improve their businesses.

Write About the Text I used the notes from my chart to help me write an informative paragraph about the women of Zanzibar.

Student Model: *Informative Text*

The women of Zanzibar took many steps to improve their community and their lives. First, they learned from scientists how to bring the oyster populations back to healthy levels. Next, the women learned how to turn the oyster shells into jewelry they could sell. Then they decided to work together to cultivate and sell valuable *mabe* pearls. Finally, the women visited the United States. There they learned more ways to improve their businesses.

TALK ABOUT IT

Text Evidence
Circle the sentence that shows the first thing the women learned. How did this help them improve their community?

Grammar
Underline the helping verb *could* and the main verb that follows it. What is the purpose of using the helping verb *could*?

Connect Ideas
Draw a box around the final two sentences. How can you combine the sentences to connect the ideas?

Your Turn

Explain how the women's jewelry businesses helped to increase the oyster population. Use text evidence.

>> *Go Digital!*
Write your response online. Use your editing checklist.

TALK ABOUT IT

Weekly Concept Milestones

? Essential Question
How can one person affect the opinions of others?

>> *Go Digital*

 Think about why this photo shows a milestone. Why is Sally Ride considered a trailblazer? How did she change the opinions of others? Write words about Sally Ride in the chart.

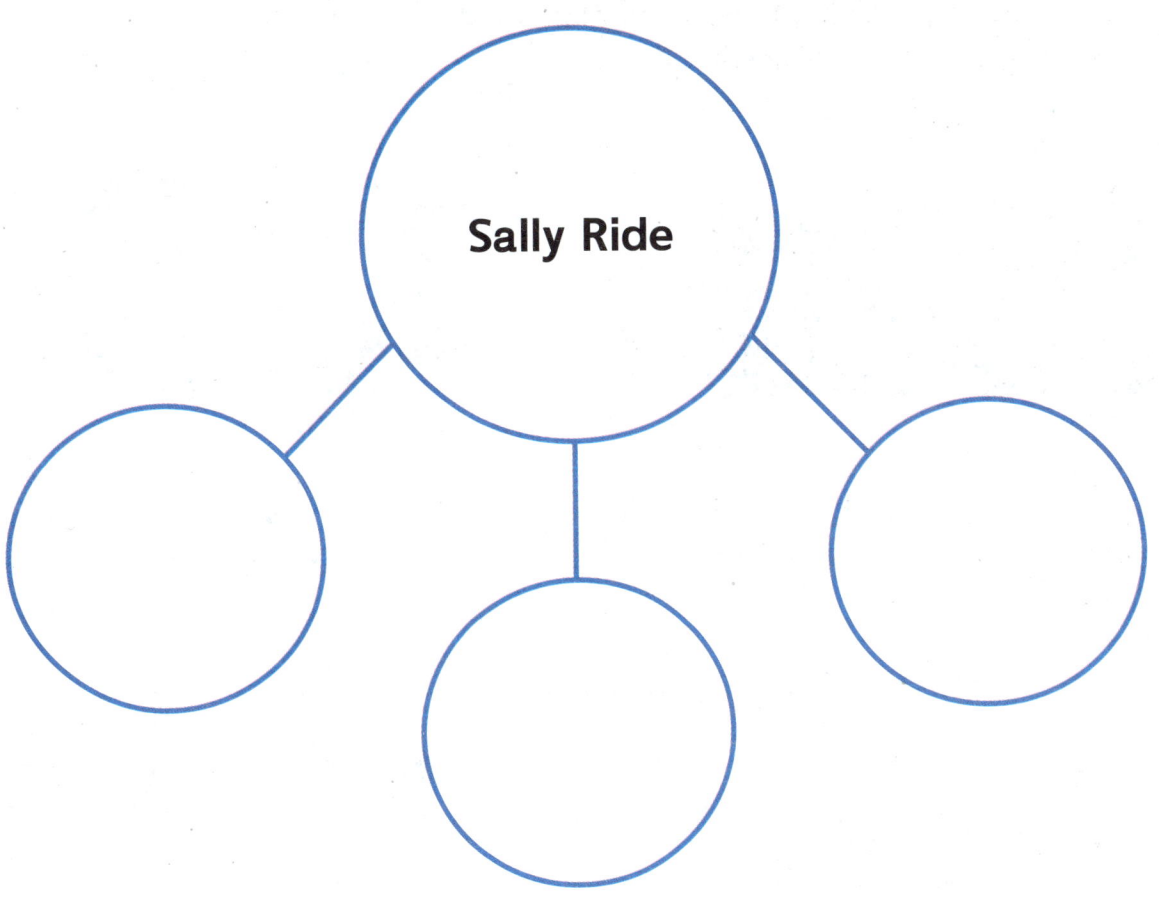

Sally Ride

Discuss why Sally Ride was a trailblazer. Use words from the chart. You can say:

Sally Ride was a trailblazer because she was the _____

_____ and the _____. She changed

opinions by _____.

More Vocabulary

 Look at the picture and read the word. Then read the sentence. Talk about the word with a partner. Write your own sentence.

audience

The **audience** cheered for the singer during the concert.

I was in the *audience* during _____

_____.

injustice

It was an **injustice** that women weren't allowed to vote until 1929.

One *injustice* I learned about in school was

_____.

enriched

Our teacher, Mrs. Williams, **enriched** our education.

_____ *enriched* my life by _____

_____.

opportunities

Students at the job fair can find many employment **opportunities**.

Some of the *opportunities* for fun in my town include _____.

perform

The singer will **perform** many of his new songs.

I would like to *perform* _____ for _____.

popularity

Using laptops to take notes in class is gaining **popularity** in schools.

_____ is gaining *popularity* in my school.

Words and Phrases
Idioms

breathed a sigh of relief = felt relieved
The driver breathed a sigh of relief after avoiding the accident.

idea could backfire = idea could have a bad result
The children want to cook dinner by themselves, but that idea could backfire.

Read the sentences below. Write the idiom that means the same thing as the underlined words.

My mother felt relieved after she passed a difficult exam.

My mother _____ after she passed a difficult exam.

Jalen wants to go camping during the storm, but that idea could have a bad result.

Jalen wants to go camping during the storm, but that _____.

» Go Digital Add these idioms to your New Words notebook. Write a sentence to show the meaning of each.

Text Evidence

Shared Read   Genre • Biography

1 Talk About It

Read the title. Look at the photograph. Talk about what you see. Write your ideas.

What does the title tell you?

_____
_____
_____
_____

What does the photograph show?

_____
_____
_____
_____

Take notes as you read the text.

MARIAN ANDERSON
STRUGGLES and TRIUMPHS

Essential Question

How can one person affect the opinions of others?

Read how the artistry of Marian Anderson changed people's minds about where African-American singers could perform.

178

A Voice of Great Promise

On February 27, 1897, a baby girl came into the world, crying with all her might. No one knew then that this voice would one day move mountains. It was not easy for an African American born at the turn of the twentieth century to follow her dream. But Marian Anderson would become one of the greatest singers of her time.

There were many opportunities for young Marian to explore her musical talent in her Philadelphia, Pennsylvania, neighborhood. She began singing in her local church choir at the age of six, but because she was such an adept singer, she was soon invited to **perform** outside of church. The Philadelphia Choral Society even awarded her $500 to take singing lessons. With such advantages, Marian was shocked by her first experience of racism.

Racism and Rejection

After graduating high school, Marian went to the admissions office of a local music school. "I want to study music here," she told the young clerk. When the clerk told her that African-American students were not accepted at the school, Marian was stunned, but she didn't argue. She wondered, "How can someone surrounded by the beauty of music be so full of hatred?"

The rejection did not stop the singer. Marian's church donated money for her to study with Giuseppe Boghetti, a famous voice teacher. In 1925, Boghetti entered Marian in a voice contest in which she competed against 300 others to win the honor of singing with the New York Philharmonic orchestra.

Unfortunately, her next big performance in New York City was not so successful. Because she was black, very few people came to hear her. Some critics found her performance to be "lacking." As a result, fewer people asked her to sing concerts.

Text Evidence

❶ Comprehension
Cause and Effect

Read the third paragraph. What was the effect of Marian asking to study at the music school?

_____

_____

❷ Specific Vocabulary

Reread the third sentence in the third paragraph. The word *stunned* means "surprised or shocked by something." Underline the sentence that tells why Marian was stunned by her rejection to the music school.

❸ Sentence Structure

Read the second sentence of the last paragraph. Circle the comma. Underline the dependent clause that tells why very few people came to hear Marian sing. Then rewrite the sentence with the dependent clause at the end.

Very few people _____

_____.

Text Evidence

1 Specific Vocabulary

Read the first paragraph. The word *discrimination* means "the act of unfairly treating people differently from others." Draw a box around one example of the discrimination that Marian Anderson faced.

2 Comprehension
Cause and Effect

Reread the first paragraph. Why did Marian choose to go to Europe in 1930?

Marian went to Europe because _____ _____ _____.

3 Sentence Structure

Read the first sentence in the third paragraph. Underline the word that tells you the quoted text was not spoken aloud.

It seemed that Marian's career was over. The discrimination she encountered at the music school could be found nearly everywhere in the United States. Many white audiences refused to hear African-American performers, and many concert halls would not allow black singers to perform. "If I cannot sing in America," Marian told herself, "I will go to Europe." She left in 1930, hoping that audiences overseas would give her a chance.

To Europe — And Back Again

In Europe, prominent composers and conductors praised Marian. Audiences flocked to hear her. To them, she was musical aristocracy, one of the most gifted singers ever. A man named Sol Hurok, who saw Marian perform in Paris, became her manager. Soon he had a request. "Come back to America to sing again," he pleaded.

"Will they ever respect me in America the way they do here?" Marian wondered. She decided to find out. She returned to the same concert hall where her career had nearly ended a decade before. This time, the performance was a success.

The singer's popularity grew, and Hurok began to book more recitals in the U.S. Still, like other African Americans at the time, Marian was not allowed to eat in many restaurants or stay in many hotels when she traveled—and no opera house would invite an African American to sing. But it was an act of prejudice in 1939 that gained Marian the greatest fame.

Change Did Not Come Easily

Hurok tried to arrange for Marian to sing at Constitution Hall, owned by the Daughters of the American Revolution (DAR). Though the DAR told Hurok no dates were available, they continued to book white performers. Outraged, First Lady Eleanor Roosevelt resigned from the DAR in protest.

180

Marian's supporters breathed a collective sigh of relief when a federal official offered her use of the Lincoln Memorial for a concert on Easter Sunday, 1939.

Marian was not sure what to do. The dignified woman was troubled by the drama of the situation. The prejudice barring her from Constitution Hall existed well beyond the concert hall's walls. Besides, the whole idea could backfire, and American audiences might once again reject her. On the other hand, Marian understood that the concert was not just about her; it was about helping all African Americans. Should she lend her voice so that others could prevail against injustice?

Marian decided to take the chance. The concert drew nationwide attention, and Marian was stunned when nearly 75,000 spectators attended. Millions more listened to the live radio broadcast.

Fifteen long years would pass before New York's Metropolitan Opera invited Marian to sing, but she was the first African American ever to receive such acknowledgment. On opening night, even before she sang a single note, the audience applauded for five full minutes. Her performance established Marian once more as a trailblazer who opened up opportunities for black Americans.

The celebrated conductor Arturo Toscanini said that a voice such as Marian's was "heard once in 100 years." Indeed, Marian Anderson's glorious singing, combined with her perseverance in the face of prejudice, shattered racial barriers and enriched the lives of countless people.

Make Connections

Talk about the way that Marian Anderson's singing changed the way Americans thought about African-American performers. **ESSENTIAL QUESTION**

Describe how a person you know or have read about helped changed your beliefs about something. **TEXT TO SELF**

Text Evidence

1 Specific Vocabulary

Read the third sentence in the second paragraph. The word *prejudice* means "an unfair opinion." Rewrite the sentence using the definition.

_____

_____

2 Comprehension
Cause and Effect

Read the third paragraph. What was the effect of Marian singing at the Lincoln Memorial concert?

_____

_____

3 Talk About It

Explain why Marian's concert at the Lincoln Memorial was important. Then write about it.

Marian's concert was important because _____

_____.

181

Respond to the Text

Partner Discussion Work with a partner. Answer the questions. Discuss what you learned about "Marian Anderson: Struggles and Triumphs." Write the page numbers where you found text evidence.

How did Marian Anderson show talent in her early life?	Text Evidence
As a young child, Marian _____.	Page(s): _____
In 1925, Marian _____.	Page(s): _____

How did Marian Anderson advance her career?	Text Evidence
Marian went to Europe because _____.	Page(s): _____
People in Europe _____.	Page(s): _____

How did Marian Anderson break barriers later in her career?	Text Evidence
At the Lincoln Memorial, Marian _____.	Page(s): _____
At the New York Metropolitan Opera, Marian _____.	Page(s): _____

Group Discussion Present your answers to the group. Cite text evidence to justify your thinking. Listen to and discuss the group's opinions about your answers.

Write Review your notes about "Marian Anderson: Struggles and Triumphs." Then write your answer to the Essential Question. Use text evidence to support your answer. Use vocabulary words from this week's reading in your writing.

> How did Marian Anderson affect people's opinions about African-American performers?
>
> At Marian's first concert in the United States, _____.
>
> When she traveled to Europe, Marian _____.
>
> When Marian sang at the Lincoln Memorial and the New York Metropolitan Opera, _____.
>
> Marian changed people's opinions by _____
> _____.

Share Writing Present your writing to the class. Discuss their opinions. Think about what the class has to say. Did they justify their claims? Explain why you agree or disagree with their claims.

I agree with _____ that _____.

I disagree with _____ because _____.

Write to Sources

Daniel

pages 178–181

Take Notes About the Text I took notes on this chart to answer the question: *What is the author's opinion of Marian Anderson?*

How the Author Describes the Subject of the Text
Marian Anderson was "one of the greatest singers of her time."
She was a dignified woman.
She was a trailblazer.
Her glorious singing had an effect on people.
She persevered in the face of prejudice.
She shattered racial barriers.
She enriched the lives of countless people.

Write About the Text I used the notes from my chart to write an informative paragraph about the author's opinion of Marian Anderson.

Student Model: *Informative Text*

The author feels great respect for Marian Anderson's singing and character. Anderson is praised throughout the text. She is described as "one of the greatest singers of her time," a "dignified woman," and "a trailblazer." The strongest praise appears at the end of the article. The author states that her "glorious singing, combined with her perseverance in the face of prejudice, shattered racial barriers and enriched the lives of countless people." The author admires Marian Anderson for her strong will, courage, and beautiful voice.

TALK ABOUT IT

Text Evidence
Circle the phrase that shows how Marian Anderson "shattered racial barriers." What does the author believe was accomplished by Anderson's efforts?

Grammar
Underline the prepositional phrases in sentence four. What purpose do the phrases serve?

Connect Ideas
Circle sentences four and five. How can you combine the two sentences to connect the ideas?

Your Turn

Explain how racism affected Anderson's career. Include text evidence.

>> *Go Digital!*
Write your response online. Use your editing checklist.

TALK ABOUT IT

Weekly Concept A Greener Future

? Essential Question
What steps can people take to promote a healthier environment?

>> Go Digital

 **What are the objects in the photo called? What do they create? What sources of energy do they use to do this? Write words in the chart to describe this green energy.**

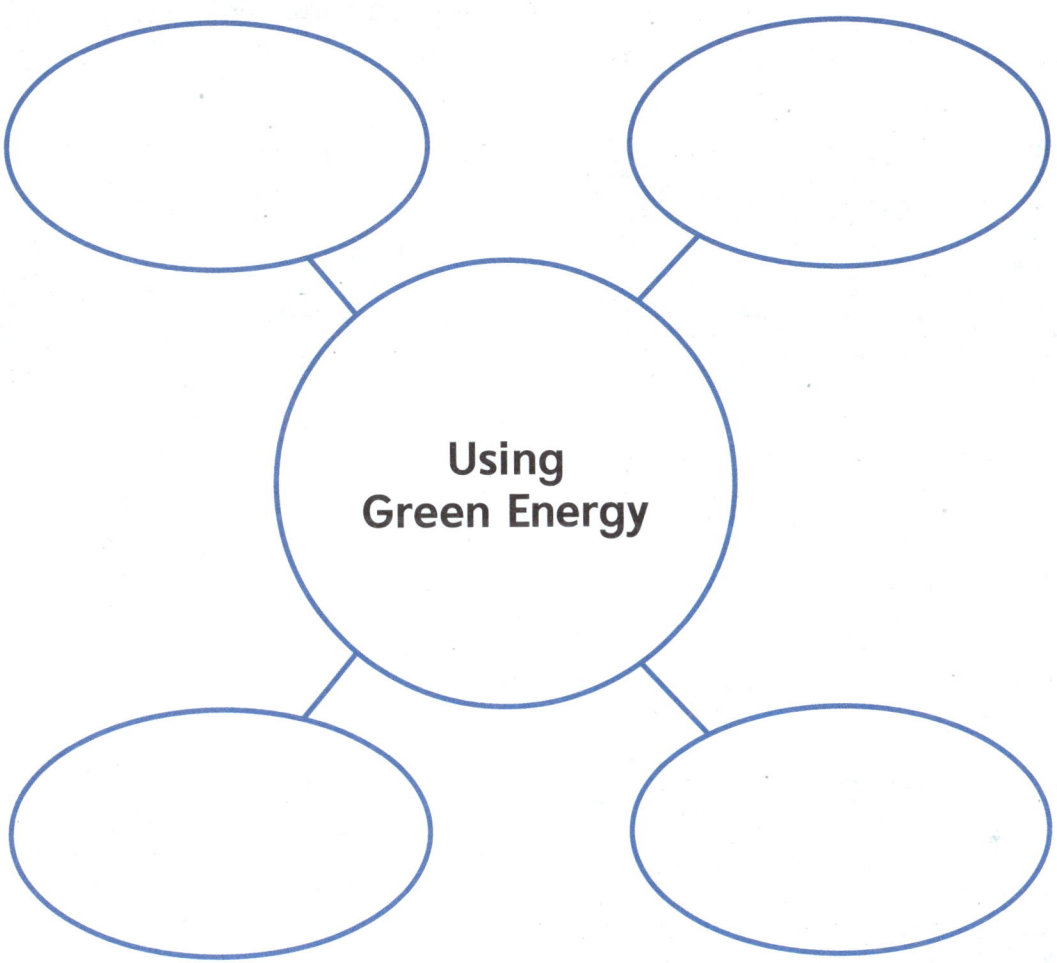

Discuss different kinds of green energy. Use words from the chart to complete the sentence.

_____ and _____ use _____ and the

_____ to make _____.

More Vocabulary

 Look at the picture and read the word. Then read the sentence. Talk about the word with a partner. Write your own sentence.

advantages

A city park is one of the **advantages** of living in a city.

One of the *advantages* of living in my town is

_____.

drawbacks

Traffic is one of the **drawbacks** of living in a city.

One of the *drawbacks* of living in my town is

_____.

features

Ryan's new laptop computer has many modern **features**.

My favorite cell phone's *features* include

_____.

process

Baking bread can be a long **process** with many steps.

_____ can also be a long *process* with many steps.

reduce

Sierra will **reduce** the weight of her backpack.

I can *reduce* the amount of _____ by _____.

retain

Studying helps me **retain** information.

Another word for *retain* is _____.

Words and Phrases
Compound Words

A compound word is made up of two words joined together to make a new word.

outdated = old, or "out of date"
A computer built in the 1980s is <u>outdated</u>.

landfills = places where the land is filled with trash
The garbage trucks take trash to the <u>landfills</u>.

Read the sentences below. Write the compound word that means the same thing as the underlined words.

The <u>places where the land is filled with trash</u> smell very bad.

The _____ smell very bad.

That steam-powered ship is <u>out of date</u>.

That steam-powered ship is _____.

» Go Digital Add these compound words to your New Words notebook. Write a sentence to show the meaning of each.

Text Evidence

Shared Read | Genre • Informational Article

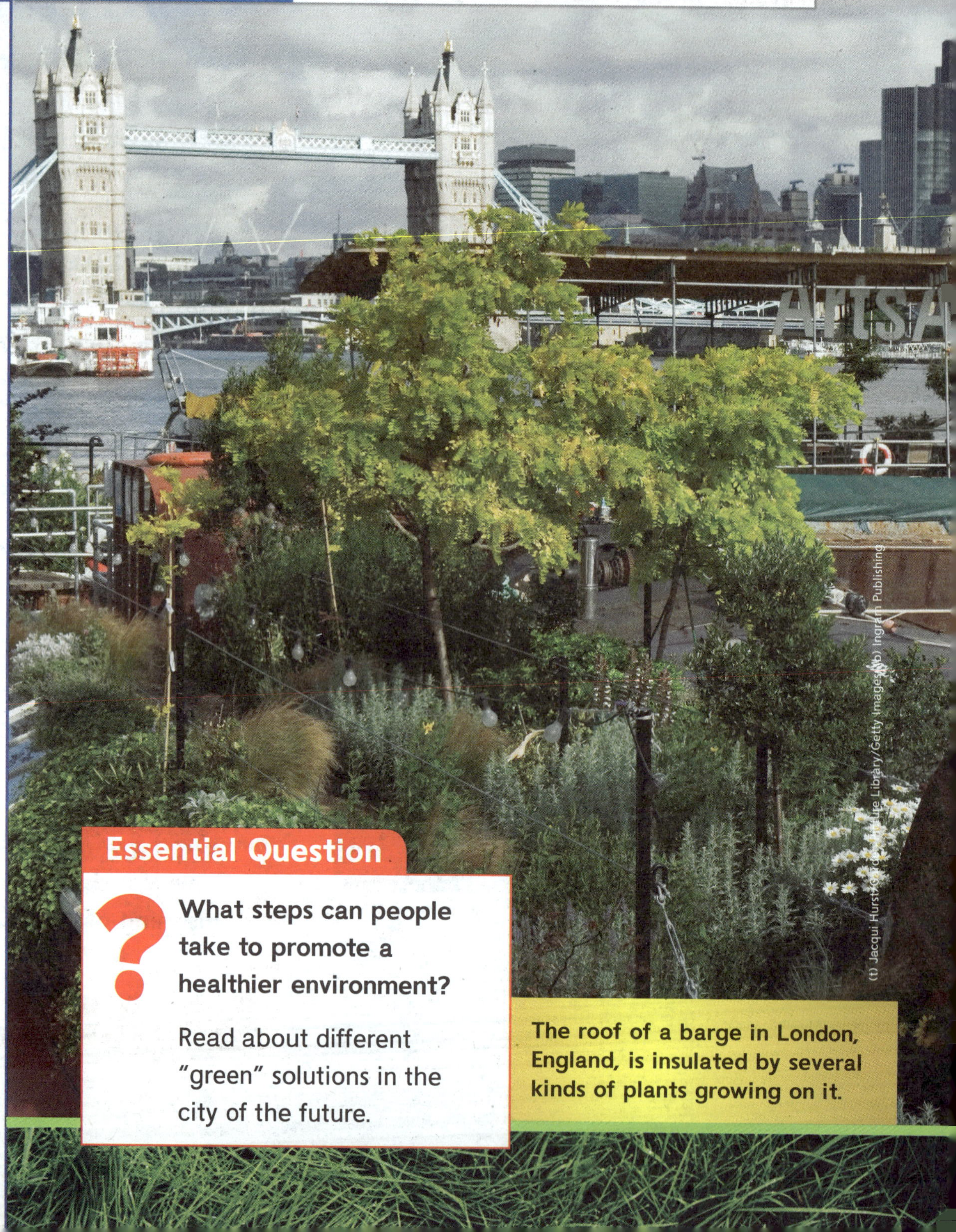

1 Talk About It

Read the title and the captions. Talk about what you see. Write your ideas.

What does the title tell you about the text? What does it mean to be "green"?

_____

_____

_____

_____

What is special about the barge shown on this page?

_____

_____

_____

_____

Take notes as you read the text.

Essential Question

? What steps can people take to promote a healthier environment?

Read about different "green" solutions in the city of the future.

The roof of a barge in London, England, is insulated by several kinds of plants growing on it.

IS YOUR CITY GREEN?

These days, people are trying to be better stewards, or caretakers, of Earth by living in a "green" way. Advocates of living in greener communities believe the advantages far outweigh any drawbacks. They think it is irrational to delay solving environmental problems. They say we can use ideas and technologies available right now to create the city of the future today.

Buildings with Green Roofs

Modern buildings in the green city of the future are designed to save water and energy. Outdated buildings of the past were not. Rooftops covered with grass and other living plants provide insulation that keeps buildings cooler. These roofs can also collect, filter, and reuse rainwater that would otherwise be wasted.

Turbines harvest the wind's energy.

Clean Energy

It is commonplace in the green city to use sources of energy that are renewable and cause no pollution. Solar panels convert the Sun's energy into electric power. Huge turbines generate electricity by harvesting the wind's energy on nearby wind farms. Even rivers are harnessed to produce electricity, and geothermal energy from deep within Earth is used to heat homes.

What you won't find in this city are gas stations on every corner. Tax breaks encourage people to use clean energy. And government agencies impose fees on the sale of fossil fuels to discourage their use.

Text Evidence

1 Specific Vocabulary

Read the first paragraph. What does it mean to be good stewards of Earth? Draw a box around the word that is a synonym for *stewards*. What do the stewards of Earth want to create today?

_____

_____

2 Comprehension
Main Idea and Key Details

Read the second paragraph. This paragraph suggests that planting gardens on rooftops is helpful. Underline two sentences that support this idea.

3 Sentence Structure

Reread the fourth sentence in the second paragraph. Underline the compound verb phrase. What can these roofs do with rainwater?

They can _____

_____.

191

Text Evidence

1 Specific Vocabulary

Read the first paragraph. Underline the sentence that helps you understand the meaning of *hybrid*. Then write the meaning in your own words.

A *hybrid* is something that _____
_____.

2 Comprehension
Main Idea and Key Details

Read the third paragraph. Why do advocates for green living believe that protecting native species is important to conserving natural spaces? Underline two details that support this idea.

3 Talk About It

Is the author's purpose for writing "Is Your City Green?" to inform, persuade, or entertain? Justify your answer.

The author's purpose is to _____
_____.

Moving Right Along

Most people in the green city of the future designate mass transit as their preferred method of travel. Since passengers who have chosen to ride trains are not driving their cars, less fuel is burned. Any private cars still in use are hybrid or plug-in electric vehicles. Hybrid cars run on both fuel and batteries. Some electric cars do not use gas at all. Instead, owners plug their cars into standard electrical outlets to charge the batteries.

In the green city, many cars, trucks, and buses burn fuels made from renewable sources rather than oil. For example, a biofuel called ethanol is made from corn and sugar cane crops. Biodiesel is made from soybean oil, animal fat, or even cooking grease!

Open Spaces

Citizens of the green city understand that protecting native species is key to conserving natural spaces.

Because native plants are original to the ecosystem, they provide the optimal habitat for local insects, birds, and other animals. Native plants that are well adapted to the local climate also require less water. Alien, or imported, plants are quickly identified and removed. Otherwise, they may become invasive and overwhelm local species.

Residents recognize that a process called *composting* helps reduce the amount of solid waste that is sent to landfills. It also increases the richness of local soil. People mix food scraps and yard waste with water and air in large bins. Helpful bacteria and fungi then break down this pile of "garbage" into an eco-friendly and economical fertilizer that improves the health of city parks and backyards.

An electric car is plugged into a recharging station.

192

HOW TO MAKE COMPOST
Cooking up some rich compost is easy when you follow these steps.

"Green" (Wet) Material (nitrogen-rich)
- grass; garden trimmings
- food scraps: fruits and vegetables (no meat, bones, dairy products, or grease)
- coffee grounds and filters; tea bags
- egg shells

"Brown" (Dry) Material (carbon-rich)
- autumn leaves
- straw
- sawdust
- shredded newspapers

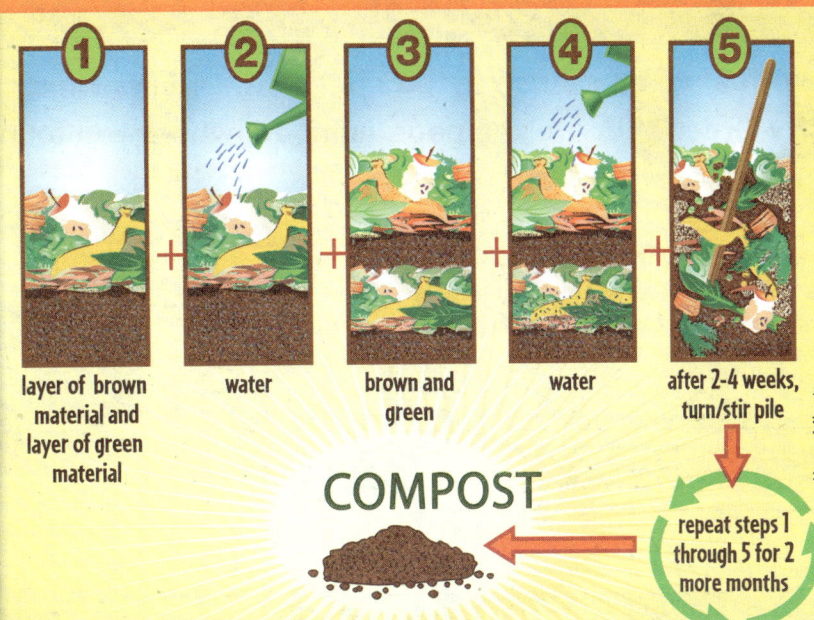

1. layer of brown material and layer of green material
2. water
3. brown and green
4. water
5. after 2-4 weeks, turn/stir pile

repeat steps 1 through 5 for 2 more months

COMPOST

Karen Minot

Your House Should Be More Passive!

I believe that all new houses should be "passive" homes. This means they would be built with materials and systems that reduce energy use. Most people think it's too expensive to do this. Actually, the savings over several years on the cost of electricity and carbon-based heating fuels soon exceed the higher initial cost of the energy-saving features. Some families are concerned that "thermal mass" floors used to retain heat in winter are too unattractive. Or they may think that keeping plants alive on the roof is too difficult. But these objections don't take into account a growing number of flooring styles and easy-to-maintain "green" roofing systems. The combined benefits of lower energy costs and less pollution from fossil fuels are reason enough to build more passive homes.

Make Connections

 Talk about the "green" solutions that people can put into practice today. **ESSENTIAL QUESTION**

Describe some of the steps you currently take to protect the environment. **TEXT TO SELF**

Text Evidence

❶ Sentence Structure

Read the first sentence of "Your House Should Be More Passive!" Circle the word with quotation marks. The author uses quotation marks to show that this idea for homes is new, or not well known. What other ideas in this paragraph are presented as new?

_____

❷ Comprehension
Main Idea and Key Details

Reread "Your House Should Be More Passive!" Underline three reasons why some people do not want to build environmentally friendly, or "passive" houses.

❸ Talk About It

Discuss why keeping a garden on the roof might be difficult. Then write about it.

_____

Respond to the Text

Partner Discussion Work with a partner. Answer the questions. Discuss what you learned about "Is Your City Green?" Write the page numbers where you found text evidence.

How are buildings different in the city of the future?

Modern buildings _____

_____.

Green buildings get energy from _____

_____.

Text Evidence

Page(s): _____

Page(s): _____

How are cars different in the city of the future?

The cars still in use are _____

_____.

Many of the cars use fuels that _____

_____.

Text Evidence

Page(s): _____

Page(s): _____

Group Discussion Present your answers to the group. Cite text evidence to justify your thinking. Listen to and discuss the group's opinions about your answers.

Write Review your notes about "Is Your City Green?" Then write your answer to the Essential Question. Use text evidence to support your answer. Use vocabulary words from this week's reading in your writing.

What steps can people take to promote a healthier environment?

People can construct buildings that _____

_____.

People can travel using _____

_____.

In their backyards, people can _____

_____.

Share Writing Present your writing to the class. Discuss their opinions. Think about what the class has to say. Did they justify their claims? Explain why you agree or disagree with their claims.

I agree with _____ that _____.

I disagree with _____ because _____.

195

Write to Sources

Fatimah

Take Notes About the Text I took notes on the idea web to answer the question: *Does the author make a successful argument for building green cities?*

pages 190–193

Detail
Plant-covered roofs naturally insulate buildings.

Detail
Plant-covered roofs collect, filter, and reuse rainwater.

Main Idea
Why should cities go green?

Detail
Solar panels convert sunlight to electricity without pollution.

Detail
Electric cars are plugged into outlets, burning no gas.

Write About the Text I used my notes from my idea web to write an argument about the author's advocacy of green cities.

Student Model: *Argument*

   I think the author makes a very strong case for building green cities. The author shows that green technologies and practices can help create a better city. For example, the author discusses green buildings. Plant-covered roofs naturally insulate buildings. They are also great at naturally collecting, filtering, and reusing rainwater. Also, the author shows that solar panels harness the energy of the Sun, making electricity without pollution. Use of electric cars is also shown to reduce fuel usage. These facts help the author show that building green cities would improve city life.

TALK ABOUT IT

Text Evidence
Draw a box around a sentence that comes from the notes. Why did Fatimah use this sentence in her writing?

Grammar
Circle the pronoun in sentence five. What noun phrase does the pronoun refer to?

Condense Ideas
Underline sentences four and five. How could you condense the ideas of these two sentences, using the phrase *while also*?

Your Turn

Explain how the author supports her argument for building energy-efficient houses. Use text evidence to support your answer.

>> *Go Digital!*
Write your response online. Use your editing checklist.

# Unit 4

Challenges

The Big Idea

How do people meet challenges and solve problems?

TALK ABOUT IT

Weekly Concept Changing Environments

 **Essential Question**
How do people meet environmental challenges?

>> *Go Digital*

 What happened to the baby bird in the photo? What are the challenges for bird rescuers? Write words to describe the challenges in the chart.

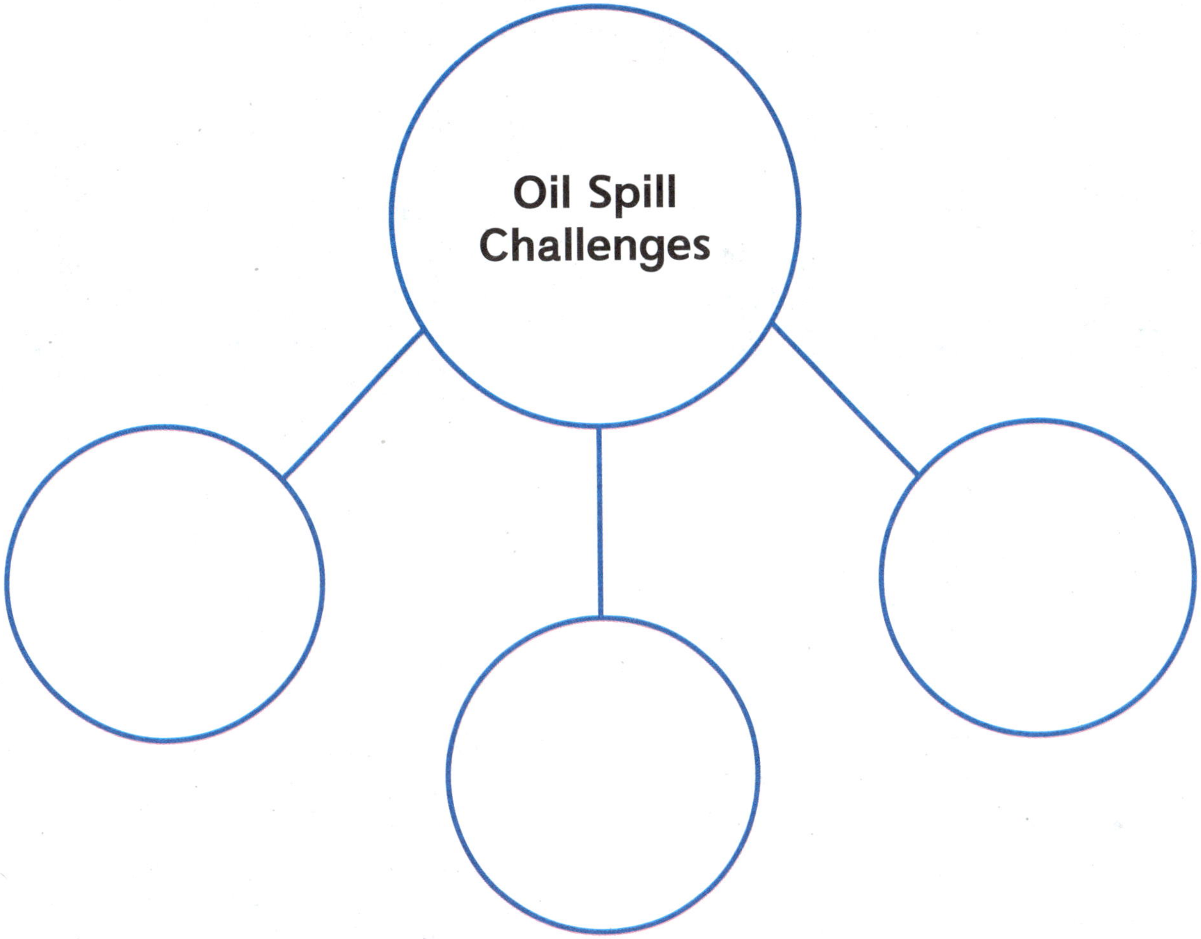

Oil Spill Challenges

Discuss the challenges of cleaning up after an oil spill. Use words from the chart. You can say:

Rescuers face the challenges of _____

_____.

More Vocabulary

 Look at the picture and read the word. Then read the sentence. Talk about the word with a partner. Write your own sentence.

collapsed

The building shook and then **collapsed** during the earthquake.

Once, I put too many things on a _____, and it *collapsed*.

frantically

Magda **frantically** tried to find her dog after it ran into the field.

When I am late for school, I *frantically* _____.

devoured

The wildfire **devoured** all the trees in its path.

Another word for *devoured* is _____.

prosperity

New buildings and parks show a city's **prosperity**.

A _____ is one sign of a school's *prosperity*.

receded

When the snow melted and **receded**, we saw the leaves on the ground.

When the ocean waves *receded*, _____
_____.

tolerate

Sara can **tolerate** the hot weather when she swims in her pool.

I can *tolerate* the winter when I have
_____.

Words and Phrases
Idioms

set the stage = made it possible
The icy sidewalk set the stage for Min to slip and fall.

closed for good = was never going to open again
After the new city pool opened, the old pool closed for good.

Read the sentences below. Write the idiom that means the same thing as the underlined words.

The empty store was never going to open again.

The empty store _____.

The team's practice made it possible for them to win the game.

The team's practice _____ for them to win the game.

» Go Digital Add these idioms to your New Words notebook. Write a sentence to show the meaning of each.

Text Evidence

Shared Read | Genre • Expository Text

1. Talk About It

Read the title. Talk about what you see. Write your ideas.

What does the title tell you?

_____

_____

What does the black-and-white photograph show?

_____

_____

Take notes as you read the text.

The Day the Dam BROKE

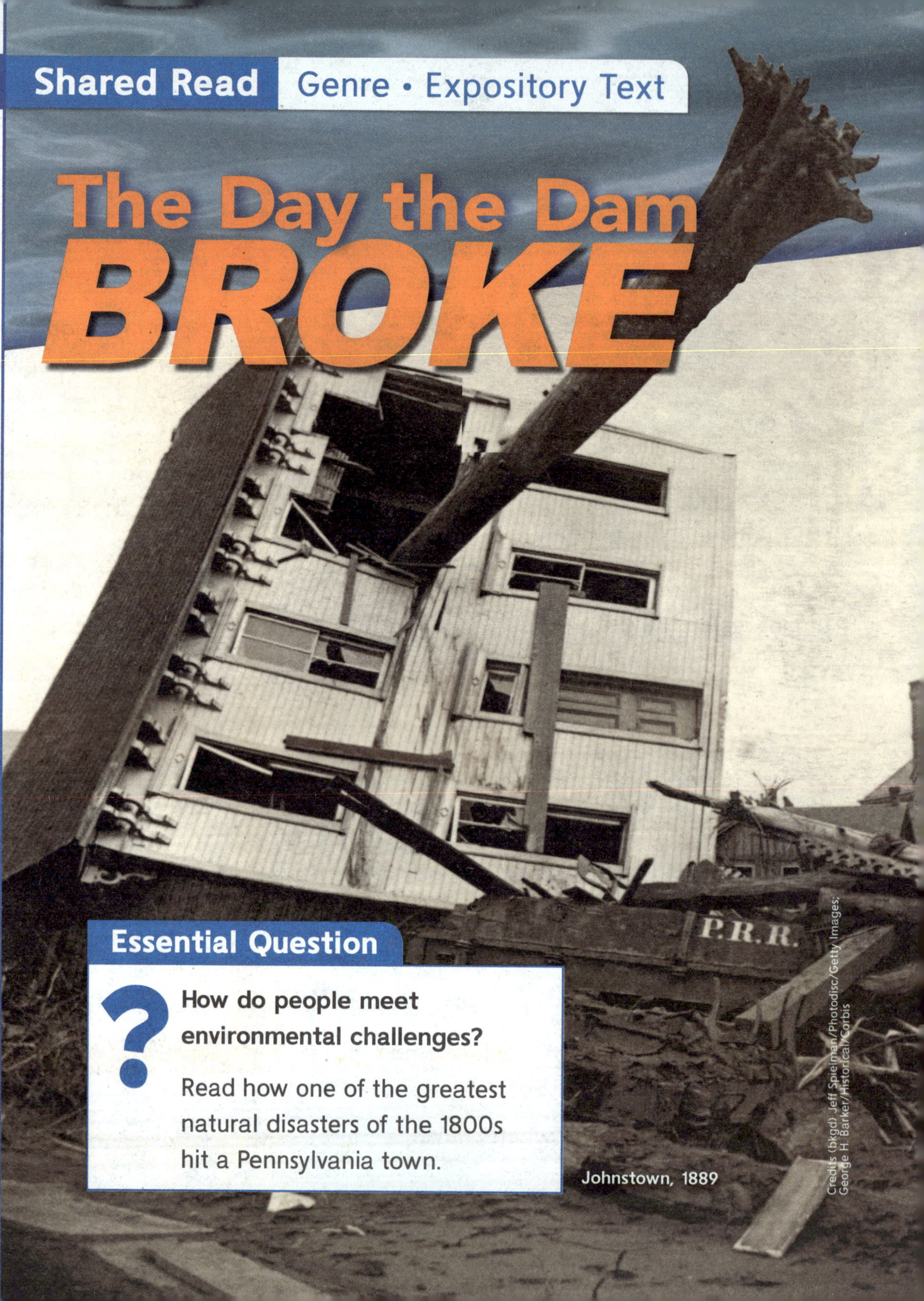

Johnstown, 1889

Essential Question

? How do people meet environmental challenges?

Read how one of the greatest natural disasters of the 1800s hit a Pennsylvania town.

204

Down in the Valley

Johnstown, Pennsylvania, lies in a beautiful valley in the Appalachian Mountains. Two rivers flank the town, so in the early 1800s people began using the water power to run grist mills for grinding flour.

By 1834, Johnstown had become a key junction on the Pennsylvania Canal System. Many new businesses were generated. The new **prosperity** was enough to offset any **hardships** caused by periodic flooding when the rivers swelled with snow melt and heavy spring rains. For Johnstown's residents, moving to higher ground until the water **receded** was an inconvenience they could **tolerate**.

The Stage Is Set

To supply water to the Canal System during dry seasons, the state built a rock-and-earth dam 14 miles upstream from Johnstown on the Conemaugh River. At the dam's base, a drain fed water into the canal. But excess water from the lake behind the dam could also run off a spillway.

By 1852, both canal and dam were abandoned when the Pennsylvania Railroad completed a line between Johnstown and Pittsburgh. In 1875, a man named Benjamin Ruff bought the property around the lake to build an exclusive resort called the South Fork Fishing and Hunting Club.

Ruff repaired the dam and stocked the lake with fish. But valves and pipes previously laid in careful alignment to control the water flow were removed, and the drain beneath the dam was filled in. The dam's lip was lowered by two feet when the road on top was widened, and the spillway was screened in from a bridge above to keep fish from escaping. Unknowingly, Ruff had set the stage for disaster.

Text Evidence

1 Specific Vocabulary ACT

Read the second paragraph. Draw a box around the word that means the opposite of *hardships*. Then describe one hardship that the residents of Johnstown faced.

One hardship was _____

_____.

2 Sentence Structure ACT

Read the first sentence of the fourth paragraph. Underline the dependent clause, which tells you in detail when the canal and dam were both abandoned.

3 Comprehension
Author's Point of View

Read the fifth paragraph. Does the author think that Ruff knew his repairs would cause a flood? Underline the sentence that tells you.

The author _____

_____.

Text Evidence

1 Specific Vocabulary

Read the third and fourth paragraphs. Here, the word *surge* means "a sudden, quick movement of water." What were the effects of the surge?

The surge _____

_____

2 Sentence Structure

Underline the quotation in the fourth paragraph. Who said this in a telegraph message?

_____

3 Comprehension
Author's Point of View

Reread the third and fourth paragraphs. Write two facts that support the idea that the 1889 Johnstown Flood is among the worst disasters in American history.

_____

_____

A Tremendous Roar

On May 30, 1889, the worst storm ever recorded in Johnstown's history hit the area. Nearly 10 inches of rain fell in just 24 hours. The next morning, the rivers around Johnstown swelled into roaring torrents. As they had so many times before, residents moved to higher ground to wait out the flood.

Upriver, South Fork Club members feared the dam would fail if the lake rose any higher. Workers **frantically** tried to strengthen the dam. Men were sent to Johnstown to warn people. But the townspeople had heard too many such alarms over the years and they ignored the warnings.

Just after 3:00 P.M., the dam **collapsed**. Club members watched in horror as a 40-foot wave, about 20 million tons of water a half-mile wide, crashed down the river valley. Within minutes, the flood **devoured** four small towns. In less than an hour, it roared into Johnstown. Most people saw nothing. They heard only a thunderous rumble. But then the water was upon them.

Those not instantly killed were swept away by the angry surge. A jumbled mass of water, houses, trees, train cars, animals, and people smashed into the stone arches of the railroad bridge downriver. Anyone still alive at that point met with prolonged torment when the debris caught fire. Many more died. That evening, a telegraph message arrived in Pittsburgh from Robert Pitcairn, railroad superintendent and a member of the South Fork Club. It said simply, "Johnstown is annihilated."

After the Flood

Response was swift as news spread. People around the world sent money,

---

Primary Sources

Sources of information are considered primary if they come from people living at the time of the event described. Examples include letters, eye-witness accounts, photographs, newspaper articles, and government documents.

There are many first-hand accounts by survivors of the 1889 Johnstown Flood. Gertrude Quinn Slattery, for example, was only six years old at the time, but she later recalled being swept away on a "raft with a muddy mattress and bedding." Like others, she remembered "holding on for dear life . . ." Thankfully, she lived to tell her story.

food, and clothing. The recently created Red Cross arrived to help survivors. Down, but not defeated, the people of Johnstown showed great tenacity. They set up tents and began to rebuild.

Facts About the 1889 Johnstown Flood
- 2,209 people killed, including 99 entire families
- 1,600 homes destroyed
- $17 million in property damage
- debris at the bridge covered 30 acres and was 40 feet high

The 1889 flood is among the worst disasters in American history. Many blamed the South Fork Club for causing the calamity with its mishandling of the dam. The people of Johnstown sued. But the courts ruled the flood an accident and awarded no money. Some club members contributed to relief efforts. Andrew Carnegie donated $10,000 and rebuilt the town's library. Other members remained silent.

When another flood hit Johnstown in 1936, the federal government paid to have the rivers re-routed. Johnstown residents rebuilt once again, believing there would be no more floods. But on July 20, 1977, nearly 12 inches of rain fell in 10 hours. Six dams burst, pouring 128 million gallons of water into Johnstown.

This time, many people moved, and businesses closed for good. Like an eclipse darkening the sky, the 1977 flood dimmed Johnstown's future.

Today, key activities help reduce the danger to Johnstown. The National Weather Service sponsors a flood watchers program, and studies are done to identify weaknesses in the flood protection systems. But there is also an emergency plan, just in case the waters overrun Johnstown again.

Make Connections

 How did the people of Johnstown respond to the challenges of flooding? **ESSENTIAL QUESTION**

Talk about a disaster you have heard or read about. Tell how people responded to the challenges they faced from the environment. **TEXT TO SELF**

Text Evidence

1 Talk About It

Read the first and second paragraphs. Explain why the effects of the 1936 and 1977 floods were different. Then write about it.

_____

_____

2 Sentence Structure ACT

Read the last sentence in the second paragraph. Circle the independent clause. Underline the phrase, which tells you the effect of the bursting dams.

3 Comprehension
Author's Point of View

Reread the third paragraph. How does the author think the 1977 flood affected Johnstown?

_____

_____

Respond to the Text

 **Partner Discussion** Work with a partner. Answer the questions. Discuss what you learned about "The Day the Dam Broke." Write the page numbers where you found text evidence.

Early on, how did people respond to floods in Johnstown?

Early on during floods, the people of Johnstown _____.

Page(s): _____

The state government _____.

Page(s): _____

Text Evidence

How did people respond after the 1889 flood in Johnstown?

People around the world _____.

Page(s): _____

The people of Johnstown _____.

Page(s): _____

Text Evidence

How did people respond to later floods in Johnstown?

After the 1936 flood, _____.

Page(s): _____

After the 1977 flood, _____.

Page(s): _____

Text Evidence

 **Group Discussion** Present your answers to the group. Cite text evidence to justify your thinking. Listen to and discuss the group's opinions about your answers.

Write Review your notes about "The Day the Dam Broke." Then write your answer to the Essential Question. Use text evidence to support your answer. Use vocabulary words from this week's reading in your writing.

How did the people of Johnstown respond to the challenges of flooding?

At first, people _____.

Following the 1889 flooding disaster, people _____
_____.

After the 1936 flood, _____.

After the 1977 flood, _____.

Based on what the people of Johnstown did over the years, I think _____
_____.

Share Writing Present your writing to the class. Discuss their opinions. Think about what the class has to say. Did they justify their claims? Explain why you agree or disagree with their claims.

I agree with _____ that _____.

I disagree with _____ because _____.

Write to Sources

Ben

Take Notes About the Text I took notes on the idea web to answer the question: *Was the South Fork Club responsible for the 1889 Johnstown Flood?*

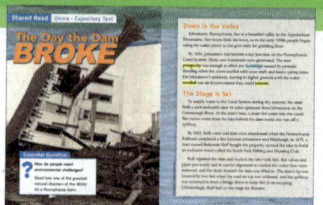

pages 204–207

Evidence
Ruff removed the valves, pipes, and drain that controlled the water flow.

Evidence
Ruff lowered the lip of the dam.

Claim
The South Fork Club was responsible for the flood.

Evidence
Ruff screened in the spillway to keep fish from escaping.

Evidence
The dam collapsed during the storm.

Write About the Text I used notes from my idea web to write an argument about whether the South Fork Club was responsible for the 1889 Johnstown Flood.

Student Model: Argument

    The South Fork Club was responsible for the 1889 Johnstown Flood. Benjamin Ruff removed the valves, pipes, and drain that controlled the water flow in the dam. He also lowered the lip of the dam. He then screened in the spillway to keep fish from escaping. As a result, the dam collapsed during a heavy storm. This would not have happened if Ruff had properly repaired the dam.

TALK ABOUT IT

Text Evidence
Draw a box around a sentence that comes from the notes. Why does Ben use this sentence in his argument?

Grammar
Circle the proper noun that the pronoun *he* refers to. Why does Ben use the pronoun *he* in two of the sentences?

Condense Ideas
Underline the sentences that describe the lip and the spillway. How can you combine these sentences to condense the ideas?

Your Turn

Should Johnstown remain a populated city? Provide evidence from the text to support your response.

>> *Go Digital!*
Write your response online. Use your editing checklist.

TALK ABOUT IT

Weekly Concept Overcoming Challenges

? Essential Question
How do people meet personal challenges?

›› *Go Digital*

 What personal challenges did Huang face? How did he meet the challenges? Write the ways in the chart.

Discuss how Huang met his personal challenges. Use words from the chart. You can say:

When Huang Guofu was 4 years old, he _____.

He paints by _____. He became a good artist by

_____.

More Vocabulary

 Look at the picture and read the word. Then read the sentence. Talk about the word with a partner. Write your own sentence.

accomplishment

The students had a feeling of **accomplishment** after they built their model volcanoes.

I had a feeling of *accomplishment* after I _____.

confidently

Peg **confidently** gave a speech to her class.

If I _____, then I can *confidently* _____.

achievement

Winning an award at the science fair was an **achievement** for Anna, Sam, and Hector.

_____ was an *achievement* for me.

determination

Lydia's **determination** will help her hit a home run.

In school, my *determination* will help me _____.

inspired

The cheering audience **inspired** the runner to finish the race.

_____ once *inspired* me to

_____.

overcome

Kim has **overcome** her fear of heights.

If I work hard, I will *overcome* _____

_____.

Words and Phrases
Subordinating Conjunctions

Though signals an idea in one part of a sentence that is different from an idea in another part of the sentence.
<u>Though</u> the dog looked old, he was just a puppy.

When tells at what time something happens.
Gia's family moved to a new home <u>when</u> Gia was ten years old.

Read the sentences below. Underline the subordinating conjunction in each sentence.

Though the weather was hot, the park was cool.

The family ate dinner when the food was ready.

Write your own sentences using *when* and *though*.

_____

_____

» Go Digital Add the conjunctions *though* and *when* to your New Words notebook. Include your sentences.

Text Evidence

Shared Read | Genre • Biography

1 Talk About It

Read the title and the caption. Talk about what you see. Write your ideas.

What does the title tell you about the text?

_____
_____
_____

What do both the photograph and caption tell you about Wilma Rudolph?

_____
_____
_____

Take notes as you read the text.

She Had to WALK Before She Could RUN

Wilma Rudolph at the 1960 Summer Olympics

Essential Question

? How do people meet personal challenges?

Read how a young woman overcame physical challenges to become an Olympic athlete.

216

In a crowded Olympic stadium, the gun sounded and Wilma Rudolph took off like a bolt of lightning. As this amazing athlete ran **confidently** around the track, she never lost her cool. Sprinting toward the finish line, Wilma used her peripheral vision to ensure that her competitors would not catch up. The crowd roared with **elation** as "the fastest woman in the world" finished more than three yards ahead of the other athletes.

Against All Odds

Though Wilma Rudolph **inspired** many during that 1960 Summer Olympics in Rome, Italy, her childhood had been riddled with hardships. Wilma was one of 22 children born to an impoverished Tennessee family. While she was a toddler, her health deteriorated because of life-threatening illnesses.

When she was four years old, Wilma contracted polio, a severe disease that causes paralysis. As a result, Wilma lost the use of her left leg. Having polio could have been devastating for Wilma. Instead, she faced this physical challenge with a positive attitude and never lost sight of her goal.

Wilma's mother taught her very early to believe she could achieve any goal, and the first was to walk without leg braces. Once a week, she drove Wilma 90 miles round-trip to Nashville for physical therapy. Her mother also instructed Wilma's siblings on how to massage their sister's legs. Done several times a day, this monotonous routine continued for several years.

An Inspiring Comeback

Wilma's doctors had little hope that she would ever be able to walk again. When she was nine years old, they decided to assess her progress. After the doctors removed the braces, they were amazed to

Text Evidence

❶ Specific Vocabulary ACT

Reread the first paragraph. The word *elation* means "joy and excitement." When did the crowd roar with elation?

_____

_____

❷ Sentence Structure ACT

Read the first sentence in the second paragraph. Circle the word *though*. Explain what relationship this subordinating conjunction shows in the sentence.

The word _____

_____.

❸ Comprehension
Author's Point of View

Reread the first two paragraphs. What is the author's point of view about Wilma Rudolph? Circle words or phrases that tell you.

The author thinks _____

_____.

217

Text Evidence

1. Specific Vocabulary

Reread the first two sentences of the second paragraph. The word *avid* means "very interested or enthusiastic." Who were avid basketball players in Wilma's family?

_____

_____

2. Sentence Structure

Read the second sentence in the third paragraph. Circle the comma. Underline the dependent clause. Box the independent clause. When did Wilma qualify for the 1956 Summer Olympic Games?

_____

_____

3. Comprehension
Author's Point of View

Reread the fourth paragraph. Underline two sentences that support the author's idea that Wilma Rudolph had to overcome many challenges to reach the Olympics.

---

see that Wilma could walk on her own. They were stunned by what this young girl could do despite having contracted a crippling disease for which there was no cure.

From then on, Wilma never looked back. To compensate for the years she had been in braces, Wilma became extremely active. As proof of her **determination**, she ran everyday. She decided never to give up, no matter what happened.

Wilma's brothers set up a basketball hoop in the backyard, and she and her siblings played all day. Wilma became an avid basketball player at school, too. A track coach named Ed Temple from Tennessee State University spotted Wilma at a basketball tournament and was extremely impressed by her athletic ability and potential. He invited her to attend a sports camp. Once again, Wilma's life changed dramatically, this time for the better.

An Olympic Champion

The minute Wilma ran on a track, she loved it. When she was just sixteen years old, she qualified for the 1956 Summer Olympic Games in Melbourne, Australia. And Wilma came home wearing the bronze medal she had won in the relay race.

After high school, Wilma was awarded a full scholarship to major in education at Tennessee State University. But once again, Wilma had to **overcome** challenges. In 1958, having put her shoulder to the wheel both in class and during track-and-field events, she became too ill to run. After she had a tonsillectomy, however, she felt better and started to run again. Unfortunately, Wilma pulled a muscle at a track meet in 1959, and Coach Temple had to implement a plan for her recovery. Wilma recovered just in time to qualify for the 1960 Summer Olympics in Rome.

Wilma displays her gold medals (above); at the 1960 games

Wilma Rudolph's Olympics Statistics

Date	Event	Time	Medal
1956	200 Meters	Not in finals	None
1956	4 x 100 Meters Relay	44.9 seconds	Bronze
1960	100 Meters	11.0 seconds	Gold
1960	200 Meters	24.0 seconds	Gold
1960	4 x 100 Meters Relay	44.5 seconds	Gold

In her individual sprints, Wilma outshone her competition and won two gold medals with ease. During the relay event, however, the team comprised of four athletes from Tennessee State found themselves in hot water. After a poor baton pass, Wilma had to pick up her pace and run like the wind to complete the last leg of the race. She successfully **overtook** Germany's last runner to win the race. Wilma became the first American woman in track and field to win three gold medals. Of her feeling of **accomplishment**, she said she knew it was something "nobody could ever take away from me, ever."

Giving Back

The summit of Wilma's career might have been her **achievements** as an Olympic athlete. Instead, she went on to accomplish much more. After graduating from college, she taught school and coached track. Soon Wilma was traveling the country, giving speeches to school audiences.

To inspire others to do their best in spite of all challenges, she would note that "the triumph can't be had without the struggle." Wilma achieved her dreams and, ever after, helped others to reach theirs.

Make Connections

Talk about how Wilma met personal challenges to become a successful athlete. ESSENTIAL QUESTIONS

Describe a time when someone you know had a personal challenge and overcame it. TEXT TO SELF

Text Evidence

1 Specific Vocabulary

Reread the first paragraph. Circle the context clues for the word *overtook*. Rewrite the sentence using a word or words that mean the same thing as *overtook*.

She successfully _____.

2 Comprehension
Author's Point of View

Read "Giving Back." What is the author's point of view about Wilma after she graduated from college? Circle one sentence in each paragraph that tells you what the author thinks.

3 Talk About It

What did Wilma mean when she said, "the triumph can't be had without the struggle"? Justify your answer.

_____

_____

Respond to the Text

Partner Discussion Work with a partner. Answer the questions. Discuss what you learned about "She Had to Walk Before She Could Run." Write the page numbers where you found text evidence.

How did Wilma Rudolph meet challenges in her childhood?

When she had polio, Wilma _____.

As a result, Wilma _____.

Text Evidence

Page(s): _____

Page(s): _____

How did Wilma Rudolph meet challenges as a young woman?

After her leg braces were removed, Wilma _____.

When she faced illness and injury, Wilma _____.

Text Evidence

Page(s): _____

Page(s): _____

How did Wilma Rudolph meet challenges as an adult?

In the relay race at the Olympics, Wilma _____.

After her Olympic medals, Wilma _____.

Text Evidence

Page(s): _____

Page(s): _____

Group Discussion Present your answers to the group. Cite text evidence to justify your thinking. Listen to and discuss the group's opinions about your answers.

Write Review your notes about "She Had to Walk Before She Could Run." Then write your answer to the Essential Question. Use text evidence to support your answer. Use vocabulary words from this week's reading in your writing.

How did Wilma Rudolph meet personal challenges throughout her life?

During her childhood, Wilma _____.

As a young woman, Wilma _____.

As an adult, Wilma _____

_____.

Based on how Wilma responded to each personal challenge, I think _____

_____.

Share Writing Present your writing to the class. Discuss their opinions. Think about what the class has to say. Did they justify their claims? Explain why you agree or disagree with their claims.

I agree with _____ that _____.

I disagree with _____ because _____.

221

Write to Sources

pages 216–219

Take Notes About the Text I took notes on the idea web to answer the question: *Who was the most powerful influence in Wilma Rudolph's life?*

Maria

Evidence
Her mother drove her 90 miles round-trip every week for physical therapy.

Evidence
Her siblings massaged her legs several times a day.

Claim
Wilma's family was her most important influence.

Evidence
Her siblings played basketball with her after her braces were removed.

Evidence
She became a great athlete.

Write About the Text I used notes from my idea web to write an argument about who was the greatest influence in Wilma Rudolph's life.

Student Model: *Argument*

Wilma Rudolph's family was the most powerful influence in her life. Wilma's mother drove her 90 miles round-trip every week for physical therapy for polio. Her brothers and sisters massaged her legs several times a day. They played basketball with Wilma after her leg braces were removed. Wilma went on to become a great athlete. She couldn't have been successful without the help of her family.

TALK ABOUT IT

Text Evidence
Underline a sentence that comes from the notes. Why did Maria include this information?

Grammar
Circle the subject pronoun and **underline** the possessive pronoun in the fourth sentence. To whom does each pronoun refer?

Connect Ideas
Underline the sentences that tell what Wilma's siblings did. How can you combine the sentences to connect ideas?

Your Turn

What qualities do you think are most important in becoming a successful athlete? Defend your argument with evidence from the text.

>> Go Digital!
Write your response online. Use your editing checklist.

TALK ABOUT IT

Weekly Concept Standing Tall

? Essential Question
When are decisions hard to make?

>> Go Digital

 What is the boy in the photo trying to decide? What choices is he thinking about? Write words in the chart to describe his choices.

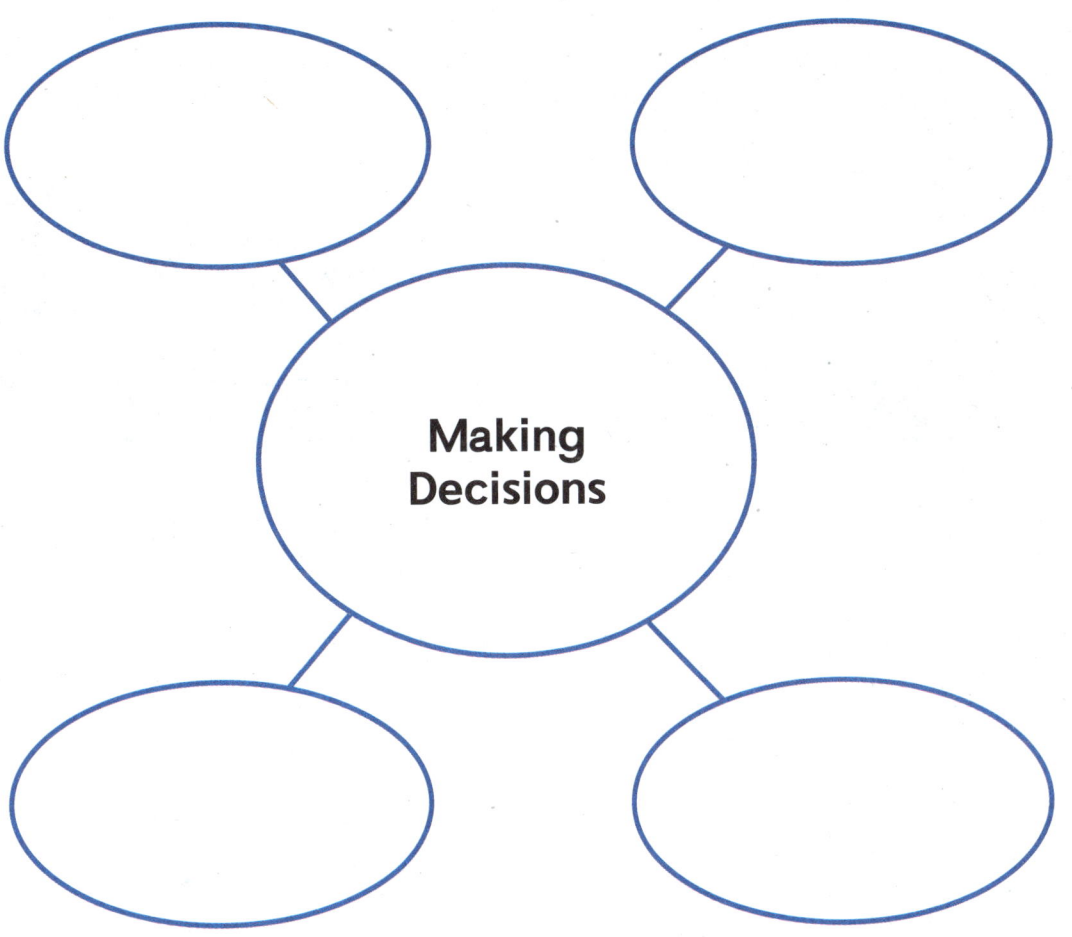

Discuss the choices the boy is thinking about. Use words from the chart. You can say:

The project will be easy if the boy chooses a topic that he is _____ with. The project will be _____ if the boy chooses a topic that he is _____ with.

More Vocabulary

 Look at the picture and read the word. Then read the sentence. Talk about the word with a partner. Write your own sentence.

debts

Alan pays his **debts** by writing checks every month.

When you have many *debts*, you _____ _____.

income

The friends receive an **income** from shoveling snow.

Another word for *income* is _____.

fortunate

The class is **fortunate** to have enough computers for all its students.

I am *fortunate* because _____ _____.

inherit

Gabe and Mark will **inherit** their grandfathers' coin collections.

When you *inherit* something, you _____ _____.

secure

The money is **secure** in the safe at the bank.

A _____ keeps you *secure* in a car.

treasures

The divers found many **treasures** on the ocean floor.

Another word for *treasures* is _____.

Words and Phrases
Phrasal Verbs

part with = sell or give away
Dad does not want to part with his old car.

tucked away = hidden
The travelers kept their money tucked away inside their shoes.

Read the sentences below. Write the phrasal verb that means the same thing as the underlined word.

Frank was sad to sell the home he had lived in for 20 years.

Frank was sad to _____ the home he had lived in for 20 years.

Emma kept her best jewelry hidden under her mattress.

Emma kept her best jewelry _____ under her mattress.

» Go Digital Add these phrasal verbs to your New Words notebook. Write a sentence to show the meaning of each.

Text Evidence

Shared Read Genre • Drama

1 Talk About It

Read the title. Talk about what you see. Write your ideas.

What does the title tell you?

_____

_____

Who are the characters?

_____

Where are the characters in this part of the story?

_____

What are they doing?

_____

_____

Take notes as you read the story.

Treasure in the Attic

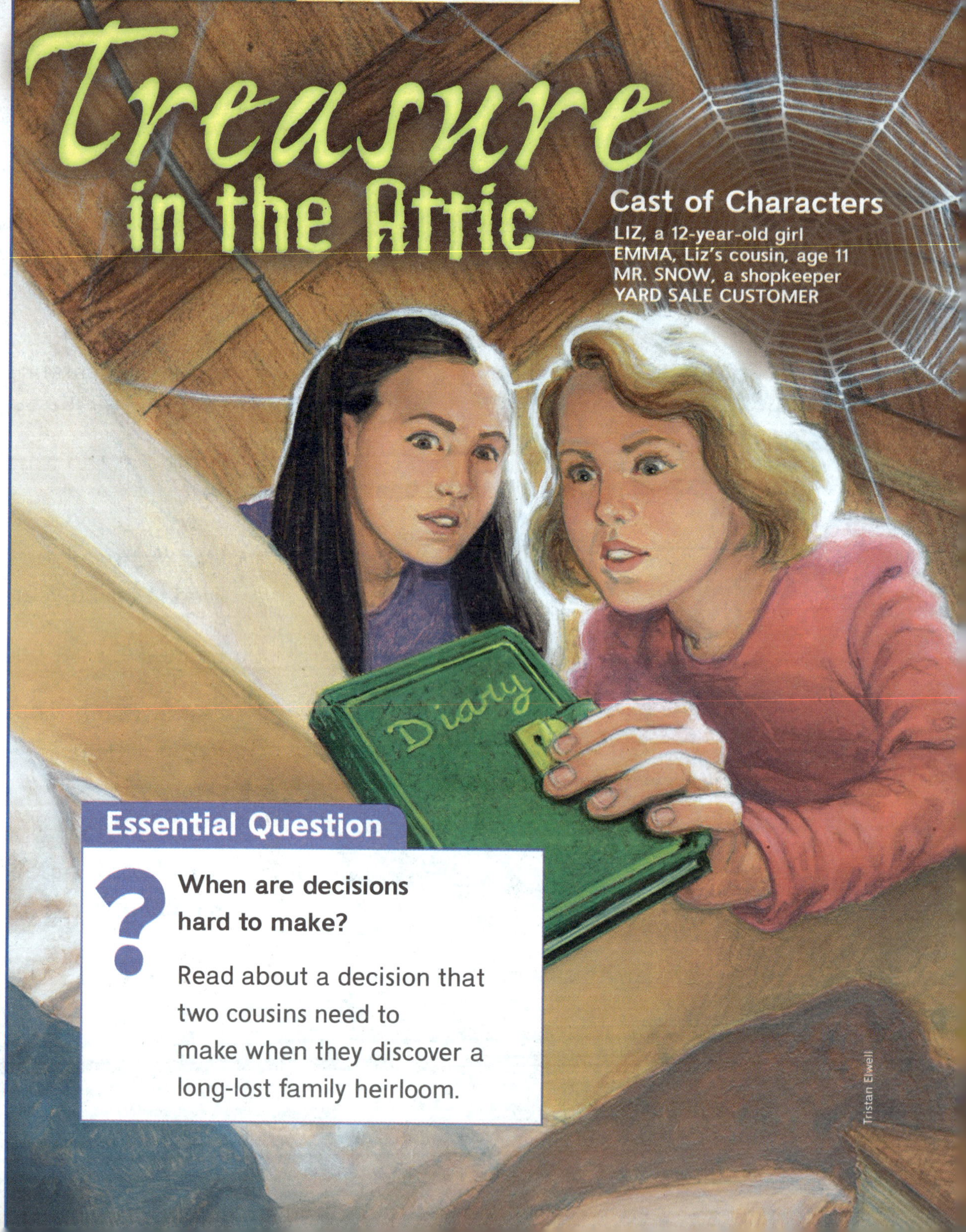

Cast of Characters
LIZ, a 12-year-old girl
EMMA, Liz's cousin, age 11
MR. SNOW, a shopkeeper
YARD SALE CUSTOMER

Essential Question

? When are decisions hard to make?

Read about a decision that two cousins need to make when they discover a long-lost family heirloom.

Tristan Elwell

SCENE 1 *The attic of Liz's house; Liz and Emma are kneeling.*

Emma (*looking through a box*): We'll never get through all this stuff!

Liz: We have to. I need twenty-five more dollars for that new bike. My dad says we can sell at a yard sale anything we find up here. You can keep half of whatever we make.

Emma (*coughing*): I know. I just didn't realize it would entail breathing in so much dust.

Liz (*with enthusiasm*): I don't think anyone has looked at Grandpa and Grandma's stuff since they moved to Florida. There's a multitude of treasures up here.

Emma: Be on the lookout for a pair of pearl earrings. Grandma says Great-Grandma forgot what she did with them. You're supposed to inherit them, since you're the oldest heir among the grandkids.

Liz: Wow. I hope they're worth a lot of money!

Emma: If I had something of Great-Grandma's, I'd never sell it.

Liz (*finding an old diary, flipping pages*): Wow, a diary! Listen to this: (reading) "October 7, 1936. I feel such empathy for Anna Snow and her family. They may have to leave us to find work elsewhere. This terrible Depression has bred such suffering for our neighbors. We are fortunate that Albert's income is not solely dependent on local business. My new endeavor is to be Anna's benefactor. If I gave her my pearl earrings, Anna could sell them to pay debts. She'd surely do the same for me. But can I? Albert would never approve if I gave away his wedding gift to me. Yet I must do it! It will be our secret—Anna's and mine...."

Emma (*excitedly*): So that's what happened to Great-Grandma's earrings! Anna Snow must have been a wonderful friend. Could hers be the same family that owns Snow's General Store?

Liz: Let's go find out.

Text Evidence

❶ Sentence Structure

Read lines 6–7, Emma's second speech. Underline the stage direction that tells what Emma is doing while she is speaking.

❷ Specific Vocabulary

Read lines 8–10, Liz's second speech. The word *enthusiasm* means "an excitement about something." Why is Liz speaking with enthusiasm?

_____

_____

_____

❸ Comprehension
Theme

Read lines 16–25, Liz's fourth speech. What secret does Liz discover from reading Great-Grandma's diary?

_____

_____

_____

Text Evidence

1 Talk About It

Read SCENE 2. Explain why Liz and Emma go to visit Mr. Snow. Then write about it.

_____

_____

2 Sentence Structure

Read lines 23-27, Mr. Snow's last speech. Reread the last sentence. Circle the comma. Underline the independent clause. Box the dependent clause. When did Mr. Snow find the envelope?

_____

_____

3 Comprehension Theme

Reread SCENE 2. Why does Mr. Snow give the envelope to Liz and Emma?

_____

_____

SCENE 2 *Snow's General Store; enter Liz and Emma.*

Mr. Snow: Good morning. May I help you young ladies?

Emma *(tentatively)*: Um… Mr. Snow, we were wondering if you might be related to Anna Snow.

Mr. Snow: Yes, I'm her grandson. Why do you ask?

Liz: We're trying to solve a mystery. Our great-grandmother, Flossie Howard, was a good friend of your grandmother's. She wrote about her in a diary she kept. *(She shows the diary to Mr. Snow.)*

Mr. Snow: Flossie Howard, you say? That name rings a bell, but I can't quite place it. There were lots of Howards in town in those days.

Liz *(with disappointment)*: Well…thanks anyway.

Mr. Snow: I do hope you solve your mystery.

SCENE 3 *Liz's yard, a few days later; the girls are setting items out for the yard sale as neighbors arrive.*

Emma: Look, Liz. Isn't that Mr. Snow from the store? I wonder what he's doing here.

Mr. Snow: Hello, girls. I think this might belong to you. *(He hands Liz a small yellowed envelope.)*

Liz *(reading)*: "For Flossie."

Mr. Snow: I knew I'd heard that name somewhere. After you left, I found that envelope tucked away in the back of the store safe.

Liz (*opens the envelope, finds a note and the pearl earrings; reading*): "Dearest Flossie, I can't tell you how much I appreciate the gesture. But I can't accept this kindest of offers. The earrings are yours and too lovely to part with."

Mr. Snow: Her brother Bert took charge of the store when she and Granddad left. In all the hubbub, I guess she forgot she'd stowed the earrings in the safe. And she never did come back.

Liz: Even so, they've been secure all these years. Thanks very much, Mr. Snow.

Yard Sale Customer: Those earrings are lovely. Would you take twenty-five dollars for them?

Liz: Twenty-five dollars? I could get my new bike.

Emma: But the earrings are family heirlooms! And we don't even know what they're worth.

Liz (*to herself, seized by indecision*): I'd really like the money for the bike. But... maybe Emma's right. They *are* Great-Grandma's earrings. (*to Yard Sale Customer*) Sorry, ma'am, they're not for sale. (*to Emma*) We should each keep one. I'll earn money for the bike some other way. Hey, I'll bet the *basement* could use an extensive cleaning out!

Make Connections

? Talk about the decisions that the characters, both past and present, find difficult to make. **ESSENTIAL QUESTION**

Talk about what you had to consider at a time when you made a difficult decision. **TEXT TO SELF**

Text Evidence

❶ Specific Vocabulary

Read Liz's first speech on this page. A *gesture* is "something you do or say to show how you feel about someone or something." What gesture did Great-Grandma make toward Anna? What did the gesture show?

_____

_____

_____

❷ Sentence Structure

Read Liz's last speech. Circle the three stage directions that help you know whom Liz is talking to. Who wants to buy the earrings from Liz?

_____

❸ Comprehension
Theme

Read lines 22–23. Underline the decision that Liz makes. How does Emma help Liz make that decision? Circle what Emma says earlier.

231

Respond to the Text

 **Partner Discussion** Work with a partner. Answer the questions. Discuss what you learned about "Treasure in the Attic." Write the page numbers where you found text evidence.

What was difficult about Great-Grandma's decision?

Great-Grandma wrote in her diary that many people suffered because of _____.

Page(s): _____

Anna Snow's family might have to _____.

Page(s): _____

Great-Grandma decided to give Anna _____.

Page(s): _____

What was difficult about Liz's decision at the end of the story?

Liz wanted to buy _____.

Page(s): _____

A yard sale customer offered _____.

Page(s): _____

Emma reminded Liz that the earrings _____.

Page(s): _____

 **Group Discussion** Present your answers to the group. Cite text evidence to justify your thinking. Listen to and discuss the group's opinions about your answers.

Write Review your notes about "Treasure in the Attic." Then write your answer to the Essential Question. Use text evidence to support your answer. Use vocabulary words from this week's reading in your writing.

> **What difficult decisions did the characters make in the story?**
>
> Great-Grandma made the difficult decision to _____
> _____.
>
> Anna Snow's difficult decision was _____.
>
> Liz made a difficult decision when she _____
> _____.

Share Writing Present your writing to the class. Discuss their opinions. Think about what the class has to say. Did they justify their claims? Explain why you agree or disagree with their claims.

I agree with _____ that _____.

I disagree with _____ because _____.

Write to Sources

Naomi

Take Notes About the Text I took notes on my idea web to respond to the prompt: *Imagine that it is October of 1936. Write a flashback scene between Flossie and Anna.*

pages 228–231

Detail
The Depression has bred suffering for Flossie's neighbors.

Detail
Anna Snow's family may have to leave to find work.

Topic
Flossie plans to help Anna Snow and her family.

Detail
Flossie wants to give Anna her pearl earrings to sell to pay debts.

Evidence
Flossie thinks it could be Anna's and her secret.

Write About the Text I used my notes from my idea web to help me write a flashback scene from 1936 between Flossie and Anna.

Student Model: Narrative Text

Anna: Flossie, times are hard for all of us. I can't let you make this sacrifice for my family.

Flossie: But it would be so sad if you left. You can sell my pearl earrings to pay your debts. Please let me do this for you and your family.

Anna: Thank you so much for your concern, Flossie. I will miss you so much.

Flossie: Then let me help you and your family. This will be our secret.

TALK ABOUT IT

Text Evidence
Draw a box around a sentence in Anna's first dialogue that comes from a detail in the notes. What is the detail in the notes?

Grammar
Circle the possessive pronouns in Flossie's first dialogue. To whom does each pronoun refer?

Connect Ideas
Underline the sentence with the phrase "times are hard." How can you combine this sentence with the sentence after it to connect the ideas?

Your Turn

Imagine that the girls discover that Anna is still alive. Write a dialogue among the three of them.

>> Go Digital!
Write your response online. Use your editing checklist.

TALK ABOUT IT

Weekly Concept Shared Experiences

? Essential Question
How do people uncover what they have in common?

>> *Go Digital*

 What is the man in the photo doing? What are the other people doing? Write words in the chart.

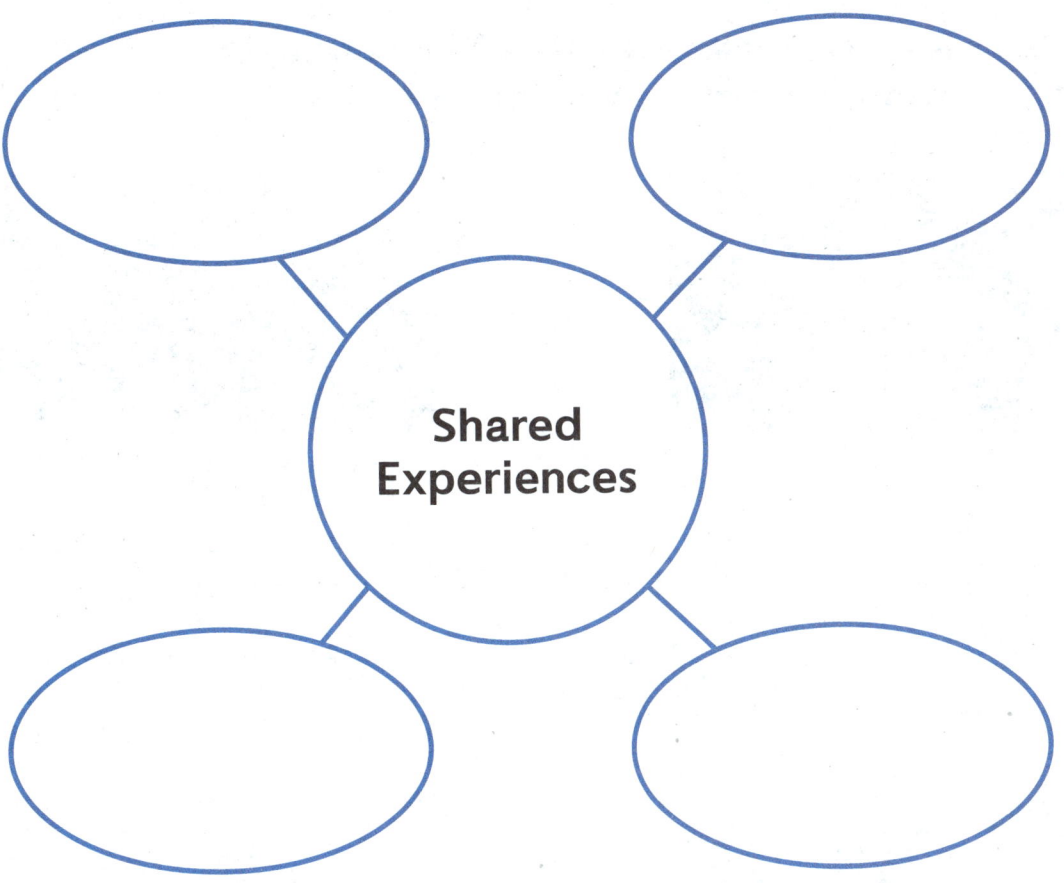

Discuss how storytelling is an experience that people share. Then talk about why sharing experiences is good. Use words from the chart. You can say:

The man is _____ that all people like to hear. Different people sit _____ and _____ to the stories. When different people share experiences, they learn about _____.

More Vocabulary

 Look at the picture and read the word. Then read the sentence. Talk about the word with a partner. Write your own sentence.

arrival

Juanita greeted her grandchildren after their **arrival** home.

I get excited by the *arrival* of _____

because _____.

disbelief

The students stared in **disbelief** as they watched the exciting basketball game.

I stared in *disbelief* when _____

_____.

automatically

The girls **automatically** smile when they meet someone new.

When you do something *automatically*, you do it without _____.

discovered

Joe **discovered** that he likes listening to country music.

I *discovered* that I _____

_____.

238

interrupts

Sometimes my brother **interrupts** me while I am reading.

I don't like when _____ *interrupts* me while I am _____.

prefer

Some people **prefer** red apples to green apples.

During the summer, I *prefer* _____ to _____.

Words and Phrases
Multiple-Meaning Words

The verb *permit* means "to allow."
My parents <u>permit</u> me to ride my bike to the park.

The noun *permit* means "license."
We need a <u>permit</u> to fish in the lake.

Read the sentences below. Circle the correct meaning of the boldfaced word.

My older sister has a **permit** to drive a car.

allow   license

Our teachers sometimes **permit** us to talk quietly before class.

allow   license

» Go Digital Add these multiple-meaning words to your New Words notebook. Write a sentence to show the meaning of each.

Text Evidence

1 Talk About It

Read the title. Talk about what you see. Write your ideas.

What does the title tell you?

_____

_____

_____

What does the photograph show?

_____

_____

_____

Take notes as you read the story.

Shared Read   Genre • Realistic Fiction

My Visit to Arizona

Essential Question

? How do people uncover what they have in common?

Read how a girl from Argentina meets the challenges of making new friends in a foreign country.

Silvina and her parents have traveled from their ranch in Argentina to one in Arizona. The trip reunites Silvina's father with his college friend, Mr. Gomez. While her parents share ideas about raising cattle, Silvina spends her days with the Gomez boys, Mike and Carl, and their grandfather.

Shocking

—*Short Sharp Shocks. Try to say it three times fast.*

My English tutor at home taught me that tongue twister. How perfectly it describes my arrival in Arizona!

Shock 1: We are staying on the hot, dusty Gomez Ranch. My family travels so much, I think we are nomadic. But usually we sleep in nice, air-conditioned hotels.

Shock 2: People here think I can ride horses. Do I tell them the only saddle I have used is on a bicycle? And that I am more inclined to read *books* about horses?

Shock 3: English lessons do not automatically prepare you to understand the way people speak in Arizona.

—*Pull up a chair and get comfy,* says Grampa G.

But the chairs are too big for me to lift. And who is *Comfy*? Must everyone here talk so fast?

Nodding and Smiling

—*Our ranch covers 150 acres,* Grampa G says. *Permit me to show you around.*

I am thinking, Show me a round *what*? but there is no time to ask, because he is pushing me toward an army of cattle.

—*Here's the finest herd in the Southwest, 'bout 200 strong.*

I think Grampa G would make an excellent mentor, if only I understood half of all he is chattering about.

Text Evidence

❶ Sentence Structure ACT

Reread the last sentence in the Introduction. The word *while* shows that two things are happening at the same time. Circle the two things that are happening at the same time.

❷ Specific Vocabulary ACT

Read "Shock 2." When you are inclined to do something, you are likely to do it. What is Silvana more inclined to do?

Silvina is more _____

_____.

❸ Comprehension
Theme

Reread "Shocking." What does Silvina say about the English lessons she took? Underline the sentence that tells you. What does Grampa G. say that Silvina doesn't understand? Circle the words.

241

Text Evidence

1 Talk About It

Explain why Silvina thinks Grampa G. is giving her a horse. Then write about it.

_____

_____

2 Specific Vocabulary

Read the third and fourth sentences in "Riding and Reading." The word *cinch* means "something that is easy to do." What does Mike say about riding? Circle the words. How does Mike say this in a different way?

_____

3 Comprehension
Theme

Read the last four paragraphs on the page. What do Carl and Silvina have in common?

They both _____.

I nod and smile and pretend I understand.

I lift my camera to take a photo of him with a big steer.

At least I am not the only one nodding and smiling now.

—Here's a sturdy fellow, says Grampa G. The strongest horse for miles.

He leads the biggest, blackest horse I have ever seen right up to me.

—Silvina, let me present Stormy to you.

I stare in **disbelief**. Is he giving me a horse?

Say something, Silvina. Say something, quick!

—Thank you, but I cannot accept such a big present, I sputter.

Grampa G laughs and laughs.

Finally, he stops laughing and tells me what is so funny.

Apparently, *PRES*ent and pre*SENT* are two different words.

I will never learn English!

Riding and Reading

It has happened: Mike **discovered** I never rode a horse.

Now he and Carl want me to ride that beast Stormy.

—Riding's a **cinch**, says Mike. Easy as falling out of bed.

Or off a cliff, I think. But I do not say that.

—He looks like the wild horse from *The Black Stallion*, I say.

—I love that book! shouts Carl.

I tell him how I read it in English class, and he forgets all about putting me on Stormy and we talk about books instead.

What a relief! I am content for the first time in days.

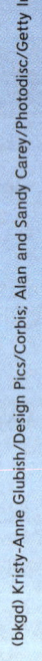

—So, Silvina, you ready to ride Stormy? *interrupts* Mike.

Goodbye, contentment. Can my camera save me again?

I point it at the brothers standing next to the black colossus.

Suddenly Carl runs to the house and brings out a camera.

—*Hey, can you show me how to work this thing?* he asks. *I got it last month and never figured it out.*

At last, something I can do!

Six weeks later, we are all sitting around a campfire, each roasting a marshmallow on a glowing ember.

—*These would go well with* dulce de leche, I say.

For once, Mike and Carl look confused instead of me.

—*A very delicious caramel*, I explain. *It is good on anything.*

Carl uses his camera to take a panoramic shot of the desert.

Then he takes one of this international group of friends, who are laughing and talking with an easy rapport.

I will place those photos in a digital scrapbook with the one of me riding Stormy.

I still prefer reading to riding, but I am glad I can do both.

My adjustment to Arizona was slow, but I learned so much!

Make Connections

Talk about how Silvina discovers what she has in common with the Gomez family. **ESSENTIAL QUESTION**

Describe a time when you learned how to adjust to new people or a new place. **TEXT TO SELF**

Text Evidence

❶ Specific Vocabulary

Read the third paragraph. The word *colossus* means "something of enormous size or importance." What does Silvina think is a colossus in this story?

_____

❷ Sentence Structure

Reread the seventh paragraph. When are Silvina and her new friends sitting around a campfire? Circle the phrase that tells you. How long has Silvina been with her new friends?

She has _____.

❸ Comprehension
Theme

Reread the last three paragraphs. Which sentence helps to tell the theme of the story? Circle it.

What did Silvina learn about adjusting to a new place?

_____

_____

243

Respond to the Text

Partner Discussion Work with a partner. Answer the questions. Discuss what you learned about "My Visit to Arizona." Write the page numbers where you found text evidence.

How does Silvina have trouble adjusting to Arizona?

Silvina thinks the Gomez ranch _____.

The Gomez family wants Silvina _____.

Silvina does not understand _____.

Text Evidence

Page(s): _____

Page(s): _____

Page(s): _____

How does Silvina try to adjust?

Grampa G. teaches Silvina about the _____.

Silvina talks with Carl about _____.

Silvina teaches Carl _____.

Text Evidence

Page(s): _____

Page(s): _____

Page(s): _____

Group Discussion Present your answers to the group. Cite text evidence to justify your thinking. Listen to and discuss the group's opinions about your answers.

 **Write** Review your notes about "My Visit to Arizona." Then write your answer to the Essential Question. Use text evidence to support your answer. Use vocabulary words from this week's reading in your writing.

> **How does Silvina uncover what she has in common with the Gomez family?**
>
> Silvina and Carl both enjoy _____.
>
> Silvina finally tries to _____.
>
> While roasting marshmallows, Silvina shares _____.
>
> Silvina uncovers what she has in common with the Gomez family by _____.

Share Writing Present your writing to the class. Discuss their opinions. Think about what the class has to say. Did they justify their claims? Explain why you agree or disagree with their claims.

I agree with _____ that _____.

I disagree with _____ because _____.

Write to Sources

pages 240–243

Take Notes About the Text I took notes on my idea web to respond to the prompt: *Write a diary entry. How would Silvina describe her experience teaching Carl how to use his camera?*

Leah

Detail
Silvina took a photo of the brothers and Stormy.

Detail
Carl asked Silvina to show him how to work his new digital camera.

Topic
Silvina describes how she taught Carl to use his camera.

Detail
Carl took a panoramic shot of the desert.

Detail
Carl took a photo of the friends around the campfire.

246

Write About the Text I used my notes from my idea web to write a diary entry from Silvina about teaching Carl to use his camera.

Student Model: *Narrative Text*

I took a photo of the brothers and Stormy today. It reminded Carl that he doesn't know how to use his new digital camera. He asked me to teach him. I showed him how to point and shoot the camera for close-up shots. I also taught him how to take panoramic shots. He will need the panoramic feature to take photos of the desert!

TALK ABOUT IT

Text Evidence
Underline the sentences that discuss panoramic shots. What detail in the notes supports these sentences?

Grammar
Circle the the prepositional phrase in the final sentence. How does this phrase add detail to the sentence?

Connect Ideas
Draw a box around the sentences describing Carl's request. How can you combine these sentences to connect ideas?

Your Turn

Write a diary entry from Silvina's perspective describing her experience of riding a horse for the first time.

>> *Go Digital!*
Write your response online. Use your editing checklist.

TALK ABOUT IT

Weekly Concept Taking Responsibility

? Essential Question
How can we take responsibility?

›› Go Digital

 **COLLABORATE** What does the photo show? Who caused the situation? Write words in the chart about what the person should do next.

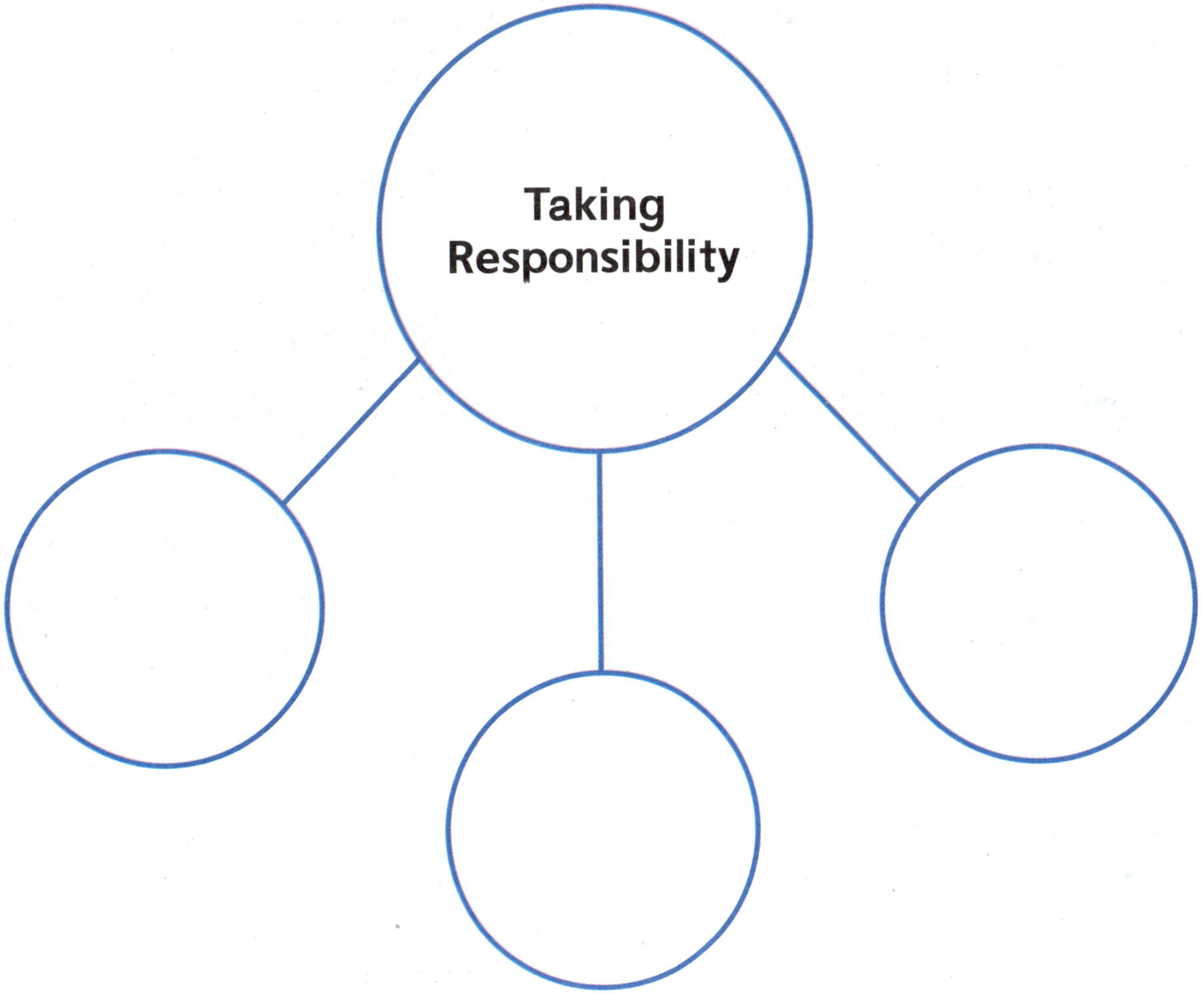

```
            ┌─────────────────┐
            │     Taking      │
            │ Responsibility  │
            └─────────────────┘
           /         |         \
      ( )         ( )         ( )
```

Discuss how the baseball player should take responsibility. Use words from the chart. For each thing, you can say:

The baseball player should take responsibility by _____

_____.

249

More Vocabulary

 Look at the picture and read the word. Then read the sentence. Talk about the word with a partner. Answer the question.

borrowed

Serena **borrowed** Mrs. Martinez's pencil to take the test.

When you borrow something, do you keep it or give it back?

clenched

The angry boy **clenched** his fist.

What word or phrase means the same thing as *clenched*?

weird

Owls turn their heads around in a **weird** way.

In what other weird ways do some animals move?

wondering

Tyra is **wondering** why the lizard is so colorful.

What are you often wondering about?

Poetry Terms

alliteration

Alliteration is the repetition of the same beginning consonant sound within a group of words.

Three grey geese were in a green field grazing.

Grey were the geese, and green was the grass.

assonance

Assonance is the repetition of the same vowel sound within a group of words.

The breeze blew through the leaves of the leaning trees.

Figurative language creates special images in a reader's mind. Idioms are a kind of figurative language. The meaning of an idiom is different from the meanings of the individual words in the idiom.

Taking the tough test

Was a **piece of cake** for Matt;

He had studied all night.

Piece of cake = easy to do

COLLABORATE

Work with a partner. Read the sentences together. Use the words below to create alliteration and assonance.

zoo   playground
Paula   do

Alliteration:

_____ picked peaches near the _____.

Assonance:

It's true. I _____ like to go to the _____.

Text Evidence

Shared Read | Genre • Poetry

Hey Nilda,

1 Literary Element
Alliteration

Read the first two lines of the poem. Circle the words that begin with the same sound. What effect does the use of these words have?

_____
_____

2 Talk About It

Reread the first stanza. Explain what the speaker did that probably seemed weird to Nilda.

_____

3 Specific Vocabulary

Reread the second stanza. When you make a beeline for something, you walk in a straight, direct line. Why would Rachel want to make a beeline for the bus?

She wanted to make a beeline for the bus because _____.

By now you're **wondering**, worrying
Why I've seemed so **weird** this week
   —not calling you, not texting,
Slipping silently past you in the hall
   at school,
Pretending to listen to music or
   checking my watch.

Outside, with classes over,
I've made a **beeline** for the bus,
Other kids, eager to leave,
Hustle and rush,
Feeling free and gleeful.
   But not me.
   I hide behind my hair.

Essential Question

? How can we take responsibility?

Read a poet's view of being responsible in a friendship.

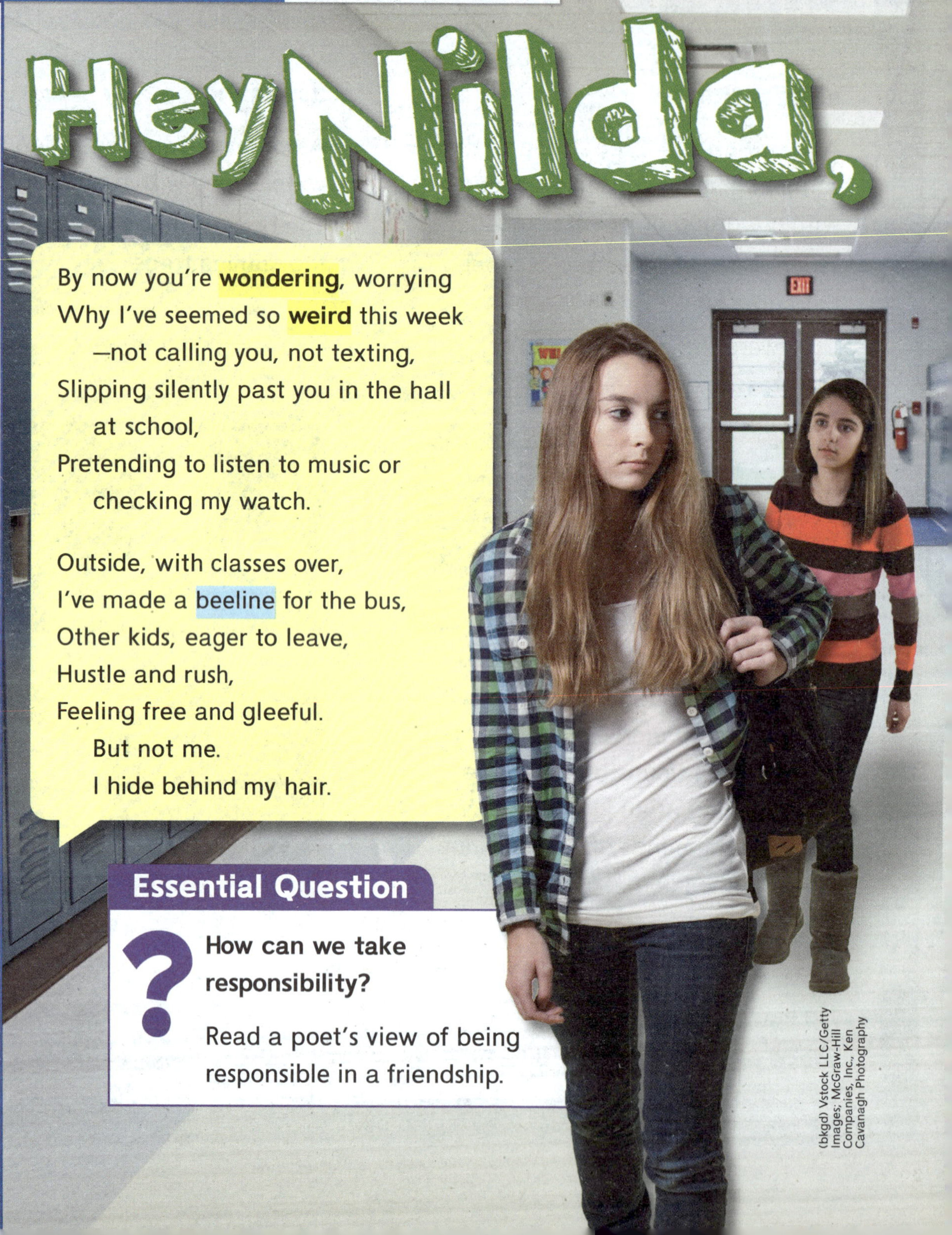

252

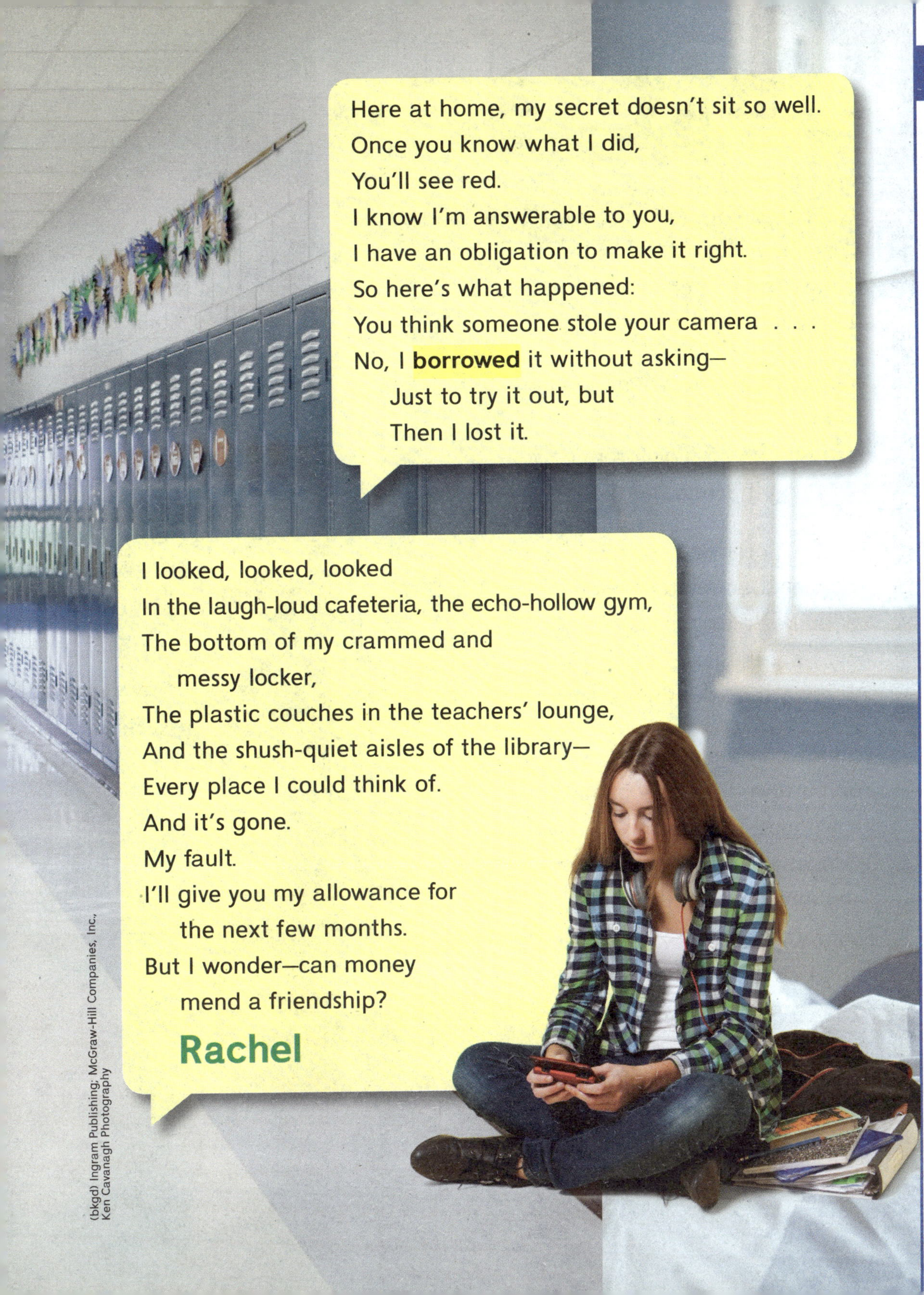

Here at home, my secret doesn't sit so well.
Once you know what I did,
You'll see red.
I know I'm answerable to you,
I have an obligation to make it right.
So here's what happened:
You think someone stole your camera . . .
No, I **borrowed** it without asking—
    Just to try it out, but
        Then I lost it.

I looked, looked, looked
In the laugh-loud cafeteria, the echo-hollow gym,
The bottom of my crammed and
    messy locker,
The plastic couches in the teachers' lounge,
And the shush-quiet aisles of the library—
Every place I could think of.
And it's gone.
My fault.
I'll give you my allowance for
    the next few months.
But I wonder—can money
    mend a friendship?

Rachel

Text Evidence

1 Sentence Structure ACT

Read the first line on this page. Circle the comma. What is the purpose of the comma here?

_____

_____

2 Talk About It

According to Rachel, what does Nilda think happened to the camera? What really happened to the camera?

_____

_____

3 Comprehension
Point of View

Who is the speaker of this poem? Explain how you know.

_____

_____

Text Evidence

❶ Literary Element
Assonance

Read the fourth line of the poem. Circle the words that have the same vowel sound.

❷ Specific Vocabulary

Read the second stanza. The word *breakable* means "easy to break." Why is Nilda glad she wasn't holding something breakable? Underline the words that tell you.

❸ Talk About It

Reread the second through fourth stanzas. Explain how Nilda feels when she first reads Rachel's text. Why does she feel this way?

_____
_____
_____

Hi Rachel,

Yep, you're right.
I wondered why you were walking around
Like you were scared or angry or
As if you'd been crying or trying to hide,
—Or all of the above.

Good thing I wasn't holding anything breakable
When I read your message,
Because I might have dropped it
—Or flung it across the room.

Instead, I dropped down into our rickety recliner
And clenched my teeth tight,
My body shaking as hard
As if I were outside
Wearing shorts in the freezing rain.

I mean, come on!
You borrowed my new camera
    without asking?
Then let me think it was stolen?
I thought I could trust you.
And I thought you would trust me enough
To tell me the truth.

254

How long have we been friends?
Since we were five, that's how long.
We may not see eye-to-eye at times,
But we have always been honest
—With each other.

Just so you know:
I found my camera yesterday,
Stuck in a big box with some
    socks in the lost and found.

Let's not blow this out of
    proportion,
Maybe just treat it as water
    under the bridge.
Start again, okay?
Still friends?
I hope so.
I've got two tickets to Friday's
    concert, and
I don't want to go by myself.

Nilda
—Lareine Interne

Make Connections

? Talk about the ways that Rachel and Nilda express their views on taking responsibility. **ESSENTIAL QUESTION**

Describe a time when you took responsibility for your actions in a friendship. **TEXT TO SELF**

Text Evidence

❶ Sentence Structure ACT

Read the fifth stanza. Find the pronoun that appears four times. Whom does this pronoun refer to? Write their names. Circle words that help you know.

_____

❷ Comprehension
Point of View

Who is the speaker of this poem? Box the speaker's name. What does she know about the camera that her friend does not know?

_____

_____

❸ Talk About It

What is Nilda's view about her friendship with Rachel at the end of the poem?

_____

_____

255

Respond to the Text

Partner Discussion Work with a partner. Answer the questions. Discuss what you learned about "Hey Nilda" and "Hi Rachel." Write the page numbers where you found text evidence.

What are Rachel's views about taking responsibility?

Rachel tells Nilda, "I know _____."   Page(s): _____

Rachel admits _____.   Page(s): _____

Rachel wants to _____.   Page(s): _____

Text Evidence

What are Nilda's views about taking responsibility?

Nilda thought Rachel would _____.   Page(s): _____

Nilda says the two friends may not see eye-to-eye at times, but they _____.   Page(s): _____

At the end of the poem, Nilda says that _____.   Page(s): _____

Text Evidence

Group Discussion Present your answers to the group. Cite text evidence to justify your thinking. Listen to and discuss the group's opinions about your answers.

Write Review your notes about "Hey Nilda" and "Hi Rachel." Then write your answer to the Essential Question. Use text evidence to support your answer. Use vocabulary words from this week's reading in your writing.

How do Rachel and Nilda take responsibility?

Rachel tells Nilda _____
_____.

Rachel takes responsibility by _____
_____.

Nilda tells Rachel _____
_____.

Nilda takes responsibility by _____
_____.

Share Writing Present your writing to the class. Discuss their opinions. Think about what the class has to say. Did they justify their claims? Explain why you agree or disagree with their claims.

I agree with _____ that _____.

I disagree with _____ because _____.

Write to Sources

Alfredo

Take Notes About the Text I took notes on my idea web to answer the question: *How does the poet of "Hey Nilda" use alliteration, assonance, and idiomatic expressions to describe an everyday experience?*

pages 252–253

Topic
Alliteration, assonance, and idiomatic expressions in "Hey Nilda"

Alliteration
the /w/ sound in *wondering, worrying,* and *weird*

Assonance
the long /e/ sound in *feeling, free,* and *gleeful.*

Idiomatic Expression
"hide behind my hair"

Write About the Text I used notes from my idea web to write a paragraph about the poet's use of alliteration, assonance, and idiomatic expressions in "Hey Nilda."

Student Model: *Informative Text*

    The poet of "Hey Nilda" uses alliteration, assonance, and idiomatic expressions to describe a familiar experience. The poet uses alliteration by repeating the /w/ sound in the words *wondering, worrying,* and *weird*. The poet uses assonance by repeating the long /e/ sound in *feeling, free,* and *gleeful*. The use of alliteration and assonance draws attention to Rachel's feelings. The poet also uses the idiomatic expression "hide behind my hair." The use of this familiar expression highlights that Rachel is ashamed she used Nilda's camera without asking her.

TALK ABOUT IT

Text Evidence
Draw a box around the examples that come from the notes. Why did Alfredo include these examples?

Grammar
Circle the verb in the fourth sentence. Why did Alfredo use the singular form of the verb?

Condense Ideas
Underline sentences 5 and 6. How could you combine these sentences to condense the ideas?

Your Turn

Write a paragraph providing three other examples of how the poet uses alliteration, assonance, and idiomatic expressions to describe a familiar experience.

>> *Go Digital!*
Write your response online. Use your editing checklist.

Unit 5

Discoveries

The BIG Idea
How can discoveries open up new possibilities?

TALK ABOUT IT

Weekly Concept Myths

? Essential Question
Why do people tell and retell myths?

>> *Go Digital*

 Who is the actor in the photo supposed to be? How do audiences recognize the character? Write words and phrases about the character in the chart.

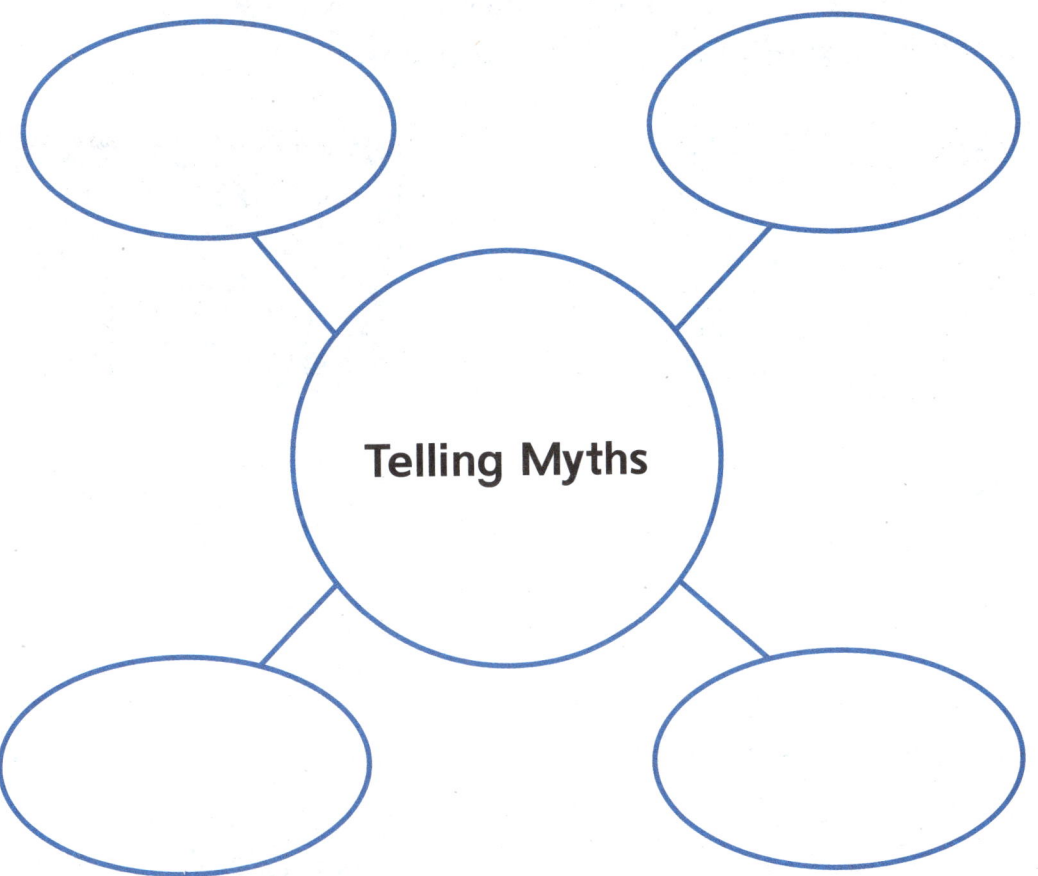

Discuss the myth the actor is retelling. Use words from the chart. You can say:

Audiences love the story because _____.

They always recognize the character because _____

_____.

More Vocabulary

 Look at the picture and read the word. Then read the sentence. Talk about the word with a partner. Write your own sentence.

demonstrate

The swimmers **demonstrate** their strength during the competition.

I *demonstrate* my _____

when I _____.

eerie

The fog around the old house was **eerie**!

Another word for *eerie* is _____

_____.

grants

The principal **grants** the students their diplomas.

I hope _____ *grants* me

_____.

murky

Lee couldn't see anything in the **murky** water.

An example of something *murky* is _____

_____.

source

Heather found the **source** of the river.

Another word for *source* is _____

_____.

victorious

The **victorious** softball team celebrated after the game.

To be *victorious*, people must _____

_____.

Words and Phrases
Connecting Phrases

The connecting phrases *one morning* and *a moment later* tell when something happened.

one morning = during the morning in the past or future
One morning, I decided to go fishing.

a moment later = very soon after something happened
A moment later, I grabbed my fishing pole and left home.

Read the sentences below. Write the connecting phrase that means the same thing as the underlined words.

In the morning a few weeks ago, I decided to start exercising.

_____, I decided to start exercising.

Very soon after that happened, I opened the door and began to run.

_____, I opened the door and began to run.

» Go Digital Add these connecting phrases to your New Words notebook. Write a sentence to show the meaning of each.

265

Text Evidence

1. **Talk About It**

Read the title. Talk about what you see. Write your ideas.

What does the title tell you?

_____

_____

_____

What does the photograph show?

_____

_____

_____

Take notes as you read the story.

Shared Read Genre • Myth

THUNDER HELPER

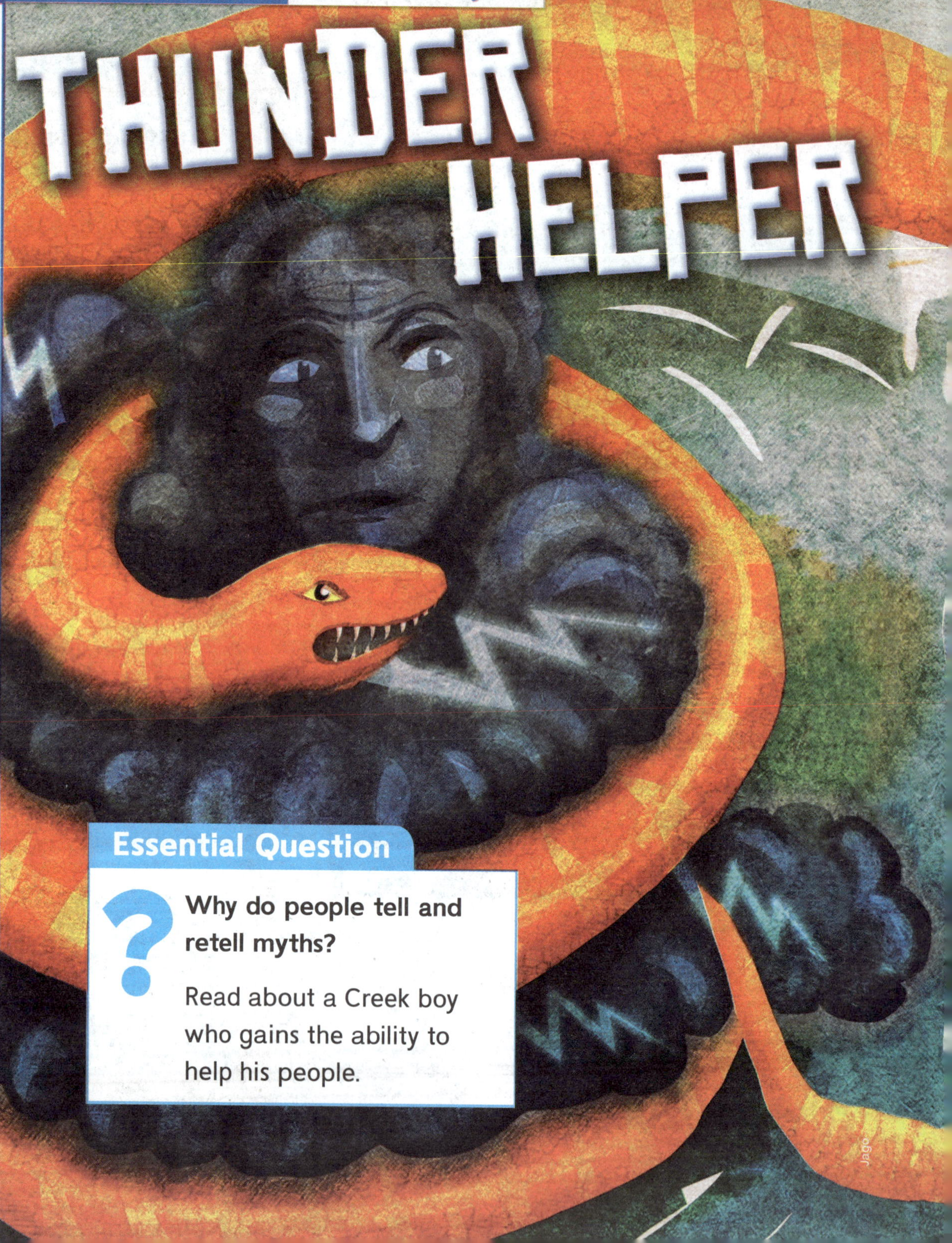

Essential Question

Why do people tell and retell myths?

Read about a Creek boy who gains the ability to help his people.

The Creek are Native Americans who come from what are now Florida, Alabama, and Georgia. Their myths, passed down from generation to generation, are often about the relationship between people and the natural world.

A long time ago, a boy and his three uncles set out from their village to go hunting. As always, the boy looked for ways to be useful to his people, so he set about catching fish in a nearby stream and gathering firewood while his uncles tracked deer. When his uncles returned, he would prepare *sofki*, a corn soup, and add the deer meat to make a mouth-watering stew.

One morning, the boy was walking toward the stream, dreaming of the tasty fish he would catch and listening to the chittering of the birds. All at once, he heard a loud roaring sound. Quickly, and as sly as a fox, he crouched, set an arrow against his bow, and readied himself for whatever might happen.

The boy crept slowly toward the **eerie** rumbling, until he reached the stream. There, towering above the rushing water, he saw two unearthly creatures locked in a terrifying struggle. One was dark and formless, yet seemed to be the **source** of the booming roar. The other, a long, wiry monster, was tightly coiled around the first.

The boy watched, his mouth **agape** with wonder. "The giant serpent must be the dreaded Tie-Snake!" he thought, remembering stories his elders told about the trickster that fooled people and drew them down into the **murky** and desolate underworld. "But who is the shapeless one? Could it be Thunder himself?" the boy wondered. In a valiant move, he raised his loaded bow and shouted to Tie-Snake, "Let go of him!"

Text Evidence

❶ Comprehension
Problem and Solution

Read the second paragraph. The boy looked for ways to be useful to his people. Circle one way he found to solve this problem.

❷ Sentence Structure

Read the third sentence in the third paragraph. Circle the adverb *quickly*. How does this adverb help you understand the sentence?

_____

_____

_____

❸ Specific Vocabulary

Reread the first sentence of the fifth paragraph. Box the word *agape*. Underline the context clue that helps you understand the meaning of *agape*.

A mouth that is agape is _____

_____.

267

Text Evidence

1. Comprehension
Problem and Solution

Read the first four paragaphs. What did the boy do when he decided not to listen to Tie-Snake's deception any longer? Underline the words that tell you.

2. Talk About It

Why does the boy choose to help Thunder instead of Tie-Snake? Justify your answer.

_____

_____

3. Specific Vocabulary

Read the fifth paragraph. Underline the context clues that help you understand the meaning of *hone*. Then rewrite the sentence below, using a synonym in place of *hone*.

He worked hard to _____ his hunting skills once he returned home.

Tie-Snake hissed back, "Boy, if you kill the evil Thunder, I will protect you always and share all the mysteries of the underworld with you!"

Thunder bellowed his response. "Listen to me, boy. Tie-Snake speaks only lies. Strike him with your arrow, and I shall **grant** you the power to be a strong, brave, and wise warrior for your people."

Without listening to more of Tie-Snake's deception, the boy took aim and let his arrow fly at the serpent. Tie-Snake fell into the stream and disappeared beneath the waters. A moment later, Thunder spoke again. "Be warned. You must tell no one the source of your new power, or it will leave you."

"I promise," said the boy solemnly, and Thunder evaporated into thin air.

The boy's uncles returned to camp that evening. Despite their questions about his time alone in the forest, the boy kept his promise, and his uncles remained oblivious of the power that Thunder had given him. But the boy was eager to employ his new abilities for worthy causes, and he worked hard to **hone** his hunting skills once he returned home. In just a few short months, to the surprise of the elders, the boy had become one of the best hunters in the village. His steadfast efforts in pursuit of food were soon recognized by all the people.

It was not long after when the Creek elders learned one of their most fearsome enemies was threatening to attack them. The boy took this opportunity to request a meeting with the village leaders. "Respected elders," the boy said boldly. "Though I am only a boy, I have the courage and cunning to fight the enemy. Will you let me perform this deed to save our people?"

The boy's audacity impressed the elders. They conferred among themselves and soon nodded their heads in agreement. The chief declared, "You have proven your strength and bravery with your hunting. Now, as you go alone to fight the enemy, you must **demonstrate** your wisdom." With determination, the boy said, "I will not disappoint my people."

That very evening, the boy set off through the forest to face the enemy. The villagers gathered to await his return, and as the hours passed with no word the Creek fell into a somber mood. Then suddenly, a deafening roar of thunder made the villagers cover their ears. Their eyes shot upward as flashes of lightning streaked the sky. Moments later, smoke filtered out through the trees, and the people sensed that the boy had been **victorious**. They rejoiced that the enemy would no longer threaten their village.

When the boy made his way out of the forest, there was much celebration in honor of his exploits. The elders called him *Menewa*, meaning "great warrior." And from that day on, whenever the Creek heard Thunder, they knew that Menewa, his helper, was at work to keep their people safe.

Make Connections

Talk about why the characters and plot of "Thunder Helper" would appeal to listeners generation after generation. **ESSENTIAL QUESTION**

Tell why a myth or story you know has special meaning to you. **TEXT TO SELF**

Text Evidence

1 Comprehension
Problem and Solution

Reread the last paragraph on page 268 and at the top of page 269. What problem confronted the Creek people? Circle the words that tell you. How did the boy want to solve the problem? Underline the words that tell you.

2 Talk About It

What happened when the boy faced the enemy? Justify your answer.

_____

_____

3 Sentence Structure

Read the first sentence of the last paragraph. *When* tells that two things happen at the same time. What happened at the same time the boy made his way out of the forest? Underline the independent clause that tells you.

Respond to the Text

 **Partner Discussion** Work with a partner. Answer the questions. Discuss what you learned about "Thunder Helper." Write the page numbers where you found text evidence.

How are myths important in this story?

The boy knew Tie-Snake was _____.

Myths helped the boy _____.

Text Evidence

Page(s): _____

Page(s): _____

What qualities did the boy show in this myth?

When he defeated Tie-Snake, the boy showed _____.

When he became a good hunter, the boy showed _____.

When he defeated the fearsome enemy, the boy showed _____.

Text Evidence

Page(s): _____

Page(s): _____

Page(s): _____

What is the purpose of this myth?

The purpose of this myth is to show _____.

Text Evidence

Page(s): _____

 **Group Discussion** Present your answers to the group. Cite text evidence to justify your thinking. Listen to and discuss the group's opinions about your answers.

Write Review your notes about "Thunder Helper." Then write your answer to the Essential Question. Use text evidence to support your answer. Use vocabulary words from this week's reading in your writing.

Why did the Creek people tell and retell myths?

Myths are important in this story because _____
_____.

The boy's actions in this myth show that the Creek people value _____
_____.

The Creek people retold myths because _____
_____.

Share Writing Present your writing to the class. Discuss their opinions. Think about what the class has to say. Did they justify their claims? Explain why you agree or disagree with their claims.

I agree with _____ that _____.

I disagree with _____ because _____.

271

Write to Sources

pages 266–269

Take Notes About the Text I took notes on the sequence chart to answer the prompt: *Continue the dialogue between the boy and Tie-Snake in the story.*

First
"The giant serpent must be the dreaded Tie-Snake!" he thought.

Next
He remembered stories his elders told about the trickster that fooled people and drew them down into the underworld.

Then
The boy raised his bow and shouted to Tie-Snake, "Let go of him!"

Last
Tie-Snake hissed back, "Boy, if you kill the evil Thunder, I will protect you and share all the mysteries of the underworld with you!"

Write About the Text I used my notes from my sequence chart to write a dialogue between the boy and Tie-Snake.

Student Model: Narrative Text

"I do not believe you!" the boy yelled.

Tie-Snake hissed. He said, "If you kill Thunder, I will give you wonderful things! I will give you sharp arrows and powerful bows."

The boy shook his head. "You are a clever trickster, Tie-Snake. Knowing this, I cannot believe anything you say."

Tie-Snake tightened his grasp on Thunder. He called to the boy once more. "Of course you can believe me. If you kill Thunder, I will give you a long life. I will give you a life longer than any human has ever lived! Now that is a fair reward for killing Thunder!"

TALK ABOUT IT

Text Evidence
Draw a box around another name for Tie-Snake that appears in the notes. How does this detail help Erin continue the dialogue?

Grammar
Circle the phrase in the third paragraph that connects ideas. Why does Erin use this phrase?

Condense Ideas
Underline the sentences in paragraph four that tell what Tie-Snake promises the boy. How can you combine the sentences to condense ideas?

Your Turn
Write a dialogue between the boy and the elders before they decide to let the boy fight the enemy alone.

» Go Digital!
Write your response online. Use your editing checklist.

TALK ABOUT IT

Weekly Concept Personal Strength

? Essential Question
How do people show inner strength?

>> Go Digital

 What is the girl in the photo doing? Why does she need to find inner strength? How can she show inner strength? Write ways in the chart.

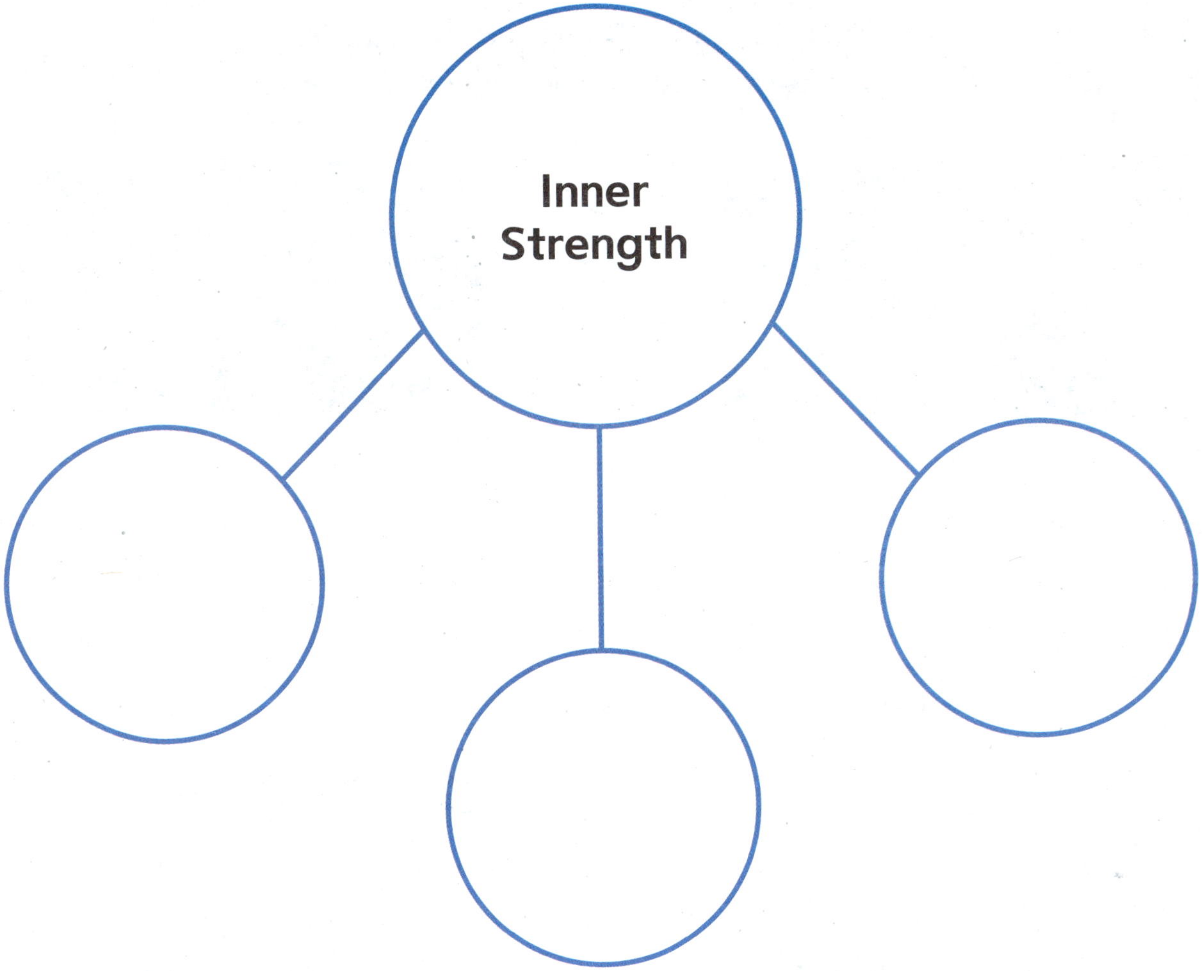

Inner Strength

Discuss how the girl can show inner strength. Use words from the chart. For each way, you can say:

The girl can show inner strength by _____

_____.

More Vocabulary

 Look at the picture and read the word. Then read the sentence. Talk about the word with a partner. Write your own sentence.

commenced

The barking **commenced** when a person walked by.

Another word for *commenced* is _____

_____.

gratitude

The thankful crowd showed their **gratitude** by clapping their hands.

When I am thankful, I can show *gratitude* by

_____.

companion

Zach's dog is his **companion** wherever he goes.

I want _____
to be my *companion* when I travel.

grave

The town was in **grave** danger during the hurricane.

Another word for *grave* is _____.

suspicion

Katie thought her friend hid behind a tree. Katie's **suspicion** was correct.

After I see lightning, my *suspicion* is _____

_____.

weary

The brave firefighter was **weary** after fighting the fire.

One thing that makes me *weary* is _____

_____.

Words and Phrases
Phrasal Verbs

spoke up = said your thoughts
The new student spoke up about the part she wanted in the play.

watched over = protected or cared for
The nurse watched over the sick man.

Read the sentences below. Write the phrasal verb that means the same thing as the underlined words.

I protected my brother while we were hiking in the woods.

I _____ my brother while we were hiking in the woods.

I said my thoughts about the kind of birthday party I wanted.

I _____ about the kind of birthday party I wanted.

» Go Digital Add these phrasal verbs to your New Words notebook. Write a sentence to show the meaning of each.

Text Evidence

Shared Read | Genre • Historical Fiction

1 Talk About It

Read the title. Look at the illustration. Talk about what you see. Write your ideas.

What does the title tell you?

_____

_____

Who are the characters in the story?

_____

_____

What are the characters doing in the illustration?

_____

_____

Take notes as you read the story.

JOURNEY TO Freedom

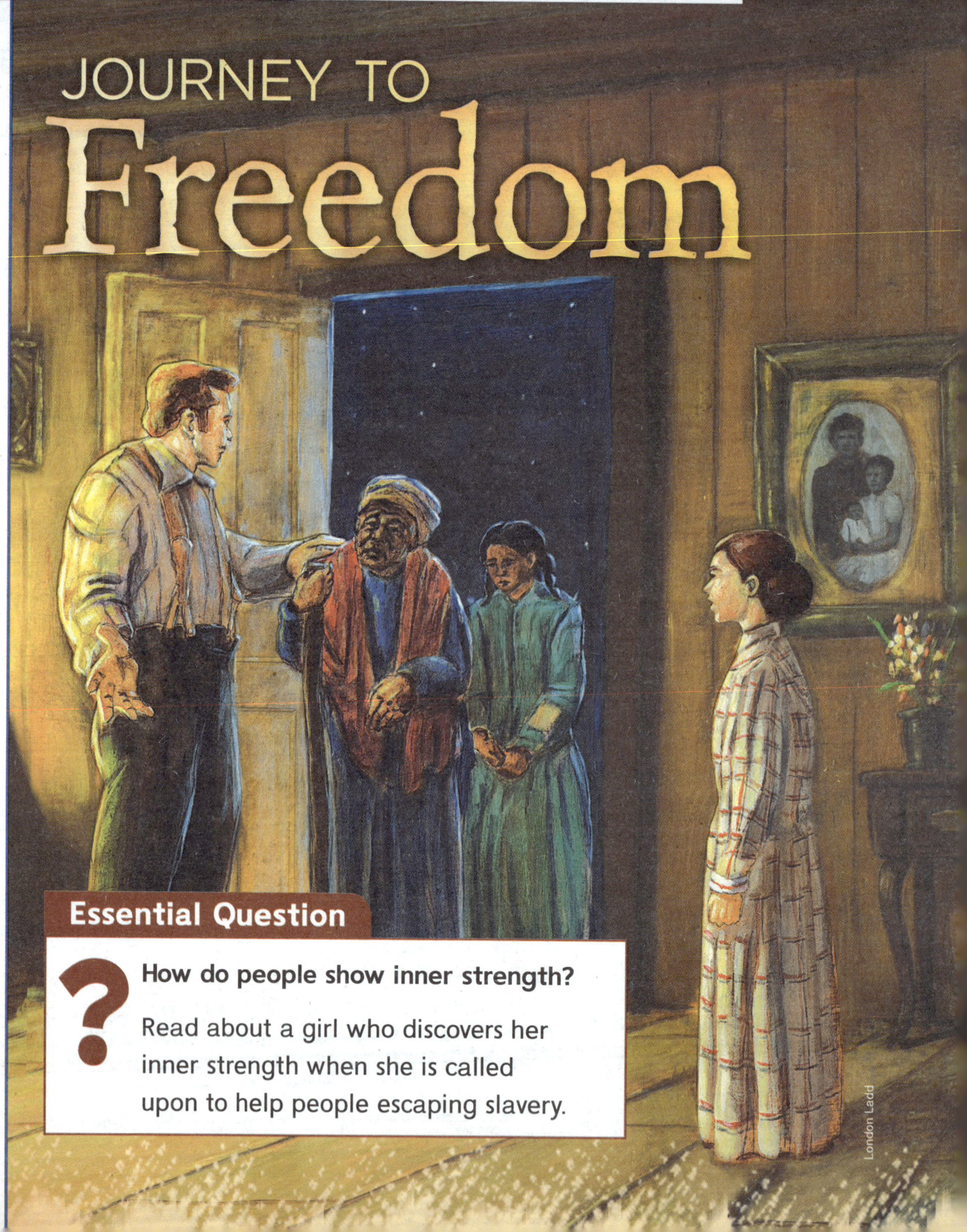

Essential Question

? How do people show inner strength?

Read about a girl who discovers her inner strength when she is called upon to help people escaping slavery.

London Ladd

278

It is early summer 1851, and 12-year-old Abigail Parker is still finding her way after the death of her mother the previous winter. Her father has recently made their Massachusetts farm a station on the Underground Railroad, and the two nervously await their first "delivery" of people on their way to Canada to escape slavery.

I could not sit for being so fretful, so I paced and sometimes paused to peer out the window. Mother often said, "Patience is bitter, but its fruit is sweet." If only I were possessed of her calm.

"I see no sign of our four guests," Papa announced as he returned from checking outdoors, fueling my fears that they had met with misfortune. Just then, a sudden knock sounded, and my heart took to pounding as Papa opened the door to two weary women on the stoop. He assisted the older one, who appeared to be about 60, to a chair by the hearth. Her companion was maybe 14. Papa directed me to poke up the fire and fetch food and drink.

When the women got back their breath, Papa asked, "What of the others? Did they not accompany you?"

"Just Nellis and me," the girl declared, and the older woman presented a letter.

Papa handed the crumpled paper to me, saying, "If you would, Abby. My eyes fail me in dim light."

I brought the letter close by a candle and commenced reading: *"Dear Jonathan, I send you Nellis and Emma, separate from their two companions, who have fallen ill with fever, one seriously. We have insufficient room to hide four until they recover, so I hope you are disposed to shelter them until further transport can be arranged. Respectfully, Jacob."*

Papa nodded and said, "We must see to their safety and comfort." I guided them to the attic hiding place and wished them a peaceful night.

Text Evidence

❶ Specific Vocabulary

Read the first paragraph. Circle words and phrases that help you understand the meaning of *fretful*. Then write a synonym below.

_____

❷ Sentence Structure

Read the third sentence in the second paragraph. Underline the adjective clause *who appeared to be about 60*. Whom does this clause describe? Circle the noun phrase that tells you.

❸ Comprehension
Cause and Effect

Read the sixth paragraph. Abigail and her father had expected four guests. Why didn't the other two guests come? Underline the words that tell you. Then write your answer below.

_____

_____

Text Evidence

1. Specific Vocabulary

Read the first paragraph. The word *gaunt* means "very thin and pale." Why is Nellis's face gaunt?

Her face is gaunt because _____

_____.

2. Talk About It

Why did Abby lie to Mr. Carrington about what she was doing?

_____

_____

3. Sentence Structure

Read the last sentence in the last paragraph. Circle the comma, which divides the sentence into two parts. What did Abigail do once Mr. Carrington nodded thanks and continued on? Underline the part of the sentence that tells you. Write a phrase that means the same thing as *once*.

_____

Come morning, afore I entered the attic, I couldn't help eavesdropping on the sound of choked coughing. Once inside, I shuddered when I saw Nellis's gaunt face—so ill she looked. "I fear it's the fever," she gasped.

I summoned Papa, pleading, "She needs a doctor!"

"Think of the risk," he scolded. "The new law allows slave catchers to come all this way north, and if we're found harboring Nellis and Emma—well, retaliation could be grave. We must tend to this ourselves."

"But I lack Mother's know-how for curing," I whispered.

"Back in Virginia, Nellis told me 'bout some fever herbs," Emma spoke up.

"You daren't go out, Emma," Papa cautioned, "but Abby can procure what you need." I felt near fainting, but he was resolved. "Remember," he said to me, "the fields have eyes, and the woods have ears. Take care how you act and speak, so as not to arouse suspicion."

I left in haste with my basket, rehearsing Emma's words about the needed herb. "Grows on edges of clearings, by streams or marshes . . . has dull white flowers, wrinkled leaves, and stout stem." My search seemed endless, but finally I spied some flowers seeming to match Emma's description. I plucked the plant and some familiar mint that I knew for sure by its smell.

As I hurried home, I met our neighbor Mr. Carrington coming opposite. "Where to in such a hurry, Miss Abigail?"

Undaunted, I spun a tale about hunting up mint for Mother's special cake recipe, and my voice was wondrous calm as I presented a sprig ". . . for the Missus." Once he'd nodded thanks and continued on, I commenced to breathe again.

At home, Emma praised my harvest as she sorted through the leaves in the basket, handing me several and bidding me to mince them fine. Then she smiled. "Mint—that's good. We'll add some to mend the taste of the fever tea."

After Nellis drank the tea, she reclined in a comfortable doze. Emma and I watched over her, and before long we fell into voicing our worries. My own desperation from missing Mother was deeply felt and true, but I could barely fathom Emma's fortitude in facing the rigors of slavery as she tell'd them. I confessed my doubt of ever being able to bear such hardships as those.

"It's why folks come together. Problems shared be problems halved," said Emma smiling. "You'll soon enough have the strength of a grown lady like your mama."

Nellis's fever broke that night. As she and Emma prepared to continue their journey, they pledged infinite **gratitude** to Papa and me. Tho' sad to see them go, I wished them safe passage, and I thanked Emma for aiding me so in my own journey.

Make Connections

 Talk about how Abigail showed inner strength in finding the healing herb on her own. **ESSENTIAL QUESTION**

Describe a time when you discovered a personal strength within you that helped you to do a difficult or demanding task. **TEXT TO SELF**

Text Evidence

❶ Specific Vocabulary

Read the second paragraph. The verb *fathom* means "understand." What could Emma hardly fathom about Emma's situation? Underline the words that tell you. Why? Circle the words that tell you.

❷ Comprehension
Cause and Effect

Read the last three paragraphs. What event caused Nellis's fever to break at the end of the story? Underline the sentence that tells you.

❸ Talk About It

Why did Abby and Emma feel grateful toward each other? Justify your answer.

_____
_____
_____

Respond to the Text

Partner Discussion Work with a partner. Answer the questions. Discuss what you learned about "Journey to Freedom." Write the page numbers where you found text evidence.

How does Abby feel about herself at the beginning of the story?	**Text Evidence**
When Abby compares herself to her mother, she _____.	Page(s): _____
When Nellis gets sick, Abby is worried because _____.	Page(s): _____

What does Abby do and feel in the middle of the story?	**Text Evidence**
When Abby's dad asks her to find the special herb, she feels _____.	Page(s): _____
When Abby meets Mr. Carrington, she feels _____.	Page(s): _____

How has Abby changed by the end of the story?	**Text Evidence**
Abby talks to Emma about _____.	Page(s): _____
Abby feels grateful to Emma because _____.	Page(s): _____

Group Discussion Present your answers to the group. Cite text evidence to justify your thinking. Listen to and discuss the group's opinions about your answers.

Write Review your notes about "Journey to Freedom." Then write your answer to the Essential Question. Use text evidence to support your answer. Use vocabulary words from this week's reading in your writing.

How does Abby show inner strength in the story?

At the beginning of the story, Abby _____

_____.

In the middle of the story, Abby _____

_____.

At the end of the story, Abby _____

_____.

Abby shows inner strength in the story by _____

_____.

Share Writing Present your writing to the class. Discuss their opinions. Think about what the class has to say. Did they justify their claims? Explain why you agree or disagree with their claims.

I agree with _____ that _____.

I disagree with _____ because _____.

283

Write to Sources

pages 278–281

Take Notes About the Text I took notes on the sequence chart to answer the prompt: *Write a letter from Jonathan to Jacob. Describe Abby's mission to get fever herbs.*

First
Abby went out to look for fever herbs for Nellis.

Next
She plucked the plant that matched Emma's description and some familiar mint.

Then
She met her neighbor Mr. Carrington.

Last
Abby said she was hunting up mint for Mother's cake recipe.

Write About the Text I used notes from my sequence chart to write a letter about Abby's mission.

Student Model: Narrative Text

Dear Jacob,

   Nellis and Emma arrived safely. But Nellis was ill with a fever by the next morning. Emma knew about some fever herbs that would help. My brave daughter Abby went out in search of the herbs. Abby found the herbs and collected a handful. On Abby's way home, a neighbor questioned her. She kept calm. She told him she was going to bake a cake! Emma brewed those herbs into a tea for Nellis. She is feeling better. I am so proud of Abby!

                              Sincerely,
                              Jonathan

TALK ABOUT IT

Text Evidence
Circle a sentence that comes from the notes and helps us learn more about Abby. How does this detail help Manuel write the letter?

Grammar
Draw a box around a phrase that provides detail about time. Why does Manuel use this phrase?

Connect Ideas
Underline the sixth and seventh sentences. How can you combine the sentences to connect ideas?

Your Turn

Write a letter from Emma to the two companions left behind where Jacob lives. Describe the situation at Jonathan's house.

>> Go Digital!
Write your response online. Use your editing checklist.

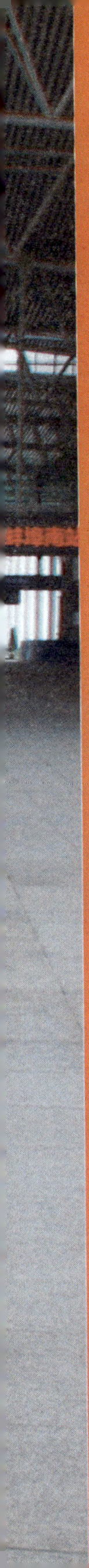

 How is the new train in the photo different from older trains? What are the benefits of the new train? Write words and phrases in the chart.

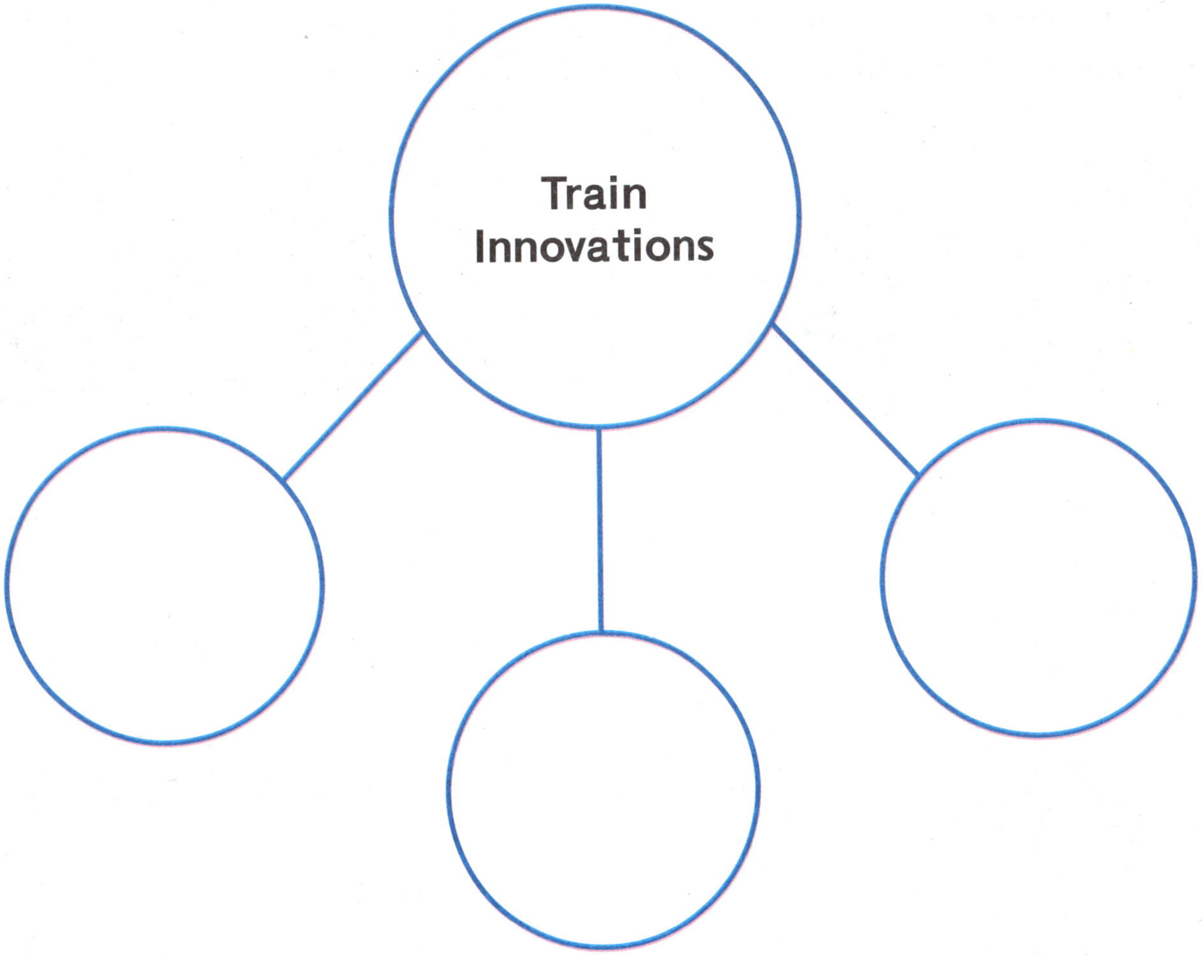

Train Innovations

Discuss the benefits of the new train. Use words from the chart. You can say:

The train has a _____. This makes the train

_____ and have a shorter _____.

More Vocabulary

 Look at the picture and read the word. Then read the sentence. Talk about the word with a partner. Write your own sentence.

innovations

Solar panels are recent **innovations** for making electricity.

Two of my favorite recent *innovations* include _____.

painstaking

Creating art can be a **painstaking** process for the artist.

_____ is a *painstaking* process for me.

mechanized

Cars are produced using a **mechanized** process.

Some other things produced using a *mechanized* process are _____.

tending

Pamela enjoys **tending** her family's garden.

I enjoy *tending* _____
_____.

288

typically

Leo's family <mark>typically</mark> eats breakfast at 7:00 every morning.

I *typically* _____

at _____.

waste

Vegetable <mark>waste</mark> can become compost for a garden.

Waste is produced when _____
_____.

Words and Phrases
Connecting Phrases

The connecting phrases *as a result* and *for this reason* are used to show cause and effect. The cause comes before the connecting phrase. The effect comes after the connecting phrase.

cause → connecting phrase → effect
I studied hard. <u>As a result</u>, I passed the test.
I studied hard. <u>For this reason</u>, I passed the test.

Read the sentences below. Combine them using a connecting phrase. Use a different connecting phrase in each sentence.

Cause: I went to bed early.
Effect: I woke up at 6:00 a.m.

_____

Cause: Jun hit a homerun.
Effect: The crowd cheered.

_____

» Go Digital Add these connecting phrases to your New Words notebook. Write a pair of sentences to show the meaning of each.

Text Evidence

Shared Read | Genre • Expository Text

1. Talk About It

Read the title. Talk about what you see. Write your ideas.

What does the title tell you about this text?

_____
_____
_____

What do you see in the photographs and diagram?

_____
_____
_____

Take notes as you read the text.

The Science of Silk

Essential Question

? How do people benefit from innovation?

Read how innovations in silk production have made this once rare cloth available to many people.

When the silk-making process was first developed five thousand years ago in China, silk was a rare and expensive luxury. Silk would still be sparse today if people had not engaged in the manipulation of a natural process. Sericulture, the breeding of silkworms to produce silk, has improved greatly over the centuries. The technologies used in making silk thread and weaving silk fabric have also benefited from important **innovations**.

A Better Silkworm

The silkworm is the larva, or caterpillar, of *Bombyx mori,* the domesticated silk moth **typically** used in silk production. (The name *Bombyx mori* means "mulberry silk moth.") This animal's life cycle has four stages: egg; larva that makes the cocoon; pupa that changes inside the cocoon; and winged adult moth. Silk is the material that the larva naturally produces to make its cocoon.

Bombyx mori is a hybrid, the result of breeding particular species over many years. This selective modification of inherited traits was done to make a stronger and more productive moth. For example, a *Bombyx mori* moth lays about 500 eggs, more than other species. The eggs are hardier than other silkworm eggs. As a result, more of them survive to develop into larvae. The larvae are also healthy. They eat enough to increase 10,000 times in size in just four to six weeks.

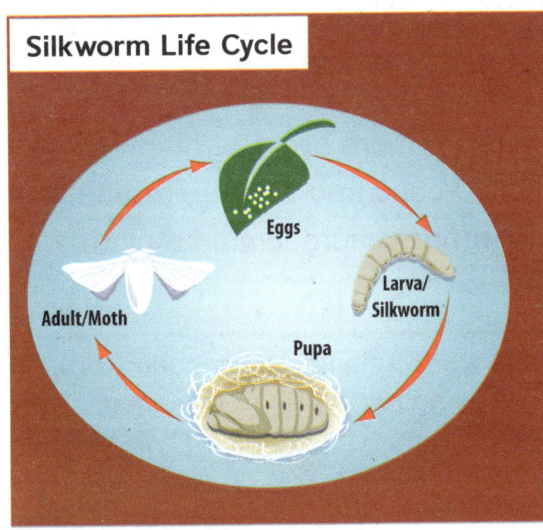

Silkworm Life Cycle

Most moths fly during their adult stage to find mates and places with plentiful food to lay their eggs. But *Bombyx mori* is a mutated species of moth that is unable to fly. For this reason, it relies entirely on humans to provide its larvae with a special diet of nutrients from the leaves of white

Text Evidence

❶ Sentence Structure

Read the second paragraph. Draw a box around the sentence in parentheses. Explain the purpose of the information in the parentheses.

_____

_____

❷ Specific Vocabulary

Read the third paragraph. The word *hardier* means "stronger; better able to live through difficult conditions." What happens when eggs are hardier?

When eggs are hardier, _____

_____.

❸ Comprehension
Cause and Effect

Read the last paragraph on this page and at the top of page 292. Why does the *Bombyx mori* moth rely on humans for its food? Underline the sentence that tells you.

291

Text Evidence

1. Talk About It

Discuss three ways in which *Bombyx mori* silk is better than silk from other moths. Then write about it.

_____

_____

_____

2. Sentence Structure ACT

Read the second full paragraph. Circle the word *they* in the last sentence. Box the noun phrase in the next-to-last sentence that *they* refers to.

3. Specific Vocabulary ACT

Read the third full paragraph. The verb *unwound* means "unwrapped." Circle the word that means the opposite of *unwound*. Then write it below.

_____

mulberry trees. Humans must also ensure that the eggs are kept at a temperature of 65° to 77° F until they hatch.

People go through this great effort because the silk of *Bombyx mori* is strong and breaks less often than "wild" silk. The filament from a single cocoon can be 3,000 feet long when it is unwound. *Bombyx mori* silk is whiter than wild silk, so it can absorb more dye. The filament is also round and smooth, resulting in a finer, more luminous cloth.

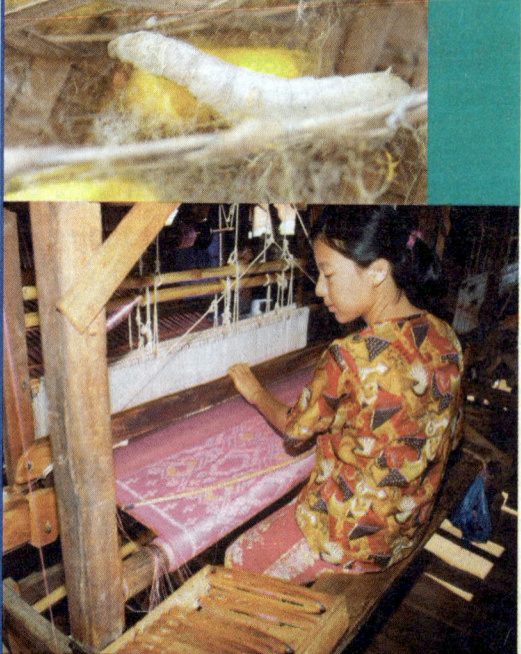

Silkworm spinning its cocoon (top); Weaving silk fabric in Myanmar

From Cocoon to Thread

For thousands of years, raising silkworms to make silk was an important part of Chinese culture. Women and girls were responsible for tending the worms, processing the cocoons, spinning the thread, and weaving fabric by hand. These painstaking chores produced beautiful results. They were also inefficient, consuming many hours per day and producing only a small amount of silk cloth.

Much of the ancient process survives in current practices. Cocoons are still harvested about eight or nine days after they form. They are placed in water so that they soften enough to be unwound without breaking the filament of raw silk. To avoid building up a surplus of unusable cocoons, a time-saving technique called *reeling* has been developed to unwind several cocoons at once. The cocoons are gently brushed to find the loose ends. Then the filaments are wound onto a reel.

A single raw silk filament is too thin to use for weaving. So the next common step in the process, called *throwing,* involves twisting several filaments together to form a thread. The thrown threads are then wound onto small spools called bobbins.

Advances in Silk Technology

Silk moth eggs and the closely guarded secret of sericulture had to be smuggled out of China before other countries could make silk. Once the basic process was known, people sought to improve the technologies used in making silk filaments into cloth. One important invention was the French reeling machine. Its great innovation was to speed up the reeling process and reduce **waste**.

About 1800, the invention of the Jacquard loom enabled silk weavers to create complex designs quickly. This **mechanized** loom required strong threads, so even better sericulture practices were developed. More recently, industrial weaving machines began using air to push the thread rapidly back and forth. This meant that fewer workers were needed to oversee the looms and that costs could be lowered. As a result, fine silk products were soon available at prices that more people could afford.

Today, China remains the leading producer of silk. But the demand for fine mulberry silk products reaches far beyond China's borders. For this reason, people will continue seeking better, more **economical** ways to produce silk.

Make Connections

Talk about the role humans play in silk production. How have innovations over time benefitted people? **ESSENTIAL QUESTION**

What other technology have you learned about that developed through innovation over time? How has this helped you? **TEXT TO SELF**

Text Evidence

❶ Comprehension
Cause and Effect

Read the second and third paragraphs. What were the effects of other countries learning the secrets of making silk? Box three effects.

❷ Specific Vocabulary

Reread the third and fourth paragraphs. The word *economical* means "using money and resources efficiently." Why will people seek more economical ways to produce silk?

_____

_____

❸ Talk About It

The author argues that the innovations in making silk are positive. Explain why. Justify your answer.

_____

Respond to the Text

Partner Discussion Work with a partner. Answer the questions. Discuss what you learned about "The Science of Silk." Write the page numbers where you found text evidence.

How did people benefit from the *Bombyx mori* moth?

The *Bombyx mori* moth is very productive because it _____ _____.

Page(s): _____

The *Bombyx mori* moth produces good silk because _____ _____.

Page(s): _____

Because of the *Bombyx mori* moth, silk cloth _____.

Page(s): _____

How did people innovate after they learned the secret of making silk?

People invented _____.

Page(s): _____

Because of industrial weaving machines, _____.

Page(s): _____

Because of technological innovation, _____ _____.

Page(s): _____

Group Discussion Present your answers to the group. Cite text evidence to justify your thinking. Listen to and discuss the group's opinions about your answers.

Write Review your notes about "The Science of Silk." Then write your answer to the Essential Question. Use text evidence to support your answer. Use vocabulary words from this week's reading in your writing.

> How did people benefit from innovations in making silk?
>
> Because the *Bombyx mori* moth is very productive, _____
> _____.
>
> The silk that these moths produce _____.
>
> Because of the reeling machine and looms, _____
> _____.
>
> People benefitted from innovations in making silk because _____
> _____.

Share Writing Present your writing to the class. Discuss their opinions. Think about what the class has to say. Did they justify their claims? Explain why you agree or disagree with their claims.

I agree with _____ that _____.

I disagree with _____ because _____.

295

Write to Sources

pages 290–293

Take Notes About the Text I took notes on the main idea and details chart to answer the question: *How does the* Bombyx mori *silk moth improve the silk-making process?*

Main Idea
The *Bombyx mori* silk moth improves the silk-making process.

Detail
The silk of *Bombyx mori* is strong and breaks less often than wild silk.

Detail
Bombyx mori silk is whiter than wild silk, so it can absorb more dye.

Detail
The filament is round and smooth, resulting in a finer, more luminous cloth.

Write About the Text I used my notes from my main idea and details chart to write a paragraph about the *Bombyx mori* silk moth.

Student Model: Informative Text

The *Bombyx mori* is a moth that is used to make silk. This silk moth improves the silk-making process. First, *Bombyx mori* silk is stronger than wild silk. It breaks less often. Second, *Bombyx mori* silk is whiter than wild silk, so it can absorb more dye. This helps create colorful silk cloth. Third, the *Bombyx mori* filament is round and smooth. Consequently, the cloth is finer and more luminous than other types of silk.

TALK ABOUT IT

Text Evidence
Underline a detail sentence that comes from the notes. Why did Roshan use this information as a supporting detail?

Grammar
Draw a box around the word that connects the last two sentences. Why did Roshan use this connecting word?

Connect Ideas
Circle the third and fourth sentences. How can you combine the sentences to connect ideas?

Your Turn

How have inventions changed silk production?

>> Go Digital
Write your response online. Use your editing checklist.

TALK ABOUT IT

Weekly Concept Breakthroughs

? Essential Question
How does technology lead to discoveries?

>> *Go Digital*

 What does the photo show? How was the picture taken? What did scientists learn? Write words to describe the technological breakthrough in the chart.

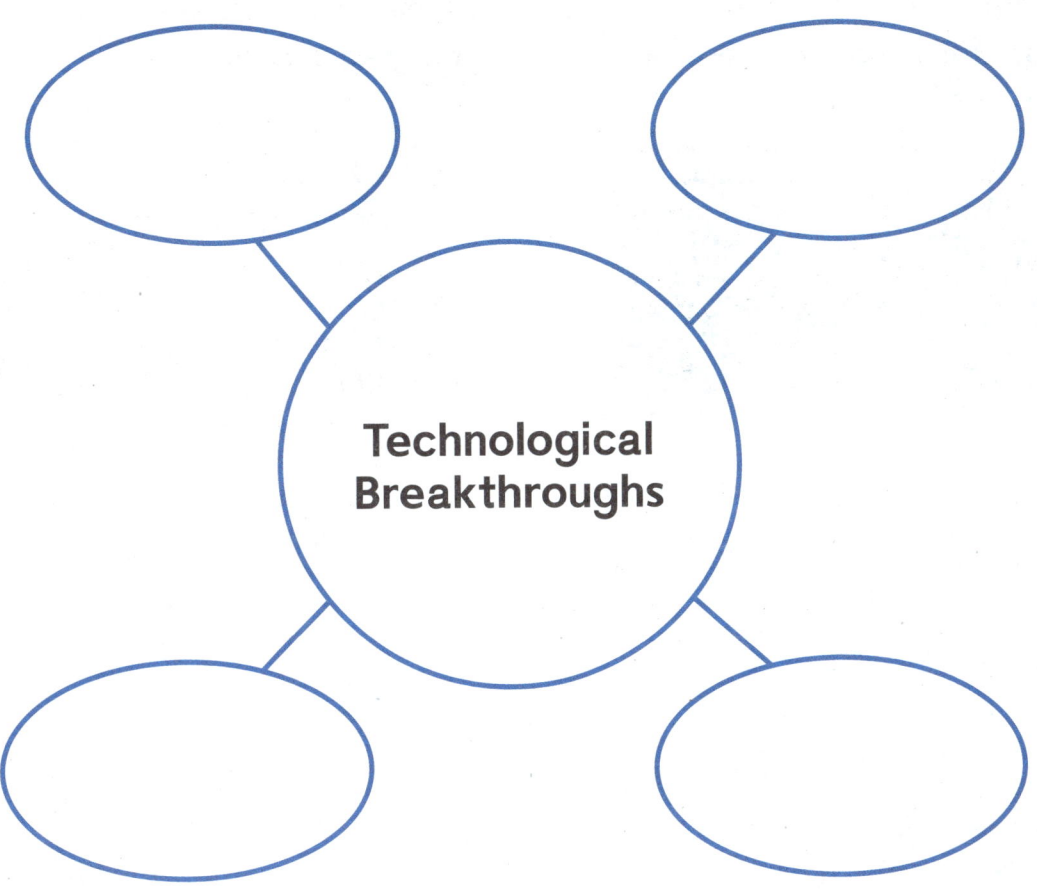

Discuss how camera technology has helped scientists. Use words from the chart. You can say:

The _____ helped scientists learn about the

_____. Scientists learned about _____.

Scientists also learned about _____.

More Vocabulary

 Look at the picture and read the word. Then read the sentence. Talk about the word with a partner. Write your own sentence.

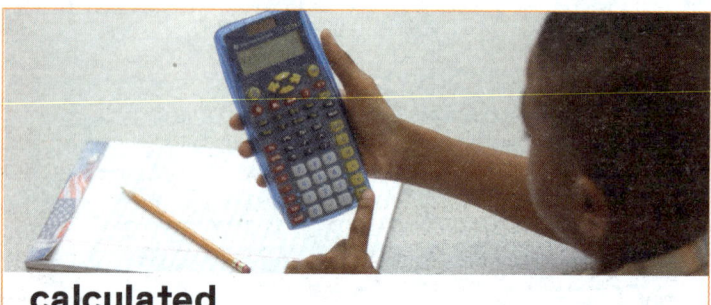

calculated

Tom **calculated** the total cost of the trip.

Recently, I *calculated* _____

_____.

method

My father and I have a good **method** for making breakfast.

I need to develop a good *method* for _____

_____.

extremely

Armani is studying an **extremely** small object under the microscope.

I am *extremely* happy when I am _____

_____.

procedure

The school follows a **procedure** during tornadoes.

My teacher follows a *procedure* for _____

_____.

300

slightly

Tomas is **slightly** shorter than his brother.

I am *slightly* _____

than _____.

viewed

Briana **viewed** a large eagle through her binoculars.

The most interesting animal I ever *viewed* was

_____.

Words and Phrases
Multiple-Meaning Words

The verb *reaches* means "stretches toward something."
John <u>reaches</u> for a hamburger whenever he's hungry.

The noun *reaches* means "faraway parts of a place."
The Vikings explored the far <u>reaches</u> of the earth.

Read the sentences below. Circle the correct meaning of the underlined word.

The ship was lost in the outer <u>reaches</u> of the ocean.

stretches toward something   faraway parts of a place

Our coach <u>reaches</u> for her whistle when she wants our attention.

stretches toward something   faraway parts of a place

» Go Digital Add these words and their meanings to your New Words notebook. Write a sentence to show the meaning of each word.

Text Evidence

Shared Read | Genre • Expository Text

1 Talk About It

Read the title and caption. Talk about what you see. Write your ideas.

What does the title tell you about the text?

_____

_____

_____

_____

What does the photograph show?

_____

_____

_____

_____

Take notes as you read the text.

Light Detectives

Essential Question

 How does technology lead to discoveries?

Read about astronomers' use of technology to find distant objects in our solar system.

Palomar Observatory, California

Astronomers use a number of technologies to analyze the light that we see reflected off the most distant objects in our solar system. These scientists often serve as "light detectives" who collect celestial clues using a variety of precision tools.

Discovering Pluto

In the 1920s, astronomers noticed something strange. The outer planets seemed to be affected by an unexplained force. Was there another planet out there with gravitational pull strong enough to tug on Uranus and Neptune? To find this object, a young scientist named Clyde Tombaugh perfected an innovative method for searching the sky.

Using a new telescope at the Lowell Observatory in Arizona, Tombaugh took wide-angle photographs of slivers of the night sky. He then viewed these images in a machine called a blink comparator. This tool was a type of microscope that superimposed two images of the exact same area taken at different times, placing one on top of the other. It blinked so rapidly back and forth between the two images that Tombaugh could see whether any objects changed position from the first time period to the next. As the months passed, Tombaugh estimated he had scanned more than a million stars. His painstaking research finally paid off in February of 1930 when he discovered Pluto and its orbital movement.

Scanning the Kuiper Belt

After Tombaugh's discovery, astronomers became more interested in the outer reaches of our solar system. In 1992, they identified a disk-like region extending up to 9.3 billion miles from the sun and named it the Kuiper Belt, after Gerard Kuiper who had theorized the existence of such a region. Estimates suggested that there were about 70,000 large, icy objects in the Kuiper Belt. Were some even larger than Pluto?

To answer this question, astronomer Michael Brown and his colleagues followed a procedure similar to the method designed by Tombaugh. But they took advantage of new technology to make their search easier and

Text Evidence

❶ Sentence Structure ⒶⒸⓉ

Read the first paragraph. Circle the phrase *these scientists* in the second sentence. Draw a box around the noun in the first sentence that this phrase refers to.

❷ Specific Vocabulary ⒶⒸⓉ

Read the second paragraph. Circle context clues that help you understand the meaning of *gravitational pull.* What did astronomers think the gravitational pull was affecting?

They thought the gravitational pull was tugging _____

_____.

❸ Comprehension
Sequence

Read the fourth paragraph. What event happened after the discovery of Pluto? Underline the sentence that tells you.

Text Evidence

1 Specific Vocabulary

Read the first five full sentences at the top of the page. Box the context clues that help you understand the meaning of *automated system*. When does this automated system run?

This automated system runs _____

_____.

2 Sentence Structure

Read the first sentence of the first full paragraph. The preposition *instead of* signals an alternative to an idea. Instead of using a blink comparator, what does Brown's team do? Underline the part of the sentence that tells you.

3 Talk About It

Explain how Brown's team uses images to identify moving objects. Then write about it.

_____

_____

---

more effective. Like Tombaugh, Brown's team takes repeated images using a telescope. Every three hours, a digital camera mounted on the Samuel Oschin Telescope at the Palomar Observatory in California snaps a picture of the night sky. A microwave link allows robots to control both the telescope and its camera. These robots follow a pre-programmed routine that moves the telescope and takes pictures. This automated system drones through the night while the astronomers sleep.

Instead of using a blink comparator, Brown's team sends the images to a bank of ten computers at the California Institute of Technology (CIT). The computers superimpose images taken at different times and identify objects that are possibly moving. Then the team analyzes the data to try to verify the movement. Most of the time, the objects identified are not breathtaking discoveries. They are simply the result of flaws in the telescope's camera. But sometimes, the computers do track down moving objects. Airplanes, satellites, and asteroids have been flagged by the system. And in 2003, the team discovered a bright shape that was moving more slowly than anything documented in our solar system. Could this be the object tugging on Uranus and Neptune?

Combining New Data with Old

The super-slow speed of this object, which was eventually named Eris, posed a problem. Brown calculated that Eris takes 560 years to orbit the sun. So it would take many years to collect enough data confirming the deduction that Eris affects planetary orbits. Rather than waiting, Brown

 ① A 161-megapixel camera mounted on the telescope.

 ② Multiple images of the night sky.

 ③ CIT computers superimpose images.

 ④ Astronomers Mike Brown, Chad Trujillo, and David Rabinowitz analyze data.

decided to check photos taken by other astronomers. Luckily, Eris appeared in photographs taken as early as 1950. By combining these images with contemporary data, the team developed a more complete view of Eris's size and movements.

The team originally estimated that Eris was 25 to 40 percent more massive than Pluto. But when they used pictures taken by the Hubble Space Telescope to confirm this hypothesis, they found out they were wrong. Eris is only **slightly** larger than Pluto. The overestimate was the result of Eris's **extremely** reflective surface. The bright, reflected light gives the impression that Eris is more substantial than it really is. Brown suggests that an atmosphere of frozen nitrogen causes Eris's high level of reflection.

As a result of Brown's discovery, astronomers reconsidered the definition of a planet. Ultimately, both Pluto and Eris were classified as "dwarf planets," rather than planets. But discoveries in the Kuiper Belt continue to sustain great interest. Conservatively, astronomers predict that new technology will allow them to identify several more dwarf planets in the Kuiper Belt. The information gained from their investigations will enrich our understanding of distant objects in other parts of the galaxy as well.

The Moon
Earth
Pluto
Eris

Relative sizes of Earth, the Moon, Pluto, and Eris

NASA

Make Connections

Talk about the technology that astronomers have used to investigate distant objects in our solar system.
ESSENTIAL QUESTION

Describe a time when using a tool (a ruler, calculator, camera, etc.) to test a hypothesis helped you answer a question. **TEXT TO SELF**

Text Evidence

❶ Sentence Structure

Read the first two full sentences at the top of the page. Circle the words *these images*. Underline the noun that *these images* refers to.

❷ Specific Vocabulary

Read the second paragraph. The noun *overestimate* means "a calculation or guess that is too large." What caused the overestimate of Eris's size? Underline the sentences that tell you.

❸ Comprehension Sequence

Read the last paragraph. What event happened after Brown's discovery about Eris's and Pluto's sizes?

_____

_____

Respond to the Text

Partner Discussion Work with a partner. Answer the questions. Discuss what you learned about "Light Detectives." Write the page numbers where you found text evidence.

How did technology help Clyde Tombaugh discover distant objects?

Clyde Tombaugh viewed images _____.

Tombaugh could see whether _____.

With this technology, Tombaugh discovered _____.

Text Evidence

Page(s): _____

Page(s): _____

Page(s): _____

How does technology help Michael Brown and his team discover distant objects in our solar system?

Today, Michael Brown and his team use computers to _____
_____.

The team used this technology to identify _____.

The team used this technology again when they reclassified _____
_____.

Text Evidence

Page(s): _____

Page(s): _____

Page(s): _____

Group Discussion Present your answers to the group. Cite text evidence to justify your thinking. Listen to and discuss the group's opinions about your answers.

Write Review your notes about "Light Detectives." Then write your answer to the Essential Question. Use text evidence to support your answer. Use vocabulary words from this week's reading in your writing.

How does technology lead to discoveries about our solar system?

Clyde Tombaugh viewed images _____.

Tombaugh discovered Pluto because _____.

Michael Brown and his team identified Eris using _____
_____.

Technology leads to discoveries about our solar system because _____
_____.

Share Writing Present your writing to the class. Discuss their opinions. Think about what the class has to say. Did they justify their claims? Explain why you agree or disagree with their claims.

I agree with _____ that _____.

I disagree with _____ because _____.

Write to Sources

Inez

Take Notes About the Text I took notes on this sequence chart to answer the question: *How does new technology help scientists find moving objects in space?*

pages 302–305

First
The Samuel Oschin Telescope at the Palomar Observatory in California snaps a picture of the night sky every three hours.

Next
Robots control both the telescope and its camera.

Then
Michael Brown's team sends the images to a bank of computers at the California Institute of Technology.

Last
The computers superimpose images taken at different times and identify objects that are possibly moving.

Write About the Text I used my notes from my sequence chart to write an informative paragraph about the Samuel Oschin Telescope.

Student Model: *Informative Text*

Michael Brown and his team use new technology to find moving objects at the outer edges of our solar system. The Samuel Oschin Telescope in California takes pictures of the night sky every three hours. Robots control the camera and the telescope. The scientists don't even have to be there. Later, the scientists send the pictures to computers at the California Institute of Technology. The computers superimpose the images. Scientists can see which objects stayed still and which objects moved. Most things they find are not big discoveries, but some are exciting.

TALK ABOUT IT

Text Evidence
Draw a box around a sentence that concerns the camera and comes from the notes. Why did Inez use this information as a supporting detail?

Grammar
Circle a word that connects events. Why did Inez use this connecting word?

Connect Ideas
Underline the sentences about superimposing images. How can you combine the sentences to connect ideas?

Your Turn

What series of events led to the discovery of Eris?

>> *Go Digital!*
Write your response online. Use your editing checklist.

TALK ABOUT IT

Weekly Concept Exploration

? Essential Question
How have tools used for exploration evolved over time?

>> *Go Digital*

COLLABORATE What does the photo show? How does this tool improve exploration? Write words in the chart.

Improving Exploration

Discuss how this tool improves exploration. Use words from the chart. You can say:

The _____ lets the scientist explore in _____ water. The scientist can _____.

More Vocabulary

 Look at the picture and read the word. Then read the sentence. Talk about the word with a partner. Write your own sentence.

aspirations

Ming has **aspirations** to go to college.

I have *aspirations* to _____

_____.

constantly

Eric is **constantly** reading a book.

Some people might say I am *constantly*

_____.

expectations

The friends have high **expectations** of enjoying the ride.

I have high *expectations* of _____

_____.

exploration

Jamie is part of an **exploration** of the rainforest.

I would like to be part of an *exploration* of

_____.

Words and Phrases
Multiple-Meaning Words

The noun *survey* means "a report about a subject."
This <u>survey</u> describes the development of computers.

The verb *survey* means "to examine in detail."
The rescuers will <u>survey</u> the ocean for the lost ship.

Read the sentences below. Circle the correct meaning of the boldfaced word.

Lucia read a **survey** about different farming methods.

a report about a subject   to examine in detail

For his class project, Mario needs to **survey** the beach for trash.

a report about a subject   to examine in detail

» Go Digital Add these words and their meanings to your New Words notebook. Write a sentence to show the meaning of each word.

indicates

The sign **indicates** where drivers must stop.

A movie schedule *indicates* _____

_____.

positions

The players take their **positions** on the field.

In basketball, players take their *positions* on

_____.

313

Text Evidence

Shared Read | Genre • Informational Article

1 Talk About It

Read the title and captions. Talk about what you see. Write your ideas.

What does the title tell you about the text?

_____

_____

_____

What is the man in the photograph doing?

_____

_____

_____

Take notes as you read the text.

Essential Question

How have tools used for exploration evolved over time?

Read how advances in technology have aided exploration.

A sextant can still be used today to navigate at sea.

Tools of the Explorer's Trade

The word *technology* sounds modern, but people have been using it for at least 300 years. Considering that one definition of *technology* is "the use of knowledge for practical purposes," we can say people have been developing new technologies since the dawn of human history. Some of them are antiquated. Others, though old, are continually improved. Stone Age axes qualify as technology, as do the wheel and the telephone. The following survey of several historical navigation techniques is one example of how technologies evolve over time.

The North Star

Sailors of early civilizations used the star Polaris, also called the North Star, to get their bearings at sea. But using the North Star for navigation had some serious drawbacks. First, it can only be seen on clear nights, so attempting to navigate through unknown waters on a cloudy night could be catastrophic. Second, Polaris can be seen only from the Northern Hemisphere. While navigating with the North Star was a good choice under certain circumstances, something better was needed.

The Astrolabe

The astrolabe was an advanced measuring tool invented in the Middle East. Though its primary application was to make computations about time and the positions of the Sun, Moon, planets, and stars, it was also employed as a technological aid to navigation. The astrolabe gave mariners a way to determine the latitude of their ships while at sea.

A Moorish astrolabe made in Andalusia, Spain

Text Evidence

❶ Specific Vocabulary

Read the first paragraph. The verb *qualify* means "to have the necessary traits to be considered something in particular." Why do Stone Age axes, the wheel, and the telephone qualify as technologies?

_____

_____

_____

❷ Sentence Structure

Read the first two sentences of the second paragraph. The first sentence says that early sailors used the North Star to navigate at sea. What contrary idea does *but* introduce in the second sentence? Underline the words that tell you.

❸ Comprehension
Author's Point of View

Read the second paragraph. Circle details that support the author's point of view that the North Star had some serious drawbacks.

315

Text Evidence

1 Sentence Structure ACT

Read the first paragraph. Circle the phrase *this technology* in the last sentence. What technology does this phrase refer to? Underline the name of this technology.

2 Comprehension
Author's Point of View

Read the second paragraph. Circle details that support the author's point of view that the compass is an important tool for navigation.

3 Talk About It

Explain what a compass uses to tell direction. Then write about it.

_____
_____
_____

The Sextant

The sextant is another tool that used the positions of the Sun and stars to find a location on Earth. First developed in Asia Minor in the late tenth century, it was used to measure the angle between a celestial object and the horizon. When navigators considered the measurement in relation to the time of day or night it was taken, they could find their ship's location on a nautical chart. Far from obsolete, this technology is still used today as a backup to modern navigation technologies.

The Compass

A compass is made by balancing a magnetic needle above a circular dial. Earth's own strong magnetic field causes the needle to swing into a north-south position. Because a compass **indicates** direction in all weather and at all times of the day or night, its importance as a navigational technology was quickly recognized. Historians are unsure who invented the compass, but we do know it was in use in China as early as the eleventh century.

A sextant (right) and how it measures angles (above)

A compass uses Earth's magnetic field to show direction.

An Opinion: Let's Keep Looking

Many characterize the ongoing story of human exploration as one of courage and creative resourcefulness. For most of history, exploration was confined to Earth's surface. But in 1930, we began diving into the ocean's depths. By 1969, we had landed on the moon. The probes that we deployed into deep space in 1977 are still transmitting valuable data back to us across billions of miles. Subsequently, we have sent robotic vehicles to survey the surface of Mars. And we have a powerful telescope in orbit that is sending us spectacular photographs of the formation of distant stars.

Exploring the unknown has clearly fueled our inventiveness, but it also inspires our imaginations. Because we are constantly elevating our aspirations, we have been able to increase our knowledge even when expectations have been the worst. Modern technologies are providing more and better tools to explore increasingly remote places. In fact, when it comes to exploration, the best is certainly yet to come. We should always resist the idea that an adventurous instinct might be foolhardy, and we should continue to value and encourage curiosity.

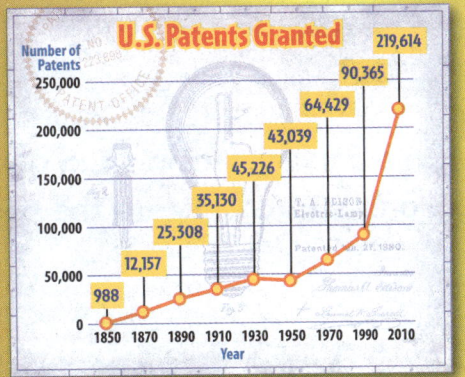

Inventing as Fast as We Can

When the U.S. government grants patents to "promote the Progress of Science and useful Arts," it gives exclusive rights to inventors for a set period of time. The number of patents issued in the years from 1850 to 2010 reveals a stunning increase in the rate of technological innovations.

Make Connections

Talk about the ways in which technologies used for exploration have developed over time. **ESSENTIAL QUESTION**

Tell how a technological tool you use in your daily life helps you learn about your community and the world. **TEXT TO SELF**

Text Evidence

1. Specific Vocabulary

Read the first paragraph. The word *confined* means "limited." How was exploration confined before 1930?

_____

_____

2. Comprehension
Author's Point of View

Read the first and second paragraphs. What are the author's points of view about exploration? Underline the sentences that tell you.

3. Talk About It

Explain how two technologies discussed in the text have been important in exploration. Justify your answer.

_____

_____

_____

317

Respond to the Text

 **Partner Discussion** Work with a partner. Answer the questions. Discuss what you learned about "Tools of the Explorer's Trade." Write the page numbers where you found text evidence.

What tools did early civilizations use to navigate?

Sailors of early civilizations used _____.

But the North Star _____.

To navigate successfully, explorers needed a _____.

Text Evidence

Page(s): _____

Page(s): _____

Page(s): _____

What other tools did explorers use to navigate?

The astrolabe and sextant worked by using _____
_____
_____.

Because the compass used Earth's magnetic field, explorers were able to _____
_____.

Text Evidence

Page(s): _____

Page(s): _____

 **Group Discussion** Present your answers to the group. Cite text evidence to justify your thinking. Listen to and discuss the group's opinions about your answers.

Write Review your notes about "Tools of the Explorer's Trade." Then write your answer to the Essential Question. Use text evidence to support your answer. Use vocabulary words from this week's reading in your writing.

> **How have navigational tools evolved over time?**
>
> On clear nights only, sailors of early civilizations used _____
> _____.
>
> New tools, such as the astrolabe and sextant, _____
> _____.
>
> After the compass was invented, _____
> _____.
>
> Tools used for exploration _____
> _____.

Share Writing Present your writing to the class. Discuss their opinions. Think about what the class has to say. Did they justify their claims? Explain why you agree or disagree with their claims.

I agree with _____ that _____.

I disagree with _____ because _____.

319

Write to Sources

pages 314–317

Take Notes About the Text I took notes on this idea web to answer the question: *Is the rapid rate of technological inventions positive or negative?*

Main Idea
Rate of technological inventions is positive.

Detail
These technologies improve communications near and far.

Detail
They aid in exploring and learning about our solar system.

Detail
Robotic vehicles study the surface of Mars.

Detail
They could help us travel to Mars and communicate with Earth.

Write About the Text I used my notes from my idea web to write an argument supporting the idea that the rapid rate of technological inventions is positive.

Student Model: Argument

The rapid rate of technological inventions is positive. People may be overwhelmed by rapidly changing technology. They get upset when a new computer is outdated within a year. They get upset when a new phone is outdated within months. These changes can be frustrating, but they improve communications near and far. New technologies aid in exploring and learning about our solar system. Robotic vehicles study the surface of Mars. Someday we might travel to Mars and communicate with Earth. The rapid rate of technological inventions makes amazing things possible!

TALK ABOUT IT

Text Evidence
Draw a box around a sentence that comes from the notes. Why did Darell use this detail to support his argument?

Grammar
Circle a word or phrase that connects ideas. Why did Darell use this word or phrase?

Condense Ideas
Underline the sentences about why people may get upset about new technologies. How can you combine the sentences to condense ideas?

Your Turn

Which early tool used for navigation was the most important invention?

>> Go Digital!
Write your response online. Use your editing checklist.

UNIT 6
Taking Action

The Big Idea

When is it important to take action?

TALK ABOUT IT

Weekly Concept Resources

? **Essential Question**
How have people used natural resources?

›› *Go Digital*

COLLABORATE What is the man in the photo doing? How is he using a natural resource? Why is this partnership special? Write words and phrases in the chart.

Natural Resources

Discuss how the man is using a natural resource. Use words and phrases from the chart. You can say:

The man and the bees are partners because _____

_____.

More Vocabulary

 Look at the picture and read the word. Then read the sentence. Talk about the word with a partner. Write your own sentence.

absorbs

The sponge **absorbs** a lot of water.

_____ *absorbs* a lot of _____

_____.

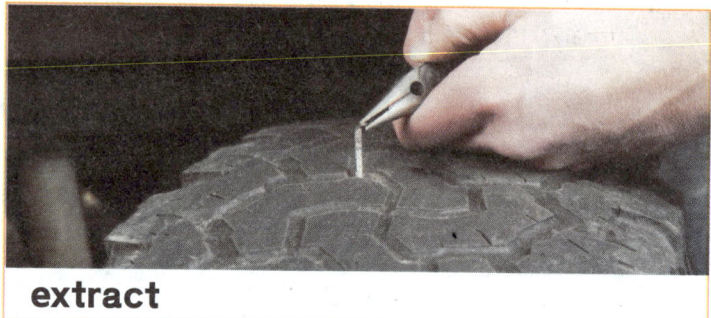

extract

Brett is trying to **extract** the nail from his car tire.

A dentist can *extract* _____

from _____.

evaporates

Water **evaporates** when the air is dry.

_____ *evaporates*

when _____.

preserve

The freezer will **preserve** the food in the store.

I usually *preserve* _____

in _____.

repel

A scarecrow can **repel** birds.

I have seen a _____

repel _____.

simulates

This video game **simulates** driving a car.

Another word for *simulates* is _____.

Words and Phrases
Multiple-Meaning Words

The noun *engineer* means "someone who designs or creates something."
The <u>engineer</u> helped design and create the new library in my town.

The verb *engineer* means "to design or create something."
I want to <u>engineer</u> a new kind of mouse trap.

Read the sentences below. Circle the correct meaning of the underlined word.

Aleena is an <u>engineer</u> for the new housing development.

someone who designs or creates something

to design or create something

Mohammed wants to <u>engineer</u> a soccer ball that will move faster.

someone who designs or creates something

to design or create something

» Go Digital Add these words to your New Words notebook. Write a sentence to show the meaning of each word.

Text Evidence

Shared Read | Genre • Expository Text

1 Talk About It

Read the title and the caption. Talk about what you see. Write your ideas.

What do the title and the caption tell you about the text?

_____

_____

_____

_____

What is the man in the photograph doing?

_____

_____

_____

_____

Take notes as you read the text.

The Fortunes of Fragrance

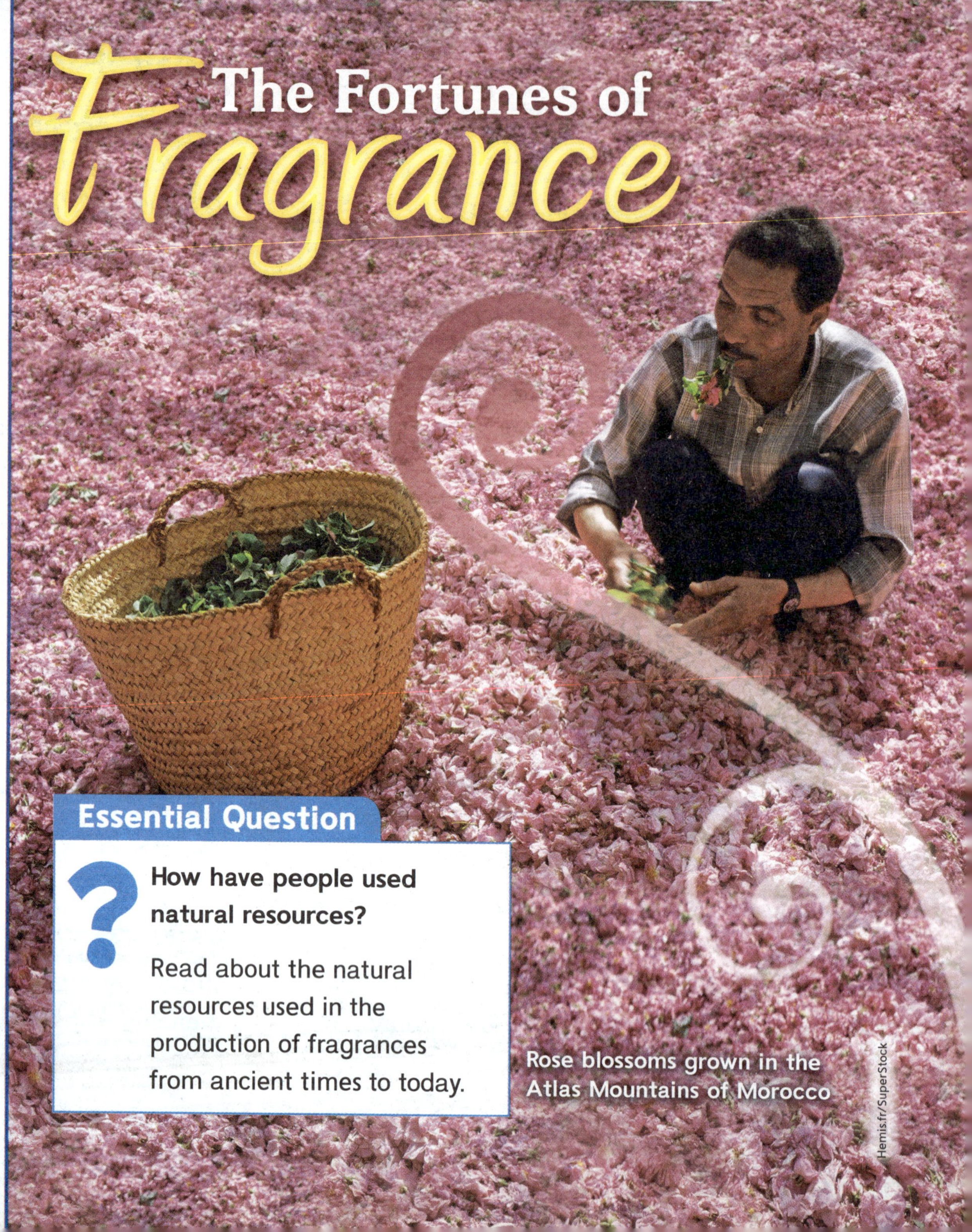

Essential Question

? How have people used natural resources?

Read about the natural resources used in the production of fragrances from ancient times to today.

Rose blossoms grown in the Atlas Mountains of Morocco

Our sense of smell plays a significant role in our survival. It helps us detect poisons, smoke from a fire, toxic gases, and other dangers. Our noses can tell us a great deal about something that is unfamiliar or questionable. For example, a piece of rotten fruit may look beautiful, but its smell lets us know it is not edible. For centuries, doctors have used their sense of smell to identify infection or disease. Fortunately, there are many pleasant odors as well. From earliest times, people have sought ways to **preserve** the lovely scents of flowers and herbs.

Capturing Aromas

Many plants contain volatile oils. These chemicals often **repel** insects, but they smell good to us. Early humans discovered them while crushing or bruising leaves, fruits, and bark. Before long, people found ways to release and use the oils. They noticed that soaking rose petals in water resulted in a scented liquid. They also learned that simply burning parts of aromatic plants would scent the air. People soon started to mix powdered resin, or tree sap, with honey to form lumps of incense. They placed the incense on hot coals or in ornate burners to produce a perfumed smoke. In fact, the word *perfume* comes from the Latin words *per* and *fumum*, meaning "through smoke."

Over time, people developed other means to capture fragrance from plants. They squeezed the rinds of citrus fruits or boiled the leaves of such plants as lavender and peppermint to obtain their oils. Later, they found that steam could extract oils from both fresh and dried plants. After the steam releases volatile oils from plant material inside a pressurized chamber, it passes through cooling tubes where the oils become a separate liquid. This technique of *steam distillation* is still widely used today.

Copper distilling chambers in use at a perfumery in Grasse, France

Text Evidence

❶ Comprehension
Main Idea and Key Details

Read the first paragraph. Look at the key details. Summarize the main idea. Then write it.

_____

_____.

❷ Sentence Structure ACT

Read the first and second sentences of the second paragraph. Underline *these chemicals* in the second sentence. What words does this phrase refer to in the first sentence? Circle the words.

❸ Specific Vocabulary ACT

Read the first two sentences of the third paragraph. The verb *obtain* means "get something through an effort." How did people obtain the oils from lavender and peppermint plants?

_____

_____

Text Evidence

Pods, Seeds
Vanilla Pod, Anise Seed

Bark
Cinnamon, Birch

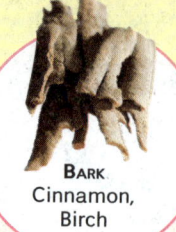
Leaves
Peppermint, Patchouli

Roots, Rhizomes
Vetiver Root, Iris Rhizome

Flowers
Jasmine, Rose

1 Talk About It

Read the first paragraph. What process other than steam distillation did people use to extract fragrances from delicate flowers?

_____

_____

_____

2 Specific Vocabulary

Read the first sentence of the second paragraph. The word *portable* means "able to be moved easily." Circle the context clue that helps you understand the meaning of this word.

3 Sentence Structure

Read the second sentence in the second paragraph. When was a treasured aromatic resource a more valuable commodity than gold or silver? Circle the phrase that tells you.

The petals of certain flowers cannot stand up to the heat of steam distillation, so people learned to press them gently into animal fat, which **absorbs** their fragrance. The fat is then washed in alcohol to draw out the fragrance molecules. After the alcohol **evaporates**, only the flower's fragrance remains as something called a *concrete*. This process, known as *enfleurage*, is both time-consuming and expensive. Today, solvent chemicals such as hexane are used to **extract** fragrance from delicate flowers.

Trading in Aromatics

Most fragrant plants are quite **portable**, so their distribution through vigorous trade was widespread throughout the ancient world. Depending on its availability, a treasured aromatic resource was often a more valuable commodity than gold or silver. Along Silk Road trade routes, Chinese merchants offered camphor for sale and purchased cinnamon and sandalwood from India. Egypt imported large quantities of myrrh. Caravans carried frankincense hundreds of miles by camel from Arabia to buyers in Greece and Rome. Eventually, Romans used so much incense that cargo ships were sent across the Mediterranean to speed up the way that supplies were replenished.

Trade in aromatics increased during the Middle Ages after people in Europe were introduced to the perfumes and spices of the Far East. But Europeans could buy these items only through merchants in the Middle East. Traders from that region had become the dominant players in the market and often charged extremely high prices. This monopoly on aromatic goods seemed impenetrable. So European explorers sought trade routes that went around the Middle East by sea.

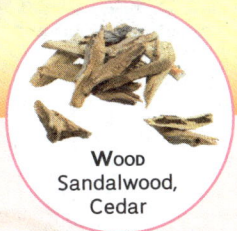
Wood
Sandalwood, Cedar

Berries
Black Pepper, Juniper Berry

Citrus Rinds
Lime, Lemon

Sap, Resins
Frankincense, Myrrh

The Enduring Power of Perfume

In the modern world, trade involving fragrance materials is as brisk as ever. But chemists are the new explorers. Over several decades, these scientists have learned to isolate the fragrant molecules in natural plant oils and engineer synthetic replacements for others. Synthetic fragrance chemicals are derived primarily from petroleum. They are usually less expensive than natural materials, because supplies are not affected by weather conditions or crop yields.

Still, many of the highest-quality perfumes require a small percentage of ingredients derived from real flowers. One perfume company maintains its own fields in the south of France to grow the special kinds of rose and jasmine needed to produce their best-selling product. Many companies use a process called *gas chromatography* to identify the molecules that make up a natural flower's fragrance. The molecules are then manufactured and blended to make a fragrance that **simulates** the real thing.

Demand for aromatics has only increased since ancient times. The production and sale of fragrance products make up an industry that is now worth billions of dollars. History has shown that, as long as people seek beautiful aromas, the fragrance market will continue to be big business.

Make Connections

Talk about the developments in technology and trade that resulted from people's demand for fragrance.
ESSENTIAL QUESTION

Describe the scent of a household product you use regularly. What do you like or dislike about it?
TEXT TO SELF

Text Evidence

COLLABORATE

❶ Talk About It

Discuss what chemists have learned to do in the fragrance business. Then write your ideas.

_____

_____

❷ Specific Vocabulary

Read the first sentence of the second paragraph. The word *derived* means "gotten from something else." For many of the highest-quality perfumes, what is still derived from real flowers?

_____

_____

❸ Comprehension
Main Idea and Key Details

Read the last paragraph. The main idea is that demand for aromatics has increased since ancient times. Underline a key detail that supports this main idea.

Respond to the Text

Partner Discussion Work with a partner. Answer the questions. Discuss what you learned about "The Fortunes of Fragrance." Write the page numbers where you found text evidence.

How did early humans make perfumes?

Early humans discovered perfumes while _____.

Text Evidence

Page(s): _____

What other processes for making perfume did people discover?

By burning incense, people _____.

They discovered other ways to capture scents, such as _____
_____.

Text Evidence

Page(s): _____

Page(s): _____

How do people make perfumes today?

Today, a widely used technique is _____.

For delicate flowers, people sometimes use _____.

Text Evidence

Page(s): _____

Page(s): _____

Group Discussion Present your answers to the group. Cite text evidence to justify your thinking. Listen to and discuss the group's opinions about your answers.

 **Write** Review your notes about "The Fortunes of Fragrance." Then write your answer to the Essential Question. Use text evidence to support your answer. Use vocabulary words from this week's reading in your writing.

How have people used natural resources to make perfume?

Early humans _____.

Then people discovered _____
_____
_____.

Today, people make perfume _____
_____.

 **Share Writing** Present your writing to the class. Discuss their opinions. Think about what the class has to say. Did they justify their claims? Explain why you agree or disagree with their claims.

I agree with _____.

I disagree with _____ because _____.

333

Write to Sources

Mateo

Take Notes About the Text I took notes on a two-column chart to answer the question: *What can I infer from the text features in "The Fortunes of Fragrance"?*

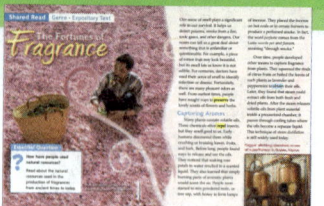

pages 328–331

Text Feature	What I Can Infer
1. Photo – Rose blossoms grown in the Atlas Mountains of Morocco	1. Many flowers are needed to make a small amount of perfume.
2. Photo – Copper distilling chambers	2. These large, copper containers are used during the process of steam distillation.
3. Illustrations – Types of flowers and plants	3. Many plants are used to make fragrances, including jasmine, peppermint, and vanilla.

Write About the Text I used my notes from my chart to write an informative text about the use of text features in the text.

Student Model: *Informative Text*

The text features in "The Fortunes of Fragrance" help me make inferences about ideas mentioned in the text. First, the photo of the field of roses shows that many flowers are needed to make even a small amount of perfume. Second, the photo of the copper distilling chambers shows the process of steam distillation, which is how many fragrances are made. Third, the illustrations show that many kinds of flowers are used to make perfume. The illustrations also show that many kinds of plants are used to make perfume. These photos and illustrations help me to better understand the information in the text.

TALK ABOUT IT

Text Evidence
Circle a sentence that comes from information in Mateo's notes. Why was this information included in the paragraph?

Grammar
Draw a box around a transition word that begins a sentence. What does this word signal?

Condense Ideas
Underline two sentences that discuss the illustrations. How can you combine these two sentences to condense the ideas?

Your Turn

How were perfumes made in the past? How are they made today? Identify the similarities and differences.

» Go Digital!
Write your response online. Use your editing checklist.

TALK ABOUT IT

Weekly Concept Witnesses

? Essential Question
How do we learn about historical events?

>> Go Digital

COLLABORATE What is the man in the photo wearing? Why is he dressed that way? How is he helping the boy learn about history? Write words and phrases in the chart.

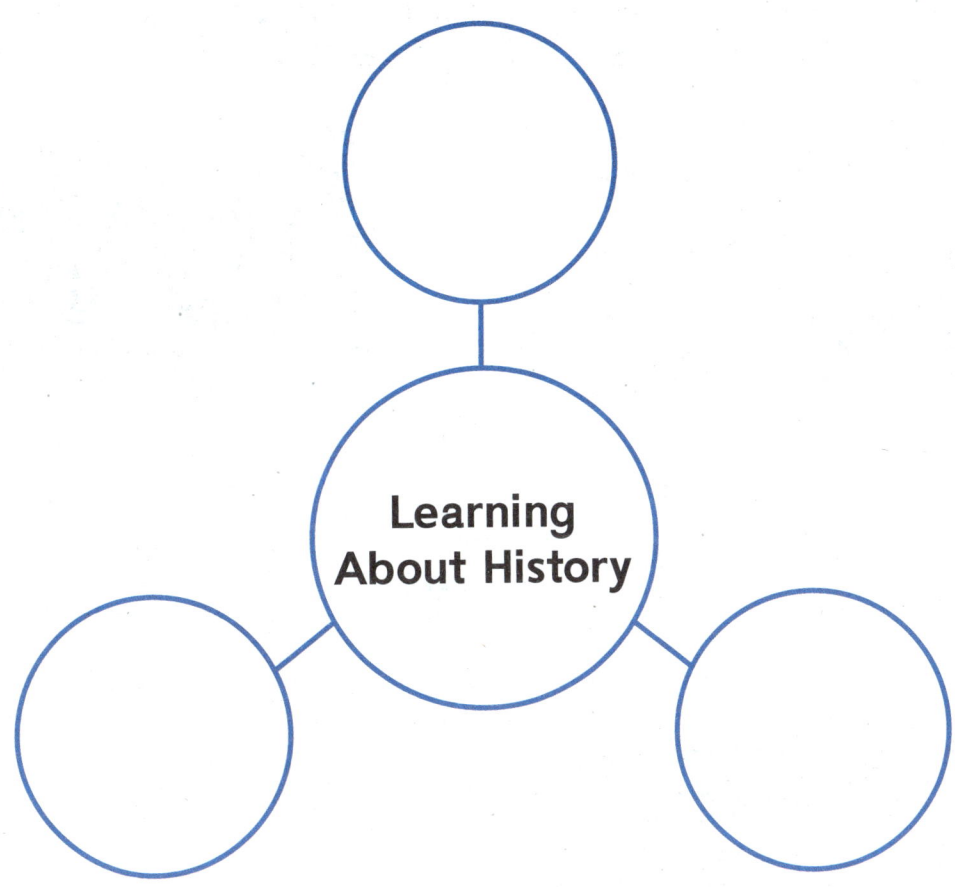

Discuss how the man is helping the boy learn about history. Use words and phrases from the chart. You can say:

The man is wearing _____.

He is dressed like a _____.

He is teaching the boy about _____.

More Vocabulary

 Look at the picture and read the word. Then read the sentence. Talk about the word with a partner. Write your own sentence.

accidental

Sam's fall from his bike was **accidental**.

_____ was *accidental*.

diligently

Jason **diligently** wrote down key ideas from the book.

To do something *diligently* means to _____

_____.

documented

Kara **documented** her entire vacation in her notebook.

The most important thing I have *documented* is _____.

insufficient

The desert has an **insufficient** amount of rainfall.

In my town, I think there is an *insufficient* number of _____.

observations

Hector and Jen wrote **observations** of the plants in their notebooks.

I told my friends about my *observations* of

_____.

recorded

The students **recorded** all the important points the teacher made.

One of the most important things I ever *recorded* was _____.

Words and Phrases
Compound Words

waterproofed = treated so that water cannot pass through

The hikers' boots were <u>waterproofed</u> with silicone spray.

firebreak = something designed to stop a fire from spreading

Firefighters cut down trees to create a <u>firebreak</u> and stop the forest fire.

Read the sentences below. Write the compound word that means the same thing as the underlined words.

The houses were torn down to create <u>something designed to stop the fire from spreading</u>.

The houses were torn down to create a _____.

The roof of the house was <u>treated so that water could not pass through it</u>.

The roof of the house was _____.

>> Go Digital Add these compound words to your New Words notebook. Write a sentence to show the meaning of each.

Text Evidence

1 Talk About It

Read the title. Talk about what you see. Write your ideas.

What does the title tell you?

_____
_____
_____

What does the illustration show?

_____
_____
_____

Take notes as you read the text.

Shared Read | Genre • Narrative Nonfiction

THE GREAT FIRE OF LONDON

Essential Question

? How do we learn about historical events?

Read how a fire that nearly destroyed the city of London in 1666 was recorded for history by those who witnessed the event.

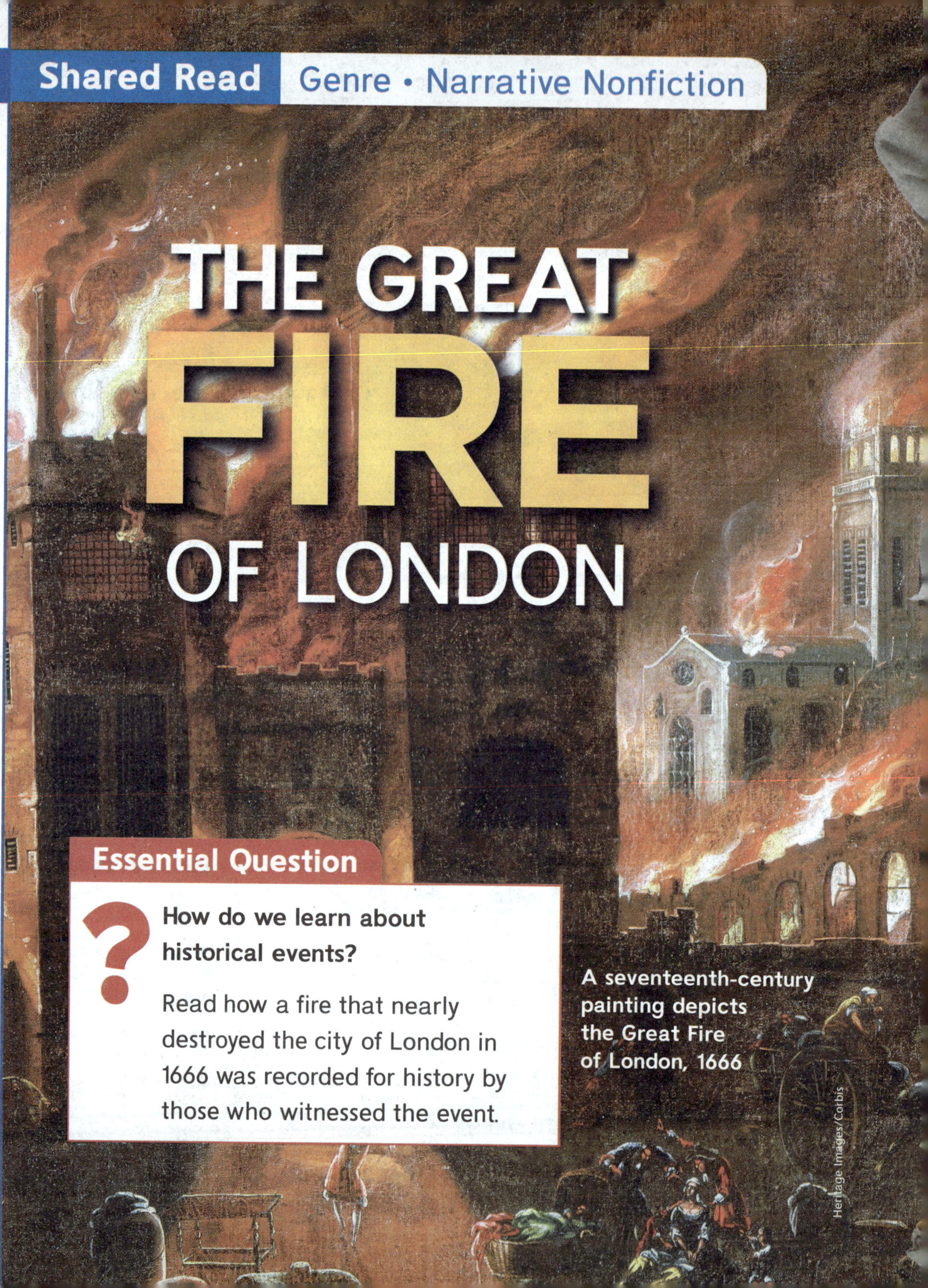

A seventeenth-century painting depicts the Great Fire of London, 1666

The incessant fire raged undiminished for four days. The *London Gazette* reported that "all attempts for quenching it however industriously pursued seemed **insufficient**." Finally, crucial relief came when the fire reached a brick wall near a law school and the winds changed direction. But by that time, four-fifths of the city had become a smoldering ruin. In all, 13,200 houses, 87 churches, and many government buildings were destroyed. Although few deaths were **recorded**, thousands were homeless.

The City Rebuilds

After the fire, people wanted someone to blame. A French watchmaker named Robert Hubert became a **scapegoat** when he said he had set the fire. Few people believed Hubert's confession. The Earl of Clarendon called him a "poor distracted wretch." Still, he was hanged. By 1667, Parliament had formally declared the fire an accident, as "nothing hath yet been found to argue it to have been other than . . . a great wind, and the season so very dry."

Where there is life there is hope, and people began to rebuild while living in nearby fields. For safety, many new buildings were constructed of stone rather than wood. The need for businesses to recover quickly even took priority over King Charles's plans for a new city design. People could also count their blessings that the fire had destroyed the city's rats and their plague-infected fleas. The plague's devastation was finally halted.

Make Connections

Talk about the ways in which personal and official records help us understand what happened during London's Great Fire. **ESSENTIAL QUESTION**

Describe an event that you and others witnessed. Tell what each of your accounts added to the overall understanding of what happened. **TEXT TO SELF**

Text Evidence

❶ Comprehension
Cause and Effect

Read the first paragraph. What two events caused the Great Fire of London to stop? Underline the sentence that tells you.

❷ Specific Vocabulary

Read the second paragraph. A scapegoat is a person who gets blamed for something he or she did not do. Why was Robert Hubert a scapegoat for the London Fire?

_____
_____
_____

❸ Talk About It

Read the last paragraph. Discuss two lasting effects of the Great Fire of London and why they were important. Then write about them.

_____
_____

Respond to the Text

Partner Discussion Work with a partner. Answer the questions. Discuss what you learned about "The Great Fire of London." Write the page numbers where you found text evidence.

What do we learn about the Great Fire from firsthand accounts?

Samuel Pepys saw _____.   Page(s): _____

John Evelyn experienced _____.   Page(s): _____

What do we learn about the Great Fire from secondhand accounts?

The London Gazette reported _____.   Page(s): _____

Parliament declared _____.   Page(s): _____

What additional information do we learn in the text?

At the beginning, we learn _____.   Page(s): _____

At the end, we learn _____.   Page(s): _____

Group Discussion Present your answers to the group. Cite text evidence to justify your thinking. Listen to and discuss the group's opinions about your answers.

Write Review your notes about "The Great Fire of London." Then write your answer to the Essential Question. Use text evidence to support your answer. Use vocabulary words from this week's reading in your writing.

> **How do we learn about historical events, such as the Great Fire of London?**
>
> We use firsthand accounts, such as _____
>
> _____
>
> _____.
>
> We use secondhand accounts, such as _____
>
> _____
>
> _____.
>
> We use what the author writes in the text to learn _____
>
> _____
>
> _____.

Share Writing Present your writing to the class. Discuss their opinions. Think about what the class has to say. Did they justify their claims? Explain why you agree or disagree with their claims.

I agree with _____.

I disagree with _____ because _____.

Write to Sources

pages 340–343

Take Notes About the Text I took notes on a two-column chart to answer the question: *Which disaster was worse, the plague or the Great Fire of London?*

The Plague	The Great Fire of London
1. The plague killed 68,000 people.	1. The Great Fire killed a few people and left thousands homeless.
2. The plague was spread by London's rats and their plague-infested fleas.	2. The Great Fire spread quickly and destroyed most of London in four days.
3. The Great Fire stopped the plague. It killed the rats and their plague-infested fleas.	3. London was rebuilt after the fire with new buildings made of stone.

Write About the Text I used notes from my chart to write an argument that explains why the plague was worse than the Great Fire of London.

Student Model: Argument

The Great Fire of London was a catastrophe. It destroyed most of London in four days, and thousands of people were left homeless. The plague, however, was even worse. About 68,000 people died of the plague, but the Great Fire killed only a few people. In addition, some positive things happened after the Great Fire. London was rebuilt after the Fire. The new buildings were safer because they were made of stone instead of wood. The Great Fire also halted the plague. It killed the rats and their plague-infested fleas. The plague was worse than the Great Fire because it killed more people and had few, if any, positive effects.

TALK ABOUT IT

Text Evidence
Circle information from the notes that tells how many people died in each disaster. Why did Gabrielle use this information in her argument?

Grammar
Draw a box around two active, past-tense verbs in this paragraph. Explain how these verbs contribute to the paragraph.

Condense Ideas
Underline two sentences that tell how the Great Fire stopped the plague. How can you combine these two sentences to condense the ideas?

Your Turn

Imagine you live in London in 1666. Can you prevent the Great Fire, or will the fire happen eventually?

>> Go Digital!
Write your response online. Use your editing checklist.

TALK ABOUT IT

Weekly Concept Investigations

? **Essential Question**
How can a scientific investigation be an adventure?

>> *Go Digital*

 Where is the scientist in the photo working? What is he studying? Why is his work an adventure? Write words and phrases in the chart.

Scientific Investigation

Discuss why this scientific investigation is an adventure. Use words and phrases from the chart. You can say:

The scientist is studying _____.

The investigation is an adventure because _____

_____.

More Vocabulary

 Look at the picture and read the word. Then read the sentence. Talk about the word with a partner. Write your own sentence.

collaboration

For their **collaboration** in the science competition, Isaiah, Deb, and Justin won a prize.

In my *collaboration* with _____,

we _____.

coordinated

Our music teacher **coordinated** a student concert.

My favorite event *coordinated* by my school

was _____.

concluded

The dentist **concluded** that Trisha's teeth were fine.

I remember when _____ *concluded*

that _____.

investigation

Marta and Ellen are conducting a scientific **investigation**.

I know about an *investigation* to _____

_____.

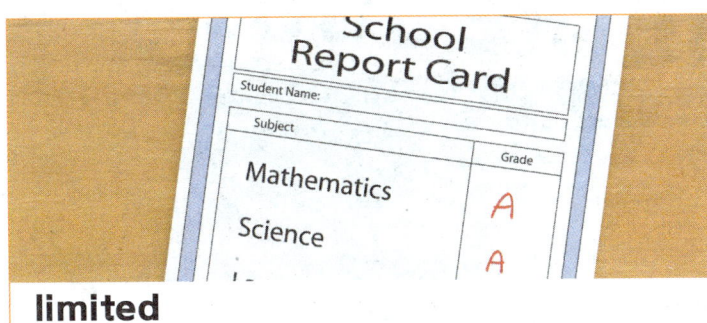
limited

Sylvia's knowledge is not **limited** to science.

My travels have been *limited* to _____

_____.

partnership

The police and fire departments in my town have a strong **partnership**.

A strong *partnership* requires _____

_____.

Words and Phrases
Idioms

to keep watch = to watch closely and carefully
The doctors will <u>keep watch</u> over the sick patient.

to spread the word = to tell many people about something
We need to <u>spread the word</u> about our school festival.

Read the sentences below. Write the idiom that means the same thing as the underlined words.

I'm going to <u>tell many people</u> about my baseball team's final game.

I'm going to _____ about my baseball team's final game.

The adult campers will <u>watch carefully</u> over the sleeping children.

The adult campers will _____ over the sleeping children.

» Go Digital Add these idioms to your New Words notebook. Write a sentence to show the meaning of each.

Text Evidence

Shared Read | Genre • Expository Text

1 Talk About It

Read the title. Talk about what you see. Write your ideas.

What does the title tell you?

_____

_____

What does the photograph show?

_____

_____

Take notes as you read the text.

RESEARCHER TO THE RESCUE

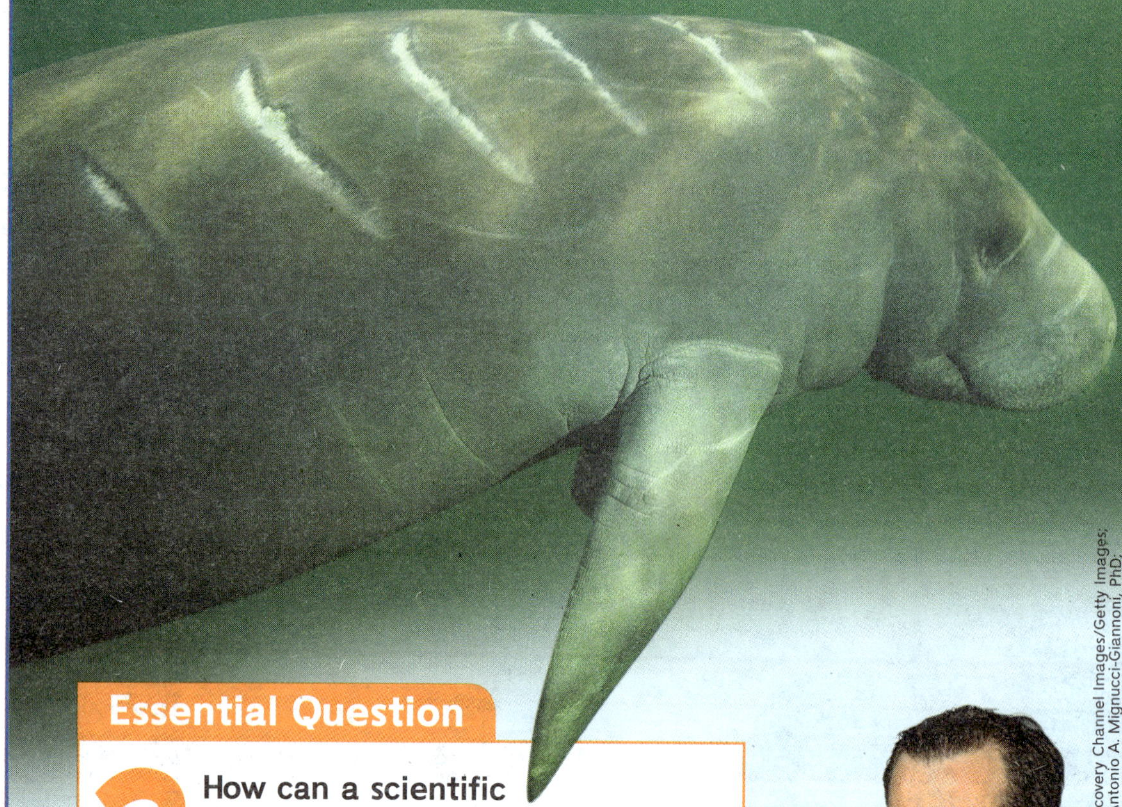

Essential Question

? How can a scientific investigation be an adventure?

Read about a biologist's efforts to find creative ways to protect marine mammals.

352

Manatee Airlift

On a sunny December day, Dr. Antonio Mignucci is in Florida to keep careful watch as a dozen crew members lift an 840-pound manatee into the cargo hold of a National Guard plane. The scene is certainly unusual, but Dr. Mignucci has learned that saving marine mammals requires uncommon **partnerships**. Today's team of scientists and military personnel don't mind that their clothes are saturated with seawater. They know their unique **collaboration** is helping to save a life.

On the aircraft, everyone calls the massive six-year-old manatee "UPC" because the wounds he received when struck by a boat resemble the bar codes on store items. When they reach the Puerto Rico Manatee Conservation Center, Dr. Mignucci renames UPC Guacara, after the river where the animal was stranded. But Guacara will get more than an alternative name. He will also take on the role of surrogate parent to younger manatees recovering at the Center.

Unlike some marine mammals, manatees cannot stay submerged for long periods of time. They lack the special protein called myoglobin that enables whales and dolphins to hold oxygen in their muscles. So manatees live in shallow water, where they eat up to 10 percent of their body weight in sea grass and other underwater foliage each day. But today these coastal waters are crowded with boats that can injure and even kill the slow-moving creatures.

Manatees are naturally resilient, but they sometimes need help to recover from injuries. As a marine biologist, Dr. Mignucci recognizes when it's time to extract manatees from tough situations. For example, he knows that Guacara's injuries make him "negatively buoyant." In other words, Guacara sinks in deep water. But he can swim safely in shallow pools at the Center. There he lives a healthy life while helping to care for the younger manatees.

Text Evidence

① Specific Vocabulary

Read the third paragraph. The term *marine mammals* means "warm-blooded animals that live in the sea." Circle the names of three marine mammals. How are manatees unlike some other marine mammals?

_____

② Comprehension
Main Idea and Details

Reread the third paragraph. Why are manatees in danger? Underline a detail that tells you.

③ Sentence Structure

Read the last sentence in the fourth paragraph. What place does the adverb *there* refer to? Circle the name of the place. What can Guacara do at this place?

_____

_____

Text Evidence

1 Specific Vocabulary

Read the first paragraph. The word *extinct* means "no longer existing or living." Circle context clues that help you understand the meaning of this word. What did the research team conclude about the Caribbean monk seal?

_____

2 Comprehension
Main Idea and Details

Read the third paragraph. The main idea of this paragraph is that collaboration has helped Dr. Mignucci solve some unusual problems. Underline a key detail that supports this main idea.

3 Talk About It

Explain why it is difficult to get an accurate internal temperature of a manatee. Then write about it.

_____

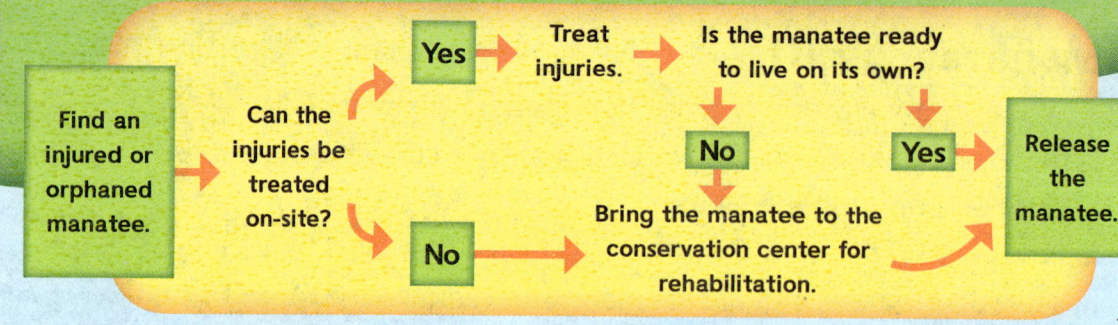

Joining Forces

Manatees are just one focus of Dr. Mignucci's work. He investigates a wide variety of marine animals. No matter what he's studying, however, he considers collaboration to be an essential part of effective research. Working with the Seal Conservation Society of the United Kingdom, Dr. Mignucci coordinated an investigation to test the hypothesis that the Caribbean monk seal is extinct. This seal once lived in the Gulf of Mexico and the Caribbean Sea. Several unconfirmed sightings suggested that a few members of this species might still be alive. The combined research team helped to prove that those sightings almost certainly correspond with a different species, the hooded seal. Regretfully, they concluded that the Caribbean monk seal truly is extinct.

Partnerships also allow researchers to share information and expand the impact of their work. In 2010, the Manatee Conservation Center joined forces with the Georgia Aquarium in Atlanta, the world's largest. These two centers now have regular dialogues and share their knowledge of animal care, veterinary procedures, and water-quality monitoring.

Collaboration has also helped Dr. Mignucci solve some unusual problems. It is important for veterinarians at the Center to get accurate internal temperature measurements, but manatees have large molars and chew on anything you put in their mouths. So oral thermometers don't work. Dr. Mignucci sought help from a company that specializes in making animal tracking devices. The company donated microchips about the size of a grain of rice. Once a chip is implanted, it can be scanned with a pocket reader to obtain the manatee's body temperature.

Singing for Support

Dr. Mignucci's scientific adventures aren't **limited** to the laboratory. He has published books for children and even ventured into the recording studio. To spread word about the plight of manatees, Dr. Mignucci turned to another unusual collaborator, musician Tony Croatto, who was well known for his versions of Puerto Rican folk songs.

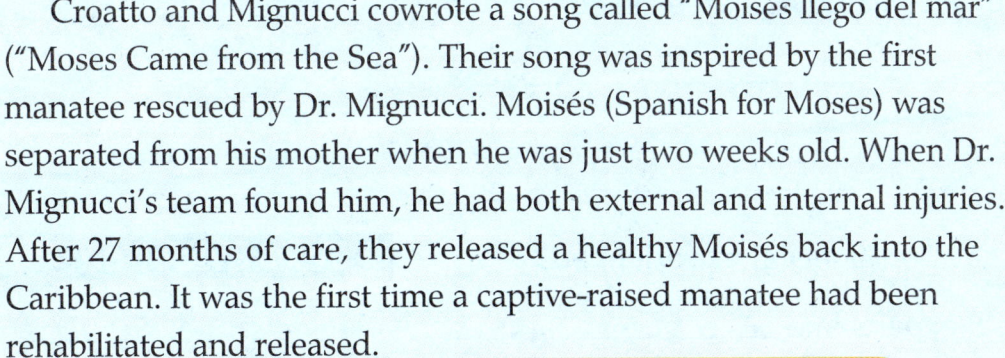

Dr. Antonio Mignucci at work

Croatto and Mignucci cowrote a song called "Moisés llegó del mar" ("Moses Came from the Sea"). Their song was inspired by the first manatee rescued by Dr. Mignucci. Moisés (Spanish for Moses) was separated from his mother when he was just two weeks old. When Dr. Mignucci's team found him, he had both external and internal injuries. After 27 months of care, they released a healthy Moisés back into the Caribbean. It was the first time a captive-raised manatee had been rehabilitated and released.

The song received plenty of airplay. Soon Moisés was a familiar icon admired by listeners around the world. Today he lives in the wild, where the Center's staff regularly monitor his progress. This was just one more way that Dr. Mignucci has brought people together to protect and care for marine life.

Make Connections

 Talk about how Dr. Mignucci and his collaborators find creative solutions to the problems facing marine mammals. **ESSENTIAL QUESTION**

Describe how you could collaborate with others to find out more about a local species that needs help. **TEXT TO SELF**

Text Evidence

1 Comprehension
Main Idea and Details

Read the second paragraph. What is the idea that expresses something about all the details in this paragraph?

The main idea is _____

_____.

2 Sentence Structure

Read the third sentence in the last paragraph. Whom do the pronouns *he* and *his* refer to? Underline the proper noun in the second sentence.

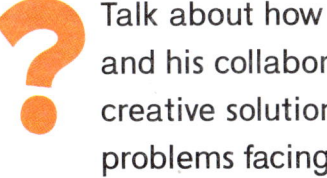

3 Talk About It

Explain how the song about Moisés can help save other manatees. Justify your response.

_____

_____

Respond to the Text

 **Partner Discussion** Work with a partner. Answer the questions. Discuss what you learned about "Researcher to the Rescue." Write the page numbers where you found text evidence.

What exciting experiences has Dr. Mignucci had?

During one manatee rescue, Dr. Mignucci _____

_____.

Page(s): _____

Dr. Mignucci created a new life for the injured manatee called Guacara by _____.

Page(s): _____

What discoveries and ventures has Dr. Mignucci experienced?

Dr. Mignucci collaborated with seal experts and _____

_____.

Page(s): _____

Dr. Mignucci collaborated to solve _____

_____.

Page(s): _____

A venture into publishing included _____

_____.

Page(s): _____

 **Group Discussion** Present your answers to the group. Cite text evidence to justify your thinking. Listen to and discuss the group's opinions about your answers.

Write Review your notes about "Researcher to the Rescue." Then write your answer to the Essential Question. Use text evidence to support your answer. Use vocabulary words from this week's reading in your writing.

How have Dr. Mignucci's scientific investigations been like adventures?

During his investigations, Dr. Mignucci has made exciting discoveries and solved problems, such as _____

_____

_____.

Dr. Mignucci has also had adventures in _____

_____.

Dr. Mignucci's scientific investigations have been like adventures because _____

_____

_____.

Share Writing Present your writing to the class. Discuss their opinions. Think about what the class has to say. Did they justify their claims? Explain why you agree or disagree with their claims.

I agree with _____.

I disagree with _____ because _____.

357

Write to Sources

pages 352–355

Take Notes About the Text I took notes on an idea web to answer the question: *Why did Dr. Mignucci cowrite a song about Moisés the manatee?*

Sarah

Detail
Moisés was separated from his mother when he was two weeks old. He had serious injuries.

Detail
Dr. Mignucci and his team cared for Moisés for 27 months; then they relased him into the Caribbean.

Topic
Song about Moisés

Detail
Dr. Mignucci and a collaborator cowrote a song about Moisés. The song received airplay and was admired.

Detail
People learned about Moisés and other marine animals.

Write About the Text I used notes from my idea web to write an informative text about Dr. Mignucci's song about Moisés.

Student Model: *Informative Text*

Dr. Mignucci cowrote a song about Moisés to raise awareness of the manatee's situation. Moisés was a baby manatee that was separated from his mother when he was two weeks old. He had terrible injuries when Dr. Mignucci's team found him. Dr. Mignucci and his team cared for Moisés for 27 months and then released him into the Caribbean. Dr. Mignucci then cowrote a song called "Moses Came From the Sea." The song was played many times on the radio. Many people learned about Moisés. Dr. Mignucci's song made Moisés famous. The song made people aware of Moisés's situation and the situation of other sea animals.

TALK ABOUT IT

Text Evidence
Circle a sentence that comes from the notes. Why did Sarah include this information in her text?

Grammar
Draw a box around each pronoun in the third sentence. To what proper noun does each pronoun refer?

Connect Ideas
Underline sentences 7 and 8. How can you use the word *because* to combine the sentences to connect ideas?

Your Turn

In what ways did Dr. Mignucci collaborate with others? Give three examples.

›› Go Digital!
Write your response online. Use your editing checklist.

TALK ABOUT IT

Weekly Concept Extraordinary Finds

? Essential Question
What can scientists reveal about ancient civilizations?

›› *Go Digital*

 **COLLABORATE** What does the photo show? What did many members of the army have? When and why was this army made? Write words and phrases in the chart.

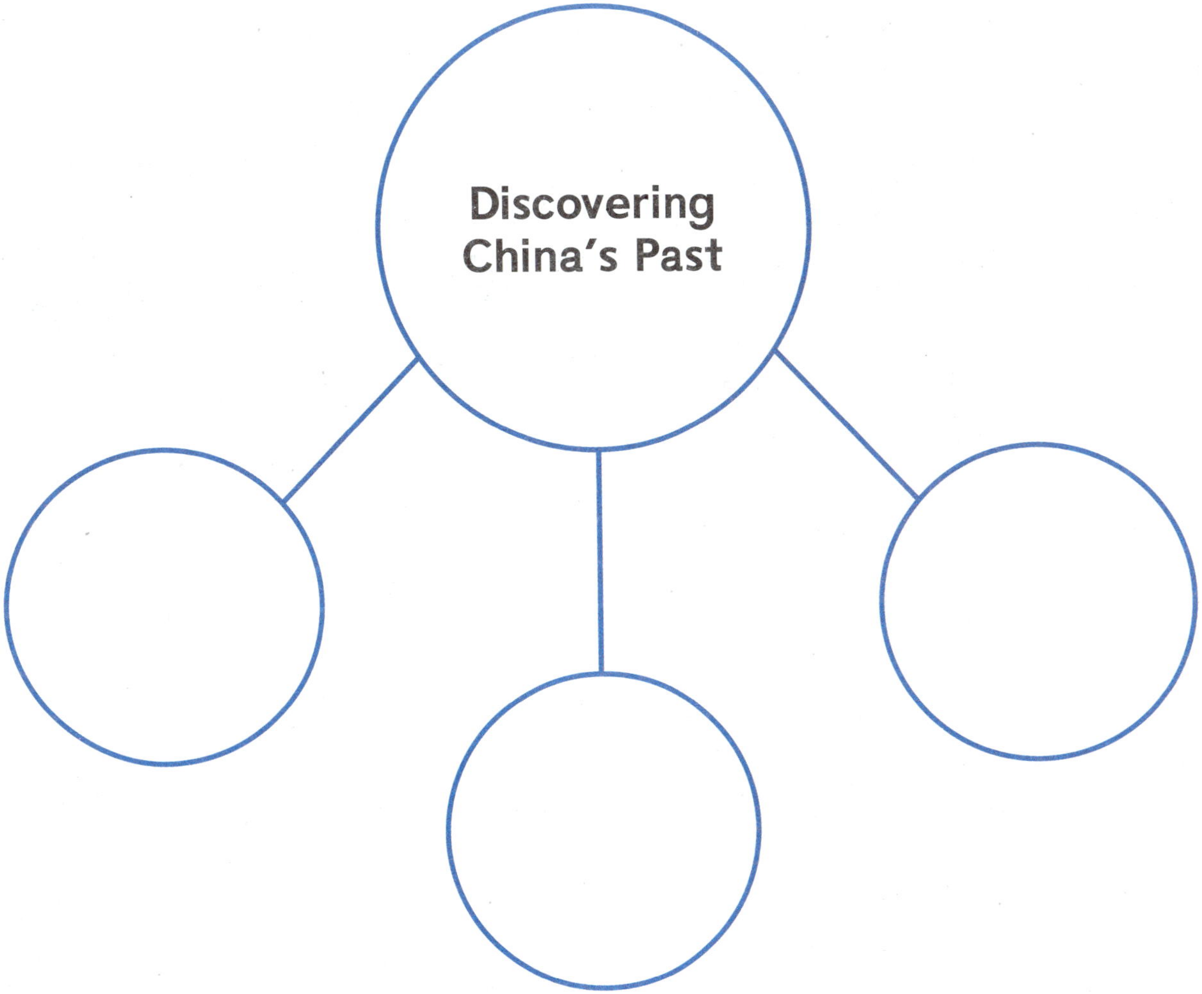

Discovering China's Past

Discuss what scientists found in the tomb of China's first emperor. Use words and phrases from the chart. You can say:

The scientists found _____.

This helped them learn about _____.

More Vocabulary

 Look at the picture and read the word. Then read the sentence. Talk about the word with a partner. Write your own sentence.

chronicle

Justine made a **chronicle** of her family's vacation.

I would like to make a *chronicle* of _____

_____.

existing

Dinosaurs are not **existing** animals any more.

An *existing* animal is one that _____

_____.

designs

Ann and Melanie enjoy creating different kinds of **designs**.

Designs can be used for _____

_____.

identifications

A uniform and a badge are two **identifications** of a police officer.

Identifications can help people _____

_____.

interpreting

Interpreting math problems can be difficult.

I sometimes have trouble *interpreting* _____

_____.

reliably

Robert **reliably** walks his dog every morning before school.

One thing I do *reliably* is _____

_____.

Words and Phrases
Multiple-Meaning Words

The noun *date* means "a specific month, day, or year."
I was born on this date: April 6, 2004.

The verb *date* means "to figure out how old something is."
The scientists will examine and date the dinosaur bones.

Read the sentences below. Circle the correct meaning of the underlined word.

The date of the concert was September 24, 2014.

a specific month, day, or year

to figure out how old something is

We need special tools to date these rocks.

a specific month, day, or year

to figure out how old something is

» Go Digital Add these words to your New Words notebook. Write a sentence to show the meaning of each word.

Text Evidence

Shared Read · Genre • Expository Text

1 Talk About It

Read the title. Talk about what you see. Write your ideas.

What does the title tell you?

_____

_____

What does the photograph show?

_____

_____

Take notes as you read the text.

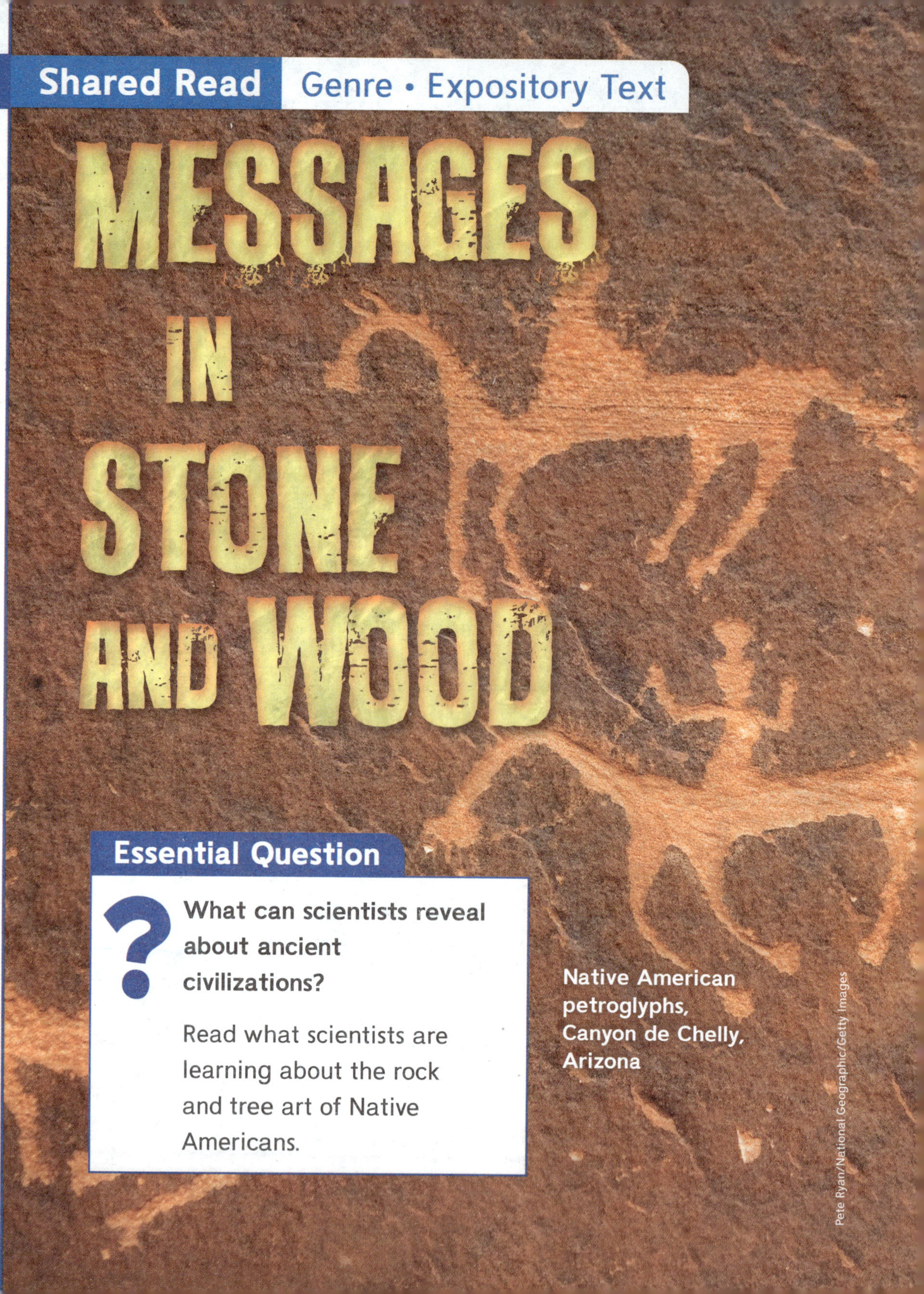

MESSAGES IN STONE AND WOOD

Essential Question

? What can scientists reveal about ancient civilizations?

Read what scientists are learning about the rock and tree art of Native Americans.

Native American petroglyphs, Canyon de Chelly, Arizona

"We Were Here"

Deep in a forest in what is now Pennsylvania, members of a hunting party were preparing to embark on their trip home. Only one task remained: creating a chronicle of their successful hunt. One of the hunters selected a broad oak tree, carefully made some cuts with his knife, and used the blade to peel back the bark. From a small leather bag, he shook out some powder he had ground from red pebbles. Then he mixed the powder with animal fat to make a thick red paint.

On the tree, the hunter meticulously painted images of a turtle and six men carrying packs and bows. Next, he drew a circle, a half circle, and six marks. Finally, he added the heads of three deer and a bear.

From then on, anyone passing this spot would see from these designs that six men of the terrapin clan had hunted here. They had camped for one and a half moons, plus six days. And they had had a successful hunt.

Mysterious Markings

The first Europeans to explore North America came across many markings like the ones on that Pennsylvania tree. At first, no one understood the meanings of these mysterious *petroglyphs* (stone carvings) and *dendroglyphs* (tree carvings and paintings). Nor did they know who had created them. As time went on, however, people studying the markings, or pictographs, began to understand that they had been made by Native Americans. They concluded that the pictographs were records of hunts, battles, and clan meetings. They seemed also to serve as directions, warnings, boundary markers, and clan identifications.

When non-native people pushed farther west during the 1800s, they discovered many more of these images. In the dry desert of the

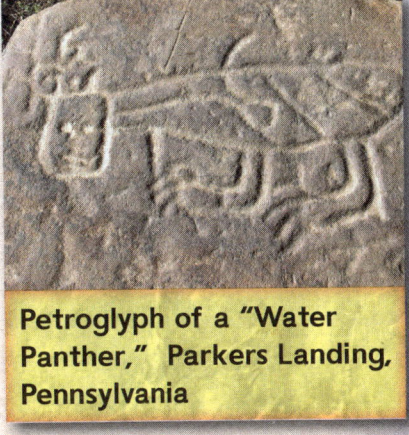

Petroglyph of a "Water Panther," Parkers Landing, Pennsylvania

Text Evidence

❶ Sentence Structure

Read the first sentence. Circle the comma, which divides the sentence into two parts. Box the part of the sentence that tells where the members of the hunting party were.

❷ Specific Vocabulary

Read the third paragraph. The word *pictographs* means "markings." Circle the names of two kinds of pictographs. What was the purpose of pictographs?

Pictographs _____

_____

_____.

❸ Comprehension
Sequence

Reread the third paragraph. What did people studying the markings start to understand about them? Underline the sentence that tells you.

Text Evidence

1 Talk About It

Read the last paragraph at the bottom of page 365 and at the top of page 366. Explain how weather affects pictographs in different parts of the country. Then write about it.

_____

_____

2 Sentence Structure ACT

Read the second sentence of the first full paragraph. Circle the commas. Underline the three actions archaeologists could not do.

3 Comprehension
Sequence

Read the first full paragraph. What could scientists do after they learned to use radiocarbon dating?

_____

_____

Southwest, exquisite pictographs on rocks and cave walls appeared to be freshly made. This was especially true of carvings protected from direct sunlight. In the East, however, moisture decomposes dead tree trunks and winter ice damages rocks. Pictographs generally survive this wetter and colder climate only in sheltered spots. These spots are often outcroppings of bedrock that have been covered over by soil or moss. As a result, the only remaining records of many vanished pictographs are copies that were sketched by early explorers and historians.

Reading the Messages

For a long time, archaeologists made little progress in studying the rock art of Native Americans. They could not reliably date the pictographs, relate them to other human artifacts, or even agree on their meanings. But as technology improved, scientists learned much more about these intriguing images. For example, they used radiocarbon dating to measure the decay rate of carbon in the paint of dendroglyphs. By analyzing how rock surfaces had weathered, they estimated that some petroglyphs were nearly a thousand years old.

Although dating is now more reliable, understanding the meanings of rock images remains difficult. It is generally accepted that the people who made pictographs in open areas wanted to mark borders or record significant events. But interpreting images hidden in sheltered areas or caves has been more challenging.

Archaeologist Rex Weeks, an Echota Cherokee from Alabama, has brought an intrinsic cultural perspective to the scientific study and interpretation of Native American rock images. Dr. Weeks suggests that petroglyphs in secluded locations were purposely made at sites that would not be accessible to outsiders. The images were intended primarily for ceremonial use. Elders may also have used them to teach young people the beliefs and history of their clan. Weeks's research has shown that many of the symbols employed in pictographs link the cultures of ancient peoples to existing oral traditions of Native Americans. And by conducting experiments with hammer and chisel stones, Weeks has been able to demonstrate his theories about the techniques used to create rock carvings.

Preserving the Past

Today, many pictographs are in danger of being destroyed by natural forces before they can be documented and studied. Others are damaged when careless excavation by non-professionals defaces them or leaves them exposed to the elements. So experts have developed a system called the Rock Art Stability Index to assess in a methodical way which sites are most at risk. They also enlist trained volunteers, including native people, to record and manage newly discovered sites. One such site, a cave in the Appalachian mountains, contains fragile rock art that is more than a thousand years old. Educating the public about the importance and vulnerability of these sites is critical if the efforts of archaeologists such as Dr. Weeks are to succeed in preserving these rich cultural resources for future generations.

Courtesy of Rex Weeks

Make Connections

Talk about what archaeologists have learned from studying the pictographs of early Native Americans. **ESSENTIAL QUESTION**

Compare pictographs to the methods you use today to deliver messages and record events in your life. **TEXT TO SELF**

Text Evidence

❶ Specific Vocabulary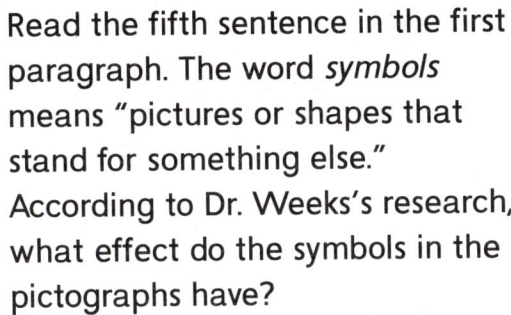

Read the fifth sentence in the first paragraph. The word *symbols* means "pictures or shapes that stand for something else." According to Dr. Weeks's research, what effect do the symbols in the pictographs have?

_____

_____

❷ Sentence Structure

Read the second sentence in the second paragraph. What noun does the pronoun *others* refer to?

_____

❸ Talk About It

Read the second paragraph. Explain why it is important to educate the public about protecting pictographs. Then write about it.

_____

367

Respond to the Text

 **Partner Discussion** Work with a partner. Answer the questions. Discuss what you learned about "Messages in Stone and Wood." Write the page numbers where you found text evidence.

How has technology helped in the dating of rock and tree art?

Scientists can measure _____.

Scientists can analyze _____.

The data tells scientists _____.

Text Evidence

Page(s): _____

Page(s): _____

Page(s): _____

What has Dr. Rex Weeks learned by studying Native American pictographs?

Dr. Weeks says the rock images were used for _____.

Dr. Weeks conducted experiments to learn about _____.

Text Evidence

Page(s): _____

Page(s): _____

 **Group Discussion** Present your answers to the group. Cite text evidence to justify your thinking. Listen to and discuss the group's opinions about your answers.

Write Review your notes about "Messages in Stone and Wood." Then write your answer to the Essential Question. Use text evidence to support your answer. Use vocabulary words from this week's reading in your writing.

> **What have scientists revealed about ancient Native American civilizations?**
>
> Using technology, scientists have learned that some petroglyphs _____
> _____.
>
> The symbols in pictographs link _____
> _____.
>
> From the rock and tree art of Native Americans, scientists have learned _____
> _____.

Share Writing Present your writing to the class. Discuss their opinions. Think about what the class has to say. Did they justify their claims? Explain why you agree or disagree with their claims.

I agree with _____.

I disagree with _____ because _____.

Write to Sources

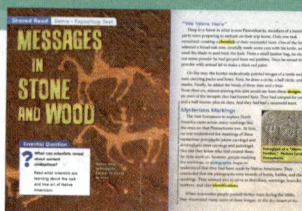

pages 364–367

Take Notes About the Text I took notes on the sequence chart to answer the question: *How has our understanding of Native American pictographs changed over time?*

First
Early European explorers did not understand the carvings and pictures they had found.

Next
People studied the pictographs. They figured out that they had been created by Native Americans and told of battles, hunts, and meetings.

Then
Technology improved. Scientists estimated that some of the pictographs were 1,000 years old. An archaeologist named Dr. Weeks studied the carvings. He connected them to Native American oral traditions.

Write About the Text I used my notes from my sequence chart to write an informative text about how people's understanding of Native American pictographs has changed.

Student Model: *Informative Text*

Many years ago, Native Americans carved and painted pictures on trees and in caves. Early European explorers did not understand these pictographs. As time went on, people studying them learned that the pictographs told stories of hunts, battles, and clan meetings. As technology improved, scientists found that many were over 1,000 years old. An archaeologist named Dr. Weeks brought a personal cultural perspective to understanding the pictographs. Dr. Weeks is an Echota Cherokee. He also connected the pictographs to Native American oral traditions.

TALK ABOUT IT

Text Evidence
Draw a box around a sentence that comes from the notes. Why did Amanda use this information in the text?

Grammar
Circle time phrases that begin sentences. How do these phrases help to organize the text?

Condense Ideas
Underline sentences 5 and 6. How can you condense the ideas by combining the sentences?

Your Turn

Why are some pictographs in danger? Why is it important to preserve the pictographs?

>> *Go Digital!*
Write your response online. Use your editing checklist.

TALK ABOUT IT

Weekly Concept Taking a Break

? Essential Question
Why is taking a break important?

>> *Go Digital*

 **COLLABORATE** What have the friends in the photo been doing all day? Why are they sitting now? What do they have to do later? Write words and phrases in the chart.

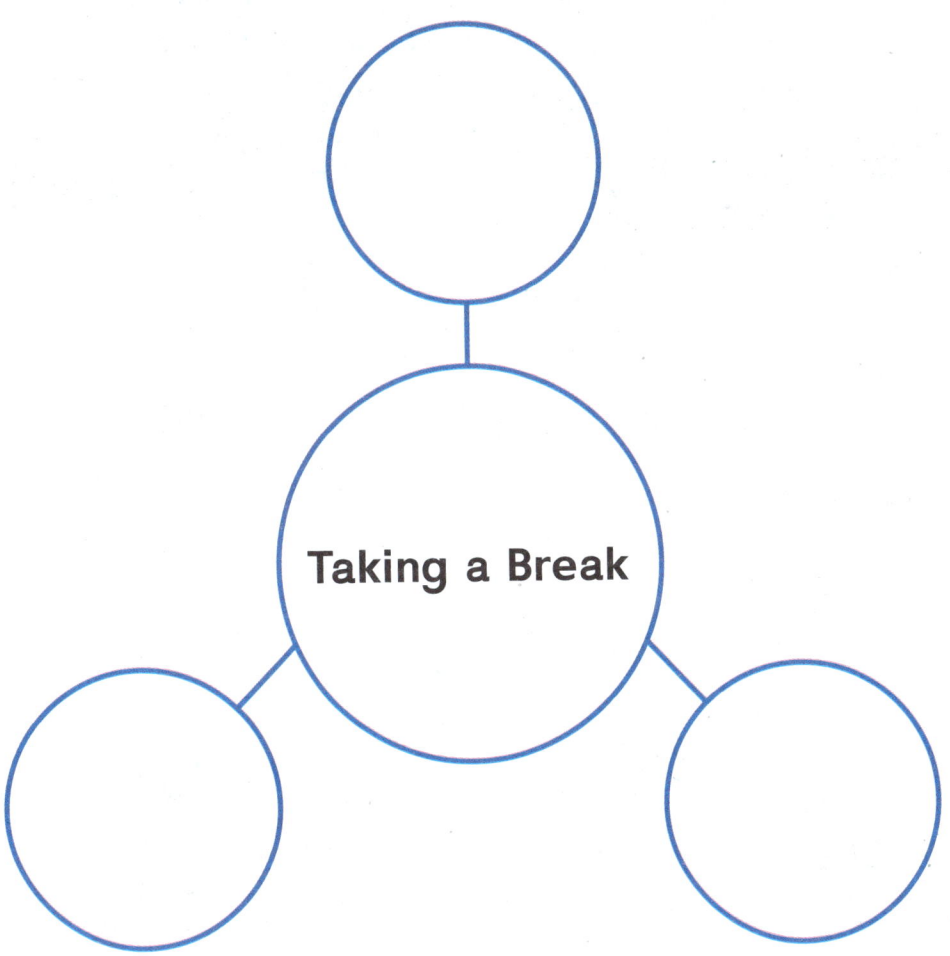

Taking a Break

Discuss why it is important for the friends to take a break. Use words from the chart. You can say:

The friends have been _____. Now they want to

_____. This will help them _____.

More Vocabulary

Look at the picture and read the word. Then read the sentence. Talk about the word with a partner. Write your own sentence.

dispersing

The police are **dispersing** the crowd.

Why might the police be dispersing the crowd?

lashing

A powerful and dangerous hurricane is **lashing** the city.

When and where have you seen rain lashing something?

revealing

Trevor opened the box, **revealing** his birthday present.

What do you like revealing about your favorite movies?

rustling

The children are **rustling** the leaves.

During which season have you seen children rustling leaves?

Poetry Terms

imagery

Imagery is language that helps to paint a picture in the reader's mind. Imagery helps readers feel, taste, smell, see, or hear something.

The sweet and juicy watermelon was cold and wet in her mouth.

repetition

Repetition is the use of the same words or sounds more than once. Poets use repetition to emphasize something.

Kind hearts are gardens,
Kind thoughts are roots,
Kind words are blossoms,
Kind deeds are fruits.

hyperbole

Hyperbole is unrealistic language that you are not supposed to believe. Hyperbole emphasizes a point.

Her smile is a mile wide.

COLLABORATE

Work with a partner. Choose the words that create imagery, repetition, and hyperbole. Read the sentences together.

**run   drip   mountain
mice   sweat   carrots**

Imagery

The heat made the runner _____ with _____.

Repetition

Three blind mice.
Three blind _____.

See how they run.
See how they _____.

Hyperbole

He ate a _____ of _____.

Text Evidence

Shared Read | Genre • Poetry

How Many Seconds?

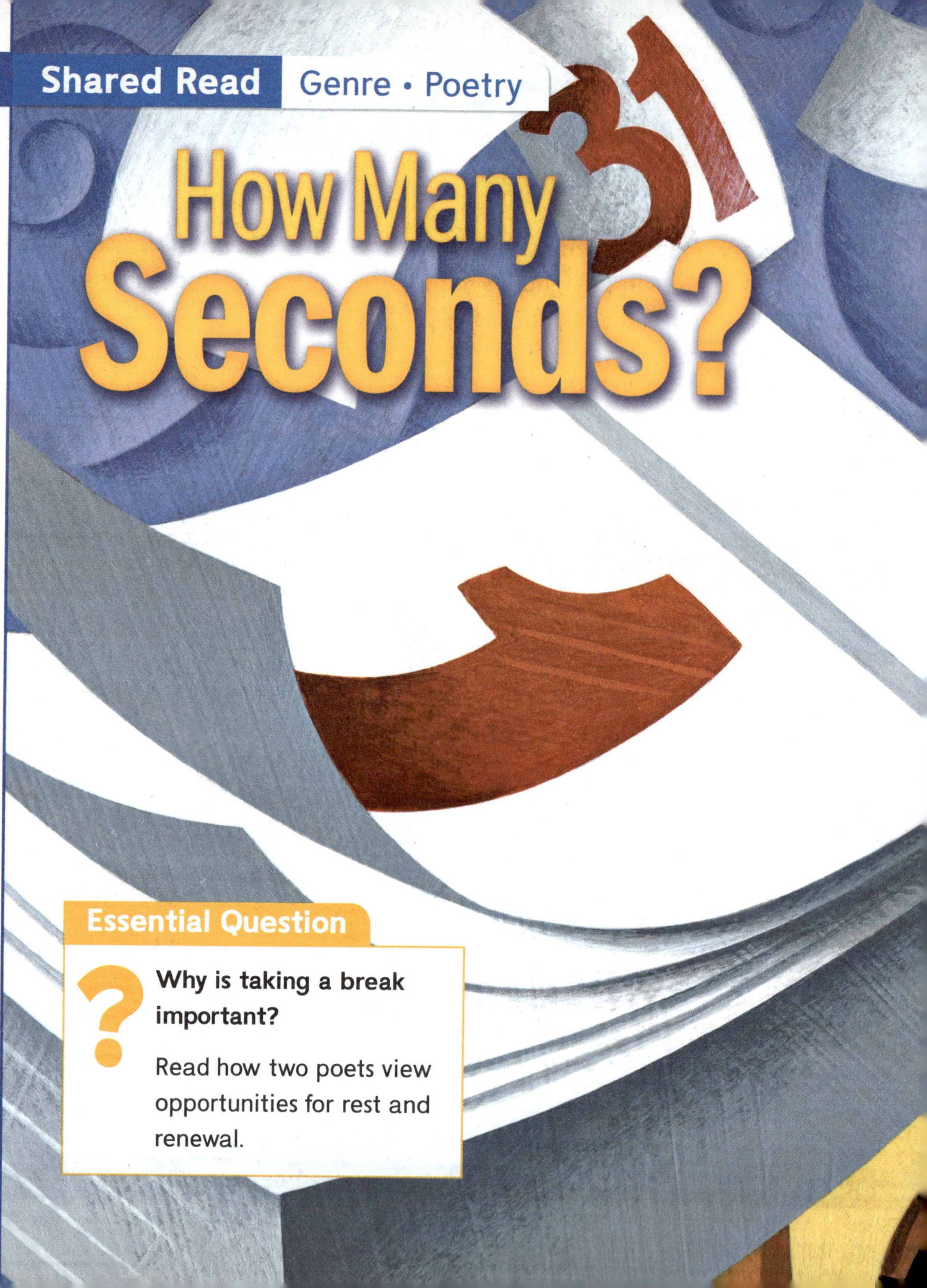

1 Talk About It

Read the title. Look at the illustration. What measures of time do you see? Write them from smallest to largest.

The measures of time from smallest to largest are _____

_____.

2 Literary Element
Repetition

Read the first two stanzas. Underline the words and phrases the poet repeats. Why does the poet repeat the words and phrases?

_____

_____.

3 Specific Vocabulary

Read the second stanza. A *shower* is "light rain falling during a short time." Circle a word that means the opposite of *shower* and helps you understand the meaning of *shower*.

Essential Question

Why is taking a break important?

Read how two poets view opportunities for rest and renewal.

376

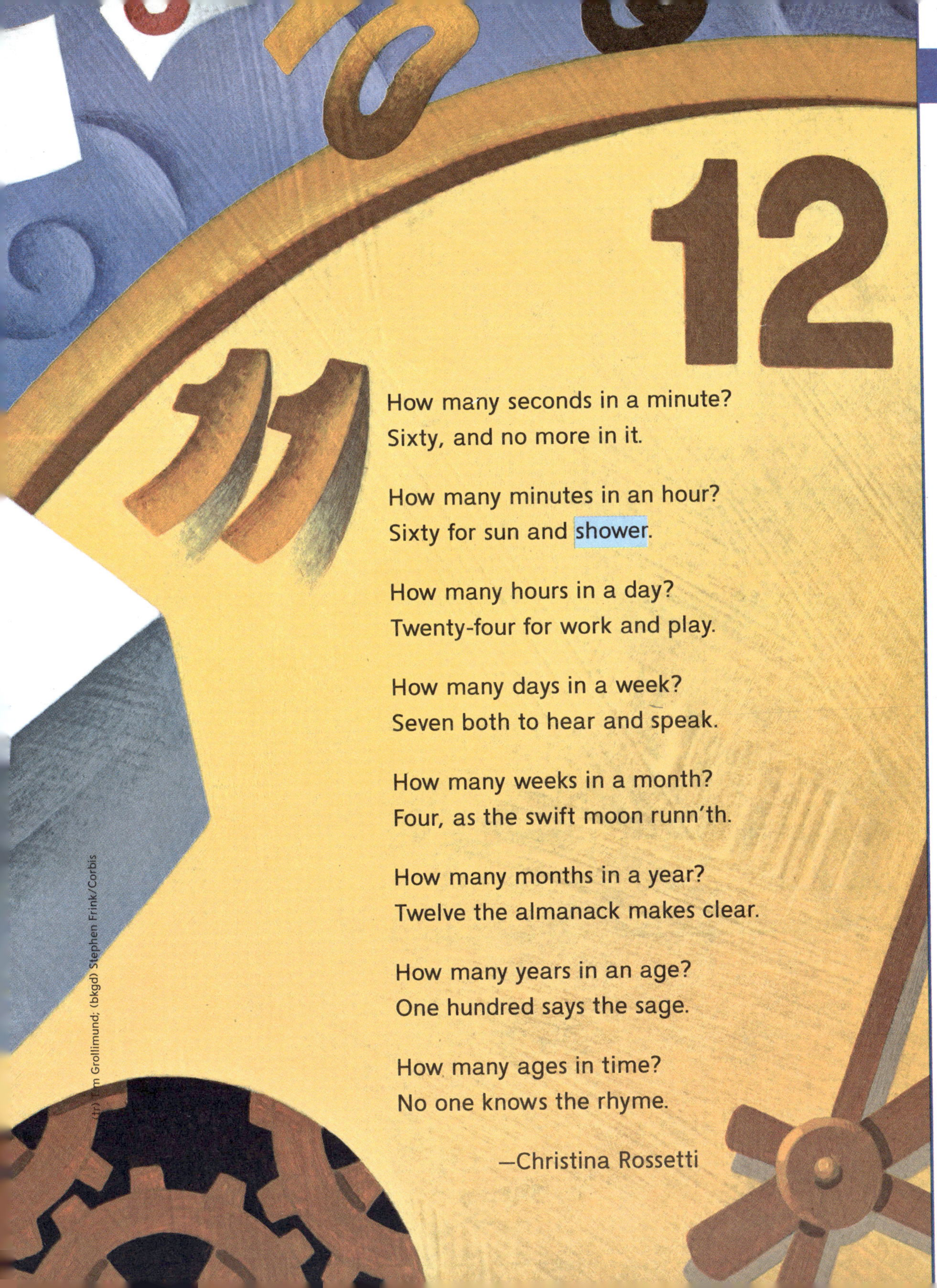

How many seconds in a minute?
Sixty, and no more in it.

How many minutes in an hour?
Sixty for sun and shower.

How many hours in a day?
Twenty-four for work and play.

How many days in a week?
Seven both to hear and speak.

How many weeks in a month?
Four, as the swift moon runn'th.

How many months in a year?
Twelve the almanack makes clear.

How many years in an age?
One hundred says the sage.

How many ages in time?
No one knows the rhyme.

—Christina Rossetti

Text Evidence

1 Sentence Structure Ⓐ Ⓒ Ⓣ

Read the third stanza. What does *twenty-four* refer to? Draw a box around the words that tell you.

2 Literary Element
Repetition

The poet repeats a pattern for each stanza in the poem. What types of sentences appear in each stanza?

In each stanza, the poet uses

_____.

3 Comprehension
Theme

Read the last two lines. Underline the words that tell the poet's message about time. In your own words, what does this mean?

_____

_____

Text Evidence

1. Sentence Structure
Read the first stanza. What noun phrase does the pronoun *it* and the possessive pronoun *its* refer to? Write the noun phrase.

_____

2. Specific Vocabulary
Read the second line in the second stanza. Circle the synonym for *pandemonium*. Write a line from the second stanza that illustrates the wind's pandemonium.

_____

3. Literary Element
Imagery

Reread the second stanza. Underline the sensory details that help you hear the wind.

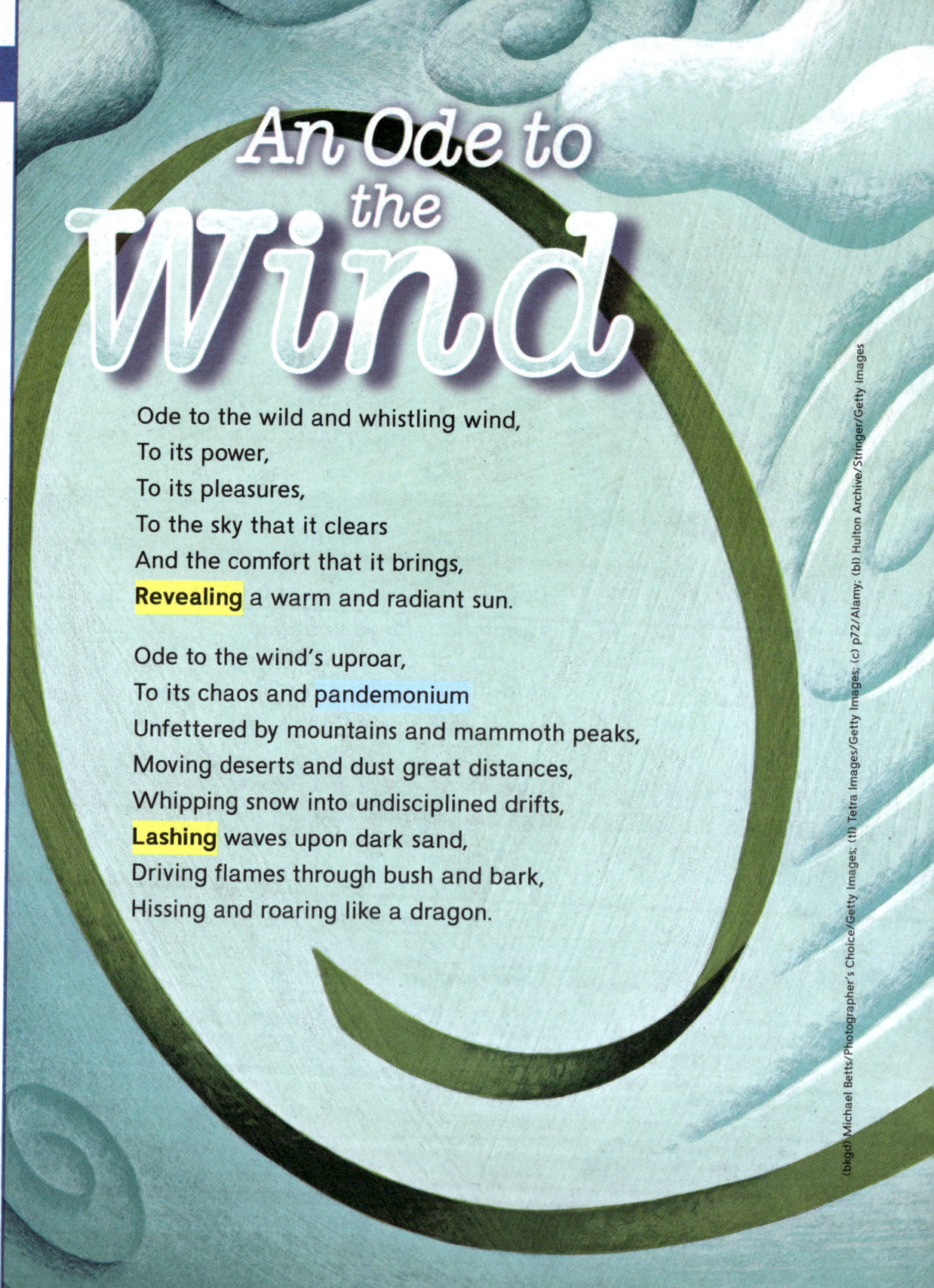

An Ode to the Wind

Ode to the wild and whistling wind,
To its power,
To its pleasures,
To the sky that it clears
And the comfort that it brings,
Revealing a warm and radiant sun.

Ode to the wind's uproar,
To its chaos and pandemonium
Unfettered by mountains and mammoth peaks,
Moving deserts and dust great distances,
Whipping snow into undisciplined drifts,
Lashing waves upon dark sand,
Driving flames through bush and bark,
Hissing and roaring like a dragon.

Ode to the wind's energy and titanic strength,
Scattering seeds as valuable as gold upon the land,
Filling square-rigged sails with billowing force,
Thrusting ships toward new horizons,
Whipping windmills to turn and generate,
Dispersing autumn leaves to replenish the earth,
To the storms it brings upon us
And the life-giving rain.

Ode to the moving air,
To the warm air rising
And the cool air that comes in to take its place,
To the sky that it cleared
And the comfort it brought,
Rustling hair, cooling fevered brows.
Wind a thousand times softer than silk
Offering a sweet incentive for recreation,
Lifting kites to the outer edge of the stratosphere.

—Jonathan Moss

Make Connections

Talk about the way each poet expresses an understanding of how people may take time to relax. **ESSENTIAL QUESTION**

How might experiencing the sensations of a windy day help when you feel the need to take a break? **TEXT TO SELF**

Text Evidence

❶ Talk About It

Read the third stanza. Discuss how the wind helps the land. Then write about it.

_____

_____

❷ Literary Element
Repetition

Read the fourth stanza. Circle the phrase the poet repeats in each stanza.

❸ Comprehension
Theme

Reread the fourth stanza. What does the poet do to connect a windy day with taking a break?

The poet uses words and phrases that _____

_____.

379

Respond to the Text

 **Partner Discussion** Work with a partner. Answer the questions. Discuss what you learned about "How Many Seconds?" and "An Ode to the Wind." Write the page numbers where you found text evidence.

What is the author's point of view in "How Many Seconds?"

The poet mostly talks about _____.

About minutes, the poet says _____.

I think this means _____.

Text Evidence

Page(s): _____

Page(s): _____

Page(s): _____

What is the author's point of view in "An Ode to the Wind"?

This poem is mostly about _____.

The poet says a windy day brings comfort by _____ _____.

I think this means _____.

Text Evidence

Page(s): _____

Page(s): _____

Page(s): _____

 **Group Discussion** Present your answers to the group. Cite text evidence to justify your thinking. Listen to and discuss the group's opinions about your answers.

Write Review your notes about "How Many Seconds?" and "An Ode to the Wind." Then write your answer to the Essential Question. Use text evidence to support your answer. Use vocabulary words from this week's reading in your writing.

Why is taking a break important?

The poet of "How Many Seconds?" says that in a day _____
_____.

The poet of "An Ode to the Wind" says a windy day offers _____
_____.

Therefore, both poets understand the importance of _____
_____.

Share Writing Present your writing to the class. Discuss their opinions. Think about what the class has to say. Did they justify their claims? Explain why you agree or disagree with their claims.

I agree with _____.

I disagree with _____ because _____.

Write to Sources

pages 376–379

Take Notes About the Text I took notes on the idea web to answer the question: *How does the poet of "An Ode to the Wind" use vivid imagery to describe the wind?*

Topic
Vivid Imagery in "An Ode to the Wind"

Evidence
"Whipping snow into undisciplined drifts"

Evidence
"Driving flames through bush and bark"

Evidence
"Hissing and roaring like a dragon"

Evidence
"Wind a thousand times softer than silk"

Write About the Text I used my notes from my idea web to write an informative text about the vivid imagery in "An Ode to the Wind."

Student Model: *Informative Text*

Jonathan Moss, the poet of "An Ode to the Wind," uses vivid imagery to describe the wind. The vivid imagery describes the wind as both fierce and gentle. For example, in Stanza 2, Moss describes the wind as "Whipping snow into undisciplined drifts." In this description, Moss appeals to the reader's sense of sight. Also in Stanza 2, Moss describes the wind as "Hissing and roaring like a dragon." With this description, Moss appeals to the reader's sense of sound. In Stanza 4, Moss describes the wind as "...a thousand times softer than silk." Here, Moss appeals to the reader's sense of touch.

TALK ABOUT IT

Text Evidence
Draw a box around details Russell used from the notes. Why did Russell use these details?

Grammar
Underline a transitional word that begins a sentence. What purpose does this word serve?

Condense Ideas
Circle the first two sentences. How can you combine the sentences to condense the ideas?

Your Turn
Write an informative text about the use of repetition in "An Ode to the Wind" or "How Many Seconds."

» Go Digital!
Write your response online. Use your editing checklist.